MURDER ON THE ROAD

ADRIANA LICIO

The Home Travellers
Press

Murder on the Road

Book 1 in *An Italian Village Mystery* Series
By Adriana Licio

Edition I
Copyright 2019 © Adriana Licio
ISBN: 978-88-32249-09-5

Cover by Wicked Smart Design
Editing by Alison Jack

To Giovanni and Frodo,
who trust in me more than I do.

CONTENTS

PROLOGUE

M ARATEA NEWS 24

HEAVY RAINS IN THE PAST FEW DAYS
have caused rockfalls on the State Road 18
Tirrena Inferiore. The road has been
temporarily closed to traffic in the
proximity of the cemetery in Acquafredda,
municipality of Maratea.

ANAS has announced the road closure,
specifying that detour road signs have
been placed to help drivers.

Passing through Maratea, in Basilicata,

the road connects the Campania coast in the north with the Calabria coastline in the south. A number of wildfires devastated the area during the summer, making the rocky ridge unstable, and the torrential rains of the last few days have caused rockfalls to break the safety nets and land on the road.

Hotels and tourist businesses will be worst hit by the measure, but anyone driving between Maratea and Sapri will be obliged to make a long detour.

Contract works for stabilisation and maintenance have been awarded, but site assessment needs to be completed before the clearing works start. According to the Mayor of Maratea, it might take over a month, by which time the tourist season will be over. The economic damage to tourist businesses is expected to be severe.

1

A PAINFUL TRAIN JOURNEY

Giò pretended to be engrossed in her book, but it did not help.

"Oh, you should see the dress we chose for her!" the fat blonde lady sitting in front of her continued mercilessly, her voice shrill. "She looks like a Hollywood actress. I can't imagine Duccio's face when he sees her. He wanted to come along, but tradition forbids the future husband seeing the bride's dress before the wedding."

Giò nodded, trying not to seem encouraging. She'd had enough of the woman's talk, which had started as the train left Naples, and was still as lively one and a half hours later. There were another 30 long minutes to go before they reached Sapri, and there was a real risk they would end up sitting next to each other on the regional train to Maratea, Giò's hometown.

Giò did not return the woman's smile and once again pretended to be absorbed in her reading. But her travelling companion, who had introduced herself as Mrs Di Bello, didn't seem to notice and carried on as if Giò had shown great interest.

"Duccio let Dora choose the wedding venue, the menu, the decorations. He totally trusts her refined taste." Mrs Di Bello elongated her vowels, sounding like a soprano singer practising the higher notes on the scale. "He's sooo in love with heeer that he said they would go whereeever she wanted tooo for their honeymoon. He said that whereeever she chose would be nothing short of peeerfect."

For a fraction of a second, Giò visualised how difficult things had been with Dorian. Whatever she suggested "could always be improved upon", by which he meant she should put aside her own desires to leave plenty of room for his ideas and plans. But she sent the thought away. Not now. Not when she was finally going home. All she wanted was a little quiet time to let it sink in…

No, stop those thoughts! They were too painful right now. She longed to gaze at the familiar landscape, knowing that after 15 years of living abroad, she was finally coming back home, maybe for good. But she dared not raise her eyes from the book.

"And the house – he bought her the house of her dreams. It has a stunning view of the gulf. It's such a big house, too. If I think how Mr Di Bello and I started when we got married. We only had two small rooms and we weren't sure we could pay the next month's rent. But these two young ones, life has been generous to them. Duccio comes from a long line of lawyers, and he's continuing the family tradition. It is not only the money, though; he is sooo much in love with Dora. In the three years of their engagement, they've only had one major fight.

"I mean, it was about something so stupid, I can't even remember what. But Dora was so angry, she left him. And when he came to ours, tears in his eyes, begging her to reconsider, to go back to him, she said she would have to think about it. He kept sending flowers and letters and ringing her. In the end, they made up. And they've never argued since."

Giò thought she wouldn't mind asking Dora for a little womanly advice. She clearly knew about winning a man's heart. But Giò was careful not to show any sign of interest; she longed for silence and hoped there would come a point when Mrs Di Bello would run out of things to say.

Unfortunately, the woman needed no encouragement to carry on. "A week ago, they passed a jewellery shop and Dora saw a beautiful bracelet. The price was outrageous, and she did not think for a moment… she simply found it beautiful. The next morning, Duccio gave me a little box and asked me to let Dora find it with her breakfast. Oh, I've never seen a man more in love…"

The gods were determined to punish Giò further. Not only did she have a broken heart, not only had she called off her forthcoming wedding after an engagement of 10 years, not only was she leaving behind all she had built, but she was supposed to listen to this nauseating love story. Mrs Di Bello was one of those people who merely needed the sight of two ears to tell all she had to tell. She noticed none of the younger woman's hurt and carried on pitilessly.

"I can't wait for them to have kids."

"Do they plan to have any? Is Duccio happy with that?" For the first time, Giò was asking questions.

"Sure they do. Dora wants to have a couple of children if God will bless her."

"And Duccio?" Giò put her book down,

stubbornly determined to find a fault with the perfect couple.

"Oh, he is such a considerate man. He said pregnancy is so demanding on a woman that he will never put Dora under pressure. When she feels she's ready…"

"Maybe he is so understanding because he does not want any kids." *At least I can instil some doubt in her mind,* Giò thought maliciously, but Mrs Di Bello's faith was unshaken.

"Oh no, he says he'd love to be a father, but that he will let Dora choose when."

This was too much. Duccio had to be a man with no backbone, just living for his wife. He was rich; he was considerate; he was the kind of man who did not exist.

"I will show you a picture of the two, as it must seem like you know them by now." Before Giò could say anything, Mrs Di Bello had pulled out her mobile to show her the ideal couple. He looked like Prince Charming (Giò had hoped he would be repulsive) and she was pretty. Not a stunning beauty, but she had an expressive, determined little face, and she certainly knew how to use make-up.

"He's so much in love with her."

Giò raised her chin in the air. Had Agnese, her sister, been there, she would have recognised that the gesture meant trouble. Giò's lips stretched into a grin, her jaw jutting forward as if to direct the incoming storm, and most telling of all, a flash passed through her eyes, turning them from deep green to a feline yellow.

She spoke in a cold voice. "Do you think so? I hope not. Because, as the entire world knows, when a man acts like that, when he shows nothing but blind devotion, he is only doing it to reassure the bride, her family and close friends that they are living the perfect dream." Her voice rose steadily. "Beware! It's only a smokescreen to hide all kinds of treacherous things. Do you believe he hasn't got a lover? That he is not painting this cutest of family pictures so he can enjoy his misdemeanours in peace? You cannot be that naïve. If I were you, I would advise my daughter to keep her eyes wide open, to get out of this fairy tale mood, and check his mobile whenever she gets a chance. If she finds nothing incriminating, he's probably got another phone."

Mrs Di Bello stared at her as if Giò was possessed. She tried to get a few words in edgeways, but the younger woman was on a roll. Giò's voice rose so much that all the passengers in the carriage started to listen in. Two women, though clearly surprised at Giò's audacity, were nodding in approval.

"By the way, did I say *a* lover? If I did, I didn't mean there would only be one. For the scoundrel to behave so meekly, to give your daughter all that you mentioned, surely he has more than one. Tell your daughter not to waste her time on shop windows, but to check where the rest of the money goes. What does he do when he is absent? For how long is he away? Is it really for work? Because, you see," and at this point, Giò stretched out her arm, palm raised to silence her horrified companion, "every time a man comes in with a present, you can be sure he's done something bad. Every flower, every box of chocolates is a bad sign, but jewellery is the worst sign of all. Every sugary message is to sweeten up your daughter when he's just left the arms of another woman!"

Mrs Di Bello had been trying to interrupt, but now she was silent, afraid that the lunatic opposite her might harm her. She had been confiding in this madwoman, telling her all about her lovely daughter for almost two hours. Grabbing her bags, Mrs Di Bello tried to get up and go, but Giò had not finished yet. She stood up and barred the older woman's way.

"And, you didn't ask a single thing of me. You spoke for two hours about your silly daughter and her happiest of weddings. Did you stop for a second to think whether the woman in front of you had also been about to get married? Yes, in a month's time. And did you stop to think that maybe something had gone terribly wrong?" Here, Giò had to pause and draw breath, her eyes watery. But her anger was such that she held back the tears that had never come when she'd wanted them.

"Have you wondered if maybe this silent lady," and she gestured towards the pale woman sitting across the aisle, close to the opposite window, "has suffered at the hands of a bastard pretending to be the best man ever?"

The pale woman nodded vigorously in approval, and so did a few other women in the carriage.

"That's so terribly selfish of you, to think only of your own – fake – happiness and forget the misery of thousands of women around you."

The whole compartment burst into loud applause. Giò had not realised there were so many women who'd had to endure Mrs Di Bello's tales too. Somebody from behind her shouted, "Well said, sister."

Finally, all her energy left her, and she dropped back in her seat, trembling with both rage and pain. Mrs Di Bello was free to run away with her heavy luggage, searching for a safe place in another carriage. Maybe this time, she would be more careful about what she said. That is, if she said anything at all.

Giò did not have much time to think. Once the train had passed through the last tunnel, the view opened up to reveal the coastline that was so familiar to her. 10 minutes later, it arrived at Sapri station and her heartbeat quickened. The regional train was waiting on the opposite platform.

She took the first available seat next to a window, knowing full well that Mrs Di Bello would be careful to avoid entering the same carriage. The train started and her eyes gazed at the most dramatic coastline she had ever seen, despite her many wanderings. High, rocky mountains in unique pinkish colours loomed like walls, plunging down into the sea beneath. A few pine forests and scattered clumps of vegetation faced the Policastro Gulf, watched over by the majestic profile of Mount Bulgheria. The Statue of Christ the

Redeemer, the symbol and protector of her seaside town, Maratea, was not yet in sight, but a few more tunnels and she would be home.

~

"AUNTIEEE!" A LITTLE RED-HAIRED girl with two pigtails ran at full speed along the platform and dived into Giò's arms. They squeezed each other tightly.

"I thought you wouldn't recognise me," Giò said, laughing.

"I did, and I spotted you long before all the others." Lilia proudly indicated the rest of the family, who were coming along the platform behind her.

"They're all here? My goodness."

"When Mum said she was coming, we all said we'd come too. Uncle Valerio could not make it, though, he is very busy," Lilia explained.

Luca, Lilia's brother, reached them. He was 12 by now and wanted to uphold a certain image, but when his auntie twinkled at him, he just had to hug her. It wasn't bad to be a kid every now and then.

"Granny!" Giò shouted.

"My little child!" Only Granny could call her that. In her arms, Giò recognised the familiar perfume of violets and face powder that had comforted her since childhood. Granny had pure white wavy hair, with a few rebel bangs hanging around her heart-shaped face, a nicely pointed chin and lively grey eyes, and she was as thin as her granddaughter.

"Such a stupid man. How could he hurt my little flower?" Granny added, caressing Giò's face.

"Granny, you promised!" Agnese chastised her. "Not here, not now."

Granny sighed; Giò tried to smile.

"And I'd say she's more of a cactus than a flower, anyway."

Giò pretended to be shocked, and Lilia laughed.

"You're just as skinny as ever. Not even the UK could give you a few curves." Agnese continued looking at her sister's slender figure and compared it with her own plumpness, but the arms that closed around Giò spoke of softness, understanding, happiness finally to be able to comfort her in person rather than over a Skype call.

"Can I welcome my sister-in-law?" asked Nando. Pulling all the others away, he hugged Giò in his massive arms. "I've only got this moment, you see," he added, looking at the rest of the family. "Give them five minutes, and she and her sister will be teasing me as usual."

They all laughed.

"Granny has made some delicious spaghetti alle vongole. For the second course, we're having stuffed squid," Lilia giggled.

"And I'm sure there will be dessert from Panza," Luca added. Family meals were a serious thing here in Southern Italy.

"Is this all the luggage you have?" asked Nando, lifting Giò's bag. It was large, but still only a single bag.

"A courier will deliver six boxes of stuff during the week. All the rest I left in a storage unit. I've rented the space for three months with the possibility of renewal. I'll see to that."

"What a waste of money. This time you're here to stay!" Granny said.

Agnese stared at her with such intensity that the 80-year-old lady fell silent, which was unusual for her.

"Was your journey OK?" Agnese changed the subject.

"I'd rather answer another question." Giò laughed guiltily, feeling suddenly ashamed of what she had done.

"Why, Auntie?" asked Lilia.

"Let's say I had a very chatty companion, and maybe I overdid it in order to keep her quiet!" Giò raised her brows comically until they almost reached her hairline. Everyone laughed, both at her funny face and because they knew all about her temper.

DINNER WAS A FAMILY OCCASION, and was great fun, with Agnese and Granny competing to refill Giò's dishes as she finished each course. They were all laughing and joking, recalling childhood memories, and Giò realised how stupid she had been. Dorian had not liked her family, nor Maratea.

"It's a good place for a day trip, but my goodness, I'd go out of my mind if I were to hang around here for longer than 24 hours," he used to say. So she had not gone home for the last few Christmases, as she used to. She knew her family had felt a mixture of disappointment and relief whenever she'd announced she would visit them, but no, Dorian could not make it.

Her family had never liked Dorian, she was positive about that, but they had always welcomed him so as not to hurt her. Well, except for Granny. Every now and then, a few harsh words would come out of her mouth, and Agnese would try to justify them.

"She's just protective; she's afraid he might not make you happy."

Or had Agnese been speaking her own mind too? None of this mattered any longer. In the future, no man would ever keep Giò away from her family, no matter what.

"I want to visit Sapri tomorrow morning. Should I use the train since the road is closed?" Giò asked while helping her sister to tidy up the kitchen.

"You said you wanted to stop at Mum and Dad's, so you'd be better off driving. Once you've finished there, park where they closed the road, just above the cemetery. You catch the bus to Sapri on the other side. I've left a timetable on your desk."

"Can I walk across the closed road?"

"Technically you can't, but everyone does, especially the folks in Acquafredda. There are too few trains. If you want company, we could go together on Sunday."

"No, I need some time alone. I also need a new SIM card. I'll be fine."

Giò went up to the attic above her sister's house. The same main doorway on the street led to three independent apartments: Granny lived on the ground floor, Agnese on the first floor. The second floor was a two-room attic with a sunny terrace. Agnese used to rent it to tourists, but it was to be Giò's space till she decided what to do next.

"You should live here forever," Lilia had said.

From her terrace, Giò could see a few lights from the fishermen's boats out at sea. Putting on a shawl, because on a September night the temperature could drop in Maratea, she went out to smell the fresh air. The silence was absolute. The air was sweet. She was home.

2

ROCKFALLS AND LIPSTICKS

The next morning, the slim figure of Elena Errico hurried across the cobblestones, despite her high heels. Her boss's wife, Mrs Rivello, had called her the night before; Mrs Rivello didn't feel well, but she needed to hand in some documents to the school office. The closed road was a pain; it meant Elena leaving Mrs Rivello's car in Acquafredda and taking the bus to Sapri. Better get it over with as soon as possible.

She got in the car and drove along the state road, passing through Cersuta. Here the coastline was particularly wild and the houses were few, mostly hidden by the vegetation. The rock walls plunged into the sea from a vertiginous height, making it an area of outstanding natural beauty in any weather. Maybe soon, she would be able to buy a house here. Her own house. Yes, later she would meet him, and she would talk to him. Well, it would be more of a reminder than a talk.

She reached Acquafredda, went through the rocky tunnel and stopped the car in front of the closed road. On the left-hand side there was a parking space containing three cars. The area on the right had to be left free for work vehicles and staff. But Mrs Rivello, who went to Sapri almost every morning, had her own parking space on that side. After all, it was a partner firm of Mr Rivello's company that had been awarded the road securing works.

Today there were no workers, though. Following the geotechnical site assessment, the firm was waiting for the last of the bureaucratic procedures to be completed. Then work would start on rock scaling: removing loose rocks from the slope, laying new catch fences to intercept rockfalls, cleaning the road, and finally repairing it.

A small niche on the right, half hidden by the vegetation, was free for Mrs Rivello's car. Elena parked, switched off the engine and searched for her bag on the passenger seat to check she had everything. She had not even removed her seatbelt when a movement from the mountain above startled her. By instinct, her hand grasped the door handle, but the seatbelt held her captive. She could not escape.

Elena did not have time to think: she just felt adrenaline bursting through her body. Could it even be called pain? A huge rock had fallen on the top of Mrs Rivello's car and crushed the life out of her.

WHEN GIÒ GOT UP THAT MORNING,

she went out onto the terrace, the beauty of the gulf overwhelming her. *I had paradise at my fingertips, yet I decided to leave it behind. How baffling!*

Agnese had left some milk in the fridge and a couple of freshly baked cornetti in a food bag on the table. Giò prepared the Moka pot for the espresso, taking the coffee jar from the fridge – a trick many Italians use to preserve the coffee aroma – and opening it. The smell of ground coffee permeated the air, reminding her of childhood when she went with her mother to the Bottega del Caffé, where a deep velvety aroma would envelop them. They would choose their favourite variety of coffee beans, and the severe man who served them every time would grind them. Giò would wait behind, and the severe man would finally smile and offer her a chocolate candy. Just one – Mum would not approve of more – but she could still recall the nutty taste of that gianduiotto.

She filled up the small Moka pot with water, just up to the valve, gently pressed the black powder in the filter, and tightened it closed. She switched on the gas and waited to hear the familiar gurgle, smell the scent of freshly made espresso saturating the air...

How sensory everything was in Italy. Things she would not even have noticed in the continuous rush of London were filling her up with little pleasures. She loved the UK and its funny, stubborn-but-gentle inhabitants, but there were huge differences between the two countries. Britons were practical people with a deep sense of civility. Italy, particularly Southern Italy, was the region of disorder; but also of small things, where even the preparation of coffee mattered.

And Giò had not finished yet. She warmed up the milk, happy to notice that Agnese had not forgotten to equip the kitchen with a milk frother. Giò loved her caffellatte to be as similar as possible to the drink she enjoyed in coffee bars. She had thought about going to the café in the main square, but if she did that, she would meet people. They would ask about her forthcoming wedding, or maybe they would already know it had been called off and would want to know all the details, all the hows and whys. There was no room for British discretion in Maratea; nobody would pretend not to know, or not to want to know. Nobody would be discussing the weather with her when they knew she had something far more juicy to tell. And she was not ready to talk about her failed relationship. Not yet.

Giò had a plan for the day: she needed to go to Sapri to get an Italian SIM for her mobile. She'd stay in Maratea at least till Christmas, and she needed to make local phone calls. Maybe she'd pitch articles to a few magazines. For too many years, her longest stays in Italy had been... well, very short.

This will never happen again!

GIÒ STARTED AGNESE'S CAR. THE

coast was shining with beauty and she had to stop the vehicle a couple of times to take it all in. The road was more than 100 metres above the sea: on one side, the powerful rock walls, on the other, the Mediterranean where the currents created stripes in all shades of blue, from turquoise to deep indigo. A gentle breeze was blowing through the car window, sweeping away thoughts that had been lingering in her mind. She felt light and full of desire to live her life, see what it was up to despite all the recent heartache.

Once in Acquafredda, Giò left the state road to take the little street leading to her parents' home. Agnese had wanted to come with her, as she feared her sister might be eaten up by nostalgia. As soon as Giò saw the garden, well attended by Olivo, the faithful gardener and family friend, her heart beat faster.

She left the car outside, pushed the iron gate, and was immediately submerged in a sea of memories: the trees she, Agnese and their brother Valerio used to climb.

She caressed the carob tree that had so many branches and gentle inclines, it made their job easy. Basil and geraniums filled a few pots under the front porch where, May to October, the family would consume most of their meals. She remembered her father busy at the barbecue, her mother teasing him for being too slow, but to this day, Giò hadn't eaten a barbecued fish as good as the ones Dad cooked.

"You need to wait for the coals to cool down a bit," he'd say. "A gentle heat, that's what we need." Then, seeing his family's mouths watering, he would move a few coals aside and toast some bread. His bruschette were full of personality – an unexpected herb, the sweetest tomatoes, the tastiest olives, or some other magic ingredient. Theirs had been such a happy family till tragedy had struck. A truck driver fell asleep at the wheel, swerving onto the wrong side of the road into the path of the oncoming car. Nothing Dad could do. When the ambulance had arrived, Giò's parents were already dead.

Giò inserted the key in the lock and pushed the door open. The sun was filtering through the windows of a light and cheerful living room. Mum, even in a time when dark colours were fashionable, had loved whites. She had picked bright white furniture to contrast with a few dark blue pieces, such as the cupboard and a couple of armchairs close to the fireplace.

Giò and her siblings had agreed to rent the house out during the summer months. It had been a painful but necessary decision, the only way to pay the bills and taxes. But Agnese had made sure they only played host to families and friends of friends. She made it clear it was a family home, not just another rental property, and the guests had taken good care of it.

Giò sat on the sofa and instinctively opened the drawer in the small table in front of her. There it was, the family album she and Agnese had created for their parents' twenty-fifth wedding anniversary. It followed the family story from their great-grandparents to the present day, capturing the things they had done together. She laughed when she remembered the silly jokes and pranks she, Agnese and Valerio had played as kids, while in all honesty she would have enjoyed a good cry. But tears, since the day she had broken off with Dorian, refused to come.

She visited the bedrooms and lingered in her own. On the wall, photos of her still hung: her funny face on her first day at school; climbing up a tree with Valerio; finely dressed (for once) with Agnese when she was eighteen. Her chest of drawers, inherited from her great-grandmother, was a heavy ebony thing – she simply loved the smell of the wood, and that would never change. The drawers were empty, but the familiar smell lingered. On the ancient marble top was a vase of dried flowers, artistically arranged – Agnese's doing for sure.

Giò looked at her watch. Almost a quarter past nine.

My goodness, time has flown.

It was too late for a visit to the cemetery. She'd stop on the way back. She sat in Agnese's car for a while, her pain and anger in pause mode. After the long days and sleepless nights, the healing process had finally started.

THE CAR PARK ON THE LEFT-HAND side of the road still had a couple of empty spaces. Giò took her bag and locked the car. The bus would arrive on the other side of the closed road in about 15 minutes – good timing. But could she buy a ticket on the bus? Or was she supposed to have one already?

The other parked cars were empty; nobody she could ask. She had almost reached the closed-road barrier when she saw a car half hidden in the vegetation on the right-hand side of the road. Maybe it too was empty, but she could still give it a try.

As she went closer, her eyes were

caught by something grotesque. The parked car had been smashed by a falling rock, which was still sitting on its crushed roof. How weird! Surely the road safety technicians had done a thorough inspection on this area.

Only when she was next to the car did she realise it wasn't empty. An arm was hanging out of the window; she saw the lacquered nails, the little silver watch around the thin wrist. Someone had been trapped in the car when the rock fell and was never going to walk away.

Like an automaton, Giò rang 112 to alert the emergency services.

SHE WAS NOT ALONE FOR LONG. MR Faraco, the engineer responsible for the site inspection, was the first to arrive. Not only did he live close by in Acquafredda, he was also visibly worried. And incredulous. The thin moustache on his otherwise clean-shaven face was shaking.

"We cannot do anything for the poor woman, so we'd better keep away from the area in case other rocks should fall."

The gently spoken engineer somehow calmed Giò, despite clearly being in shock himself.

"What an awful death! Poor woman, and her poor husband," he commented. "This is Mrs Rivello's car. For years, there has been a problem with rocks falling on State Road 18, but there has never been a victim."

Giò thought about the large statue of Christ the Redeemer that embraced the Maratea Gulf. Perhaps the locals thought that would protect them from what ANAS (the public company responsible for road maintenance and security in Italy) could not.

A few minutes later, an ambulance and a carabinieri car arrived, soon followed by an assistance truck from Maratea. A tanned, muscular maresciallo approached them.

"Was it you who found the smashed car

and called us?" he demanded, looking over Giò's head.

"Yes, it was me."

"I'm Maresciallo Mauro Mangiaboschi and I need you to answer a few questions. What's your name and where do you live?"

Giò answered.

"What time was it when you found the car?"

She took out her mobile and checked her outgoing calls. "I phoned the carabinieri at 9.32, immediately after finding the body. Well, one or two minutes later, I mean."

"What time did you arrive here? Do you have a car?"

"Yes, that's my car." Giò pointed. "Actually, it's my sister's car. I do not live here – yet."

"Do you plan to?" asked the maresciallo, looking at her for the first time. Did he think she had nothing better to do with her life than find dead bodies?

"I might. I've yet to decide."

The carabiniere harrumphed

contemptuously. "So what time did you arrive?"

"Well, when I parked the car, I looked at my watch to make sure I was in time for the bus and it was 9.27." She went on, reporting all that had happened, and then concluded, "When I saw the woman's arm hanging from the car window, I knew the driver must have been killed on the spot."

"Do you think the rock had already fallen when you arrived?"

"Absolutely. Mind you, I had the radio on, but I keep the volume low. I think the noise of the rock falling must have been tremendous." She indicated towards the huge boulder still sitting on the car.

"Do you know who the driver was?"

"Mr Faraco recognised her."

"I believe the car belongs to Mrs Camilla Rivello," the engineer said. "And I'm afraid it's Camilla inside."

"Yes," confirmed a second carabiniere, emerging from behind the maresciallo and speaking for the first time, "we've just confirmed the registration number, and it's definitely her car. The men at the station in Maratea are going to inform her husband."

"What an awful death!" repeated Mr Faraco in a murmur, his eyes scanning the mountains. "It has never happened before, despite the number of falling rocks."

The maresciallo clearly knew the engineer. "And you, Franco, were in charge of the closure of the road?"

"Yes, my team and I did the site assessment. I've been up there personally, and I am sure there was no danger to this side of the road. We checked the mountain square metre by square metre."

"I need to speak to *you*," the maresciallo said pointedly to Mr Faraco, which Giò took to mean he didn't want her to listen. "I would be grateful if you would wait for us a few more minutes," he added to her. "But we need to evacuate this area, so you can park at the cemetery. It will be safer there."

"OK, I'll wait for you."

"Maresciallo, should I accompany her?"

the brigadiere murmured, his short, chubby figure contrasting with his tall, fit superior. "I don't think she should drive."

The maresciallo reluctantly agreed. "But be back immediately!" he roared.

It was then that Giò realised she was shaking. It took her a while to find her keys in her bag and hand them to the brigadiere, and then she sank into the car's passenger seat, relieved to sit down.

"I'm Paolo," the carabiniere said shyly. "I know your sister, Agnese. Actually, I am a customer at her perfumery. Great place." As they drove the few hundred metres to the cemetery, he added, "I think the engineer and technicians who did the assessment are in for a tough time."

They had barely arrived when Paolo got a call on his mobile, summoning him back to the scene of the accident. Photos needed to be taken, and the owners of the other three parked cars had to be tracked down and asked to remove their vehicles, along with telling the carabinieri what they had noticed that morning.

"Shall I tell Miss Brando she can go?" Paolo asked thoughtfully. "We've already sort of questioned her, and she lives in Maratea, anyway."

The answer was positive.

"Now, Giò," Paolo said, "stay here longer to calm down if you need to, then when you feel you're OK, go home carefully. Do you think you can manage it?"

"I believe I'm already better."

"Just give me your mobile number, in case we need to question you."

"Of course."

GIÒ DROVE BACK TO MARATEA AND went directly to her sister's perfumery, hidden in one of the many little streets off the Town Hall Square. She was badly in need of the comfort only her family could give.

Agnese was busy with a customer, but as soon as she saw her sister's pale face, she raised her brows in alarm and gave Giò a "What's-happened?" look. Giò sat down in one of the two armchairs close to a small white book cabinet. She had no intention of reading anything, instead letting the comforting scent of the perfumery calm her and taking pleasure in looking around.

It was an unusual perfumery; Agnese kept a few antique cabinets, along with neat white shelving and colourful rustic cupboards all stocked with lines of perfume bottles in all shapes and sizes. The perfumes were accompanied by soaps, toiletries and other cosmetics, and a turquoise cupboard displayed scented candles, the doors open to encourage visitors to try the testers.

There were also a few objects from around the world on display, some of which Giò had bought during her travels. Wooden masks from Africa; jewellery from Morocco; lanterns and lamps from Sweden. Agnese loved the Swedes' talent for creating a cosy atmosphere at night.

And it was not just about lanterns, but also colourful pillows and small blankets, ideal for curling up to read on an armchair. For summer, Agnese sold a collection of colourful flip-flops from Spain, while in winter she opted for a selection of woollen slippers from Denmark.

Agnese was still with her customer, who seemed to be finding it difficult to make up her mind about what she wanted. Impatient to speak to her sister, Agnese went from sweet and companionable to wearing her determined look, her voice becoming firmer and her eyes fixed on the customer. She had to take control, otherwise the undecided lady could have spent the next hour contemplating all the shades of pink lipstick in the shop, despite Agnese having found her perfect match within a couple of minutes of her entering the perfumery.

"But don't you think, dear, that the one up there is a slightly warmer shade?" the lady asked, pointing towards a group of lipsticks behind the counter.

"No, I don't think so." Agnese reached for the lipstick she'd indicated and showed it to her. "It has a peach tone which I frankly doubt would suit you."

"But the one beside it...?"

"You have already made the perfect choice."

"Because, you see, I'm so used to coral, and the idea of pink scares me a little. Maybe I should return to my familiar colours; shall we have a look?"

"There are times when we need to be daring. If we do not dare with a lipstick, what's left?" Agnese smiled to sweeten her words and added, "That's 15 Euros. An excellent choice."

"Oh... if I do not dare with a lipstick... what's left?" The undecided lady chuckled, handing Agnese the money. "Just one last question: do you think I can continue using coral every now and then?"

"You will use pink when you feel daring and coral when you don't."

"Right, dear. You really are precious. Goodbye."

"Goodbye," said Agnese, finally turning towards her sister. "Oh my goodness, if she can spend hours choosing a lipstick, I wonder how she copes with the bigger problems in life. So what's happened to you? Did Dorian call you?"

"Dorian? Oh no, it's nothing to do with him at all. I just happened to find Mrs Rivello crushed to death under a rock."

And in a rush, Giò told Agnese all that had happened. Agnese put the 'Back Soon' sign on the shop door.

"You need a strong cup of coffee. Let's go to Iannini's bar."

3

WHO WAS THERE?

They reached a small bar not far from the shop. By the time they had seated themselves at one of the tables outside, rumours had already spread. It was amazing how fast news could travel in the little community. People were animated, discussing safety and the old road.

"Poor Mrs Rivello – she definitely wasn't an easy person to deal with, but what a shame she died in such a way."

"God knows when they will open the road again. It will be a pretty sad autumn for the hotels."

"At least we're at the end of September, and they were full in August."

"It will be a tough time for Franco Faraco. Had he closed the road a mere 10 metres further back, Mrs Rivello would still be alive. How could he not have recognised the risks?"

"That is strange, he is usually pretty meticulous. But after the closure, there were days of heavy rain. You cannot check the whole mountain!"

"The carabinieri are interrogating Mr Faraco; they might arrest him."

"How about Mr Rivello? I think they rang him first thing, poor man."

At that moment, Sebastiano, an employee at the municipality of Maratea, brought fresh news.

"It wasn't Mrs Rivello. Elena Errico was driving the car."

Everyone present almost gave a collective sigh of relief, before realising that a life had been crushed away all the same.

"Apparently," Sebastiano continued, his

tone grave despite him clearly being happy to be the centre of attention, "Mrs Rivello had asked Elena to go to Sapri in her place, and use her car. This is why the carabinieri thought it was her."

"Elena was too young to die... what a tragedy!"

"I wonder if Mrs Rivello will feel guilty or grateful to be alive."

"Most likely both."

"I don't think so, she's not the kind who feels guilty about a subordinate. Actually, it will probably confirm her own high opinion of herself: not even rocks dare annoy her."

This bitter comment lingered in the air for much longer than the others. There were some silent nods.

"Who was Elena?" Giò asked Agnese, the first words she'd spoken since they had reached the café. Till then, they had just been listening; you couldn't call it eavesdropping as it was a collective discussion.

"Elena is... was Mr Rivello's secretary.

She helped him on all fronts, and she occasionally ran errands for his wife too. What a shame!"

"It was you who found her?" Sebastiano asked, moving towards Giò's table.

"Yeah," she replied, surprised that he already knew that detail.

"Not a pretty sight, I guess."

"There was not much to see."

The crushed car under the rock materialised in front of her eyes: the lifeless arm hanging from the broken window; a watch around the wrist; the red fingernails...

"The carabinieri are going to question Carlo and Andrea," Sebastiano said. "It seems they parked their cars across the road before Elena arrived. But I am sure they saw nothing, otherwise they would have called for help."

"I guess it's carabinieri procedure."

When Giò had finished her tea, the two sisters headed back to the shop.

"How old was Elena?" asked Giò. "Did you know her?"

"Of course I knew her. We were not friends, just acquaintances. She was 38, like you. You were in the same year at high school. Different classes, though."

Giò thought for a while. "I think I remember her. She was a pretty brunette, rather popular with the boys. We were never close – nothing in common. But when I think of how she passed away…"

"Oh my goodness, it could have been you!" Agnese gasped, bringing her hands to her cheeks, her mouth half open in shock. Giò shivered.

"I hadn't thought of that."

"We'd better call on Granny. She knew you were going to Sapri, and as news spreads fast here, I don't want her to get worried."

Agnese's mobile rang; it was Nando. Had she heard? Had Giò gone to Sapri? She reassured him that Giò was safe and sound with her as they arrived at the perfumery.

A young girl was waiting outside. Giò said to her sister, "You'd better go in, your customers are waiting for you. I'll let Granny know I'm fine, then wait for you at home. See you at lunchtime."

"Get some rest, too. You've had a nasty shock."

"I will."

"GOOD MORNING, DEAR, SORRY TO have kept you waiting," Agnese said, searching for her keys and opening the door.

"Not at all," said the girl. Wearing her brown hair short with bangs, she was a little thing, but was so slim, she looked taller than she was. She had dreamy chestnut eyes, but there was something strong-willed in the set of her jaw.

As they entered the perfumery, Agnese switched on the lights and asked her, "What can I do for you?"

"Would you mind if I have a look around?"

"You can do more than that." Agnese handed her a few paper strips. "You can use these *touches* to spray a few perfumes and find your perfect match, if you like."

"I love perfumes, they take you away to other places," the girl replied, taking the *touches*.

"That's very true. Do you have a favourite?"

"Quite a few, but I've heard you can advise people on the perfume that's best for them. Do you think one should stick to a single perfume forever?"

"Not at all. There's a right perfume for each moment of our lives. It's similar to music: having a favourite song doesn't mean that you won't listen to any others."

"One should always try new things?"

"Of course, there might be a perfume that will remain your favourite for a lifetime. But I always suggest sticking to the old ones while searching for more. Perfumes are a thing of beauty, so it would be a pity to deny yourself the pleasure of smelling and discovering new sensations."

The girl looked at her. "I wonder what my perfect perfume would be right now."

"I can help you find it, but have a little experiment on your own first. Then we will try to find the one for you."

Agnese glanced at the ebony table. She rarely offered her perfume session so quickly, but today she had a hunch. She felt, beyond any doubt, that the girl needed her help, and she was happy to oblige. The two rarely combined!

"By the way, I'm Agnese."

"Nice to meet you, I'm Cabiria."

I'm Cabiria and I'm so sad, Agnese thought. How incredible for a young girl, no older than her mid-twenties, to have a shroud of unhappiness around her. And it was something much deeper and more meaningful than the superficial dissatisfaction of some of Agnese's richer customers.

Cabiria went around the shop, looking at and handling soaps and cosmetics, but most of her attention was on the perfumes. She sprayed, she sniffed, she smiled, she thought. Some she discarded, some *touches* she kept with her as a reminder of what she liked.

When Agnese called her over, Cabiria started as if she had been in a dream. Agnese had put the 'closed' sign on the shop door, and Cabiria took a seat in front of her at her table in a little alcove.

"I don't know many of the brands you have here, but I loved these three most of all," and Cabiria handed her three *touches*. Agnese smelled them, and then carefully put 12 different candles on the table.

"Please smell each of them. Don't think too much, just tell me which smell you'd love to have around you."

Cabiria lifted the candles to her nose one by one, squeezing her eyes every time she smelled something she liked. She selected three, and Agnese took all the others away.

"Which one is your favourite? Not for a lifetime, just now. Let go of your rational thoughts. Close your eyes and tell me..."

Cabiria sniffed the three candles again, then pointed to the one she liked the most. It had an evocative dark balsamic scent. Agnese knew it to be agarwood.

She acknowledged that choice, took the candles away and, from a drawer behind her, selected eight bottles, placing them on the table one by one. In each, she dipped a long, thin paper *touche*, and then placed it in front of the corresponding bottle.

"Smell each one and tell me which you prefer."

Cabiria, fascinated by the process, made her choice quickly.

Agnese repeated the exercise with four new bottles, and when they'd finished, she said, "Oriental woody, incense and cardamom, but also saffron and oud." She picked up a square panel, which represented one of the olfactory families she'd named with perfumes listed in circles down one side. It was the one corresponding to 'oriental woody', and she put it face down on the table.

"Life is forged by our will, the choices we make, but also by an element of chance." She handed Cabiria a small wooden spinning top, painted in lively coloured stripes, and asked her to launch it across the panel. Cabiria twirled the wooden stem using her thin fingers. When it stopped, Agnese put a pin in its position, turned the wooden panel face up and read aloud, "Dzongkha!".

I knew, she thought. She was always thrilled when the perfume game went the way her instinct had directed her; it proved to her that there was a right perfume for the right person at the right time.

"I'm going to fetch you two perfume samples. You're free to have a look around in the meantime," Agnese said, leaving the alcove. Cabiria's attention was drawn to the white book cabinet, attracted by a title. Pulling the book from the shelf, she looked at the cover, browsed a few pages, and then started to read. When Agnese came back, she found the girl sitting in the armchair, so absorbed in her reading that she decided not to interrupt her.

Around 20 minutes later, Cabiria rose from the armchair, the book still in her hands. Agnese was changing the jewellery on display on some of her favourite head mannequins.

"So you said you have two perfumes for me?" Cabiria asked.

"Yes, I've prepared a couple of samples. One is called Io, Myself. I think you know who you are, but you need to find the strength to assert it. Or maybe you need to be more aware that who you are matters, to you and to the people you love. The second one is Dzongkha! I can't explain why this one, but it's a bright and beautiful oriental. By the way, may I ask you what book you are reading?"

Cabiria turned the cover round so Agnese could see it. Agnese laughed.

"Oh, the excellent *Eat, Pray, Love*. Have you read it before, or seen the movie?"

Cabiria shook her head. "No, I've never

heard of it," she said, then added swiftly, "Do you think one can feel desperate, even if one has no real reason to?"

"Of course."

"How is that possible?" Cabiria asked, but Agnese decided not to answer. She wanted Cabiria to carry on. "I love my family. I've just taken my engineering degree, and I am going to study for a Master's in Milan. Dad is so proud of me, but I... I don't want to go. But at the same time I don't have another plan, so I can't tell my father, 'I want to do this'. I feel I'm stuck in a life that's not my own. But at the same time, I don't know what I want."

"Is your father pushing you in a direction you don't want to go?"

Cabiria shook her head again. "No, it would be unfair to say that. I've *never* told him I wanted to do something different. Actually, I never thought I *did* want to do something different. It was fine. But this summer, I came back home and for the first time in years, I was completely free. It was then I started to wonder what I'm doing with my life. When I received the news that my application for the Master's had been accepted, I felt nothing but sadness. I can't explain it further."

Agnese asked her smoothly, "Have you fallen in love, maybe?"

"Oh no, it's not that. It's something inside me. But I really don't know what it means. Maybe in Milan I will be OK; maybe it was just that I had such a lazy summer. I used to study all the time and was not prepared for a three-month break…"

Agnese smiled. Indicating the book in Cabiria's hands, she said, "Well our friend Miss Gilbert would say some 'Big Magic' has just occurred. You picked up the right book for you, and two perfumes to go with it. When is your Master's study starting?"

"In three weeks' time."

"I'm sure you're a fast reader. Use Io Myself for going out, and Dzongkha! when you're by yourself."

"Have you always lived here?"

"Yes, I have."

"It looks like you've seen a lot. You're different from other people in Maratea."

Agnese laughed. "My sister has travelled the world for me. But you get to know a lot of people very well if you live in a small village like this."

AT THAT MOMENT, SOMEBODY knocked on the closed door rather insistently. As Agnese opened the door to let Cabiria out, Mrs Lavecchia stalked in. She wore her typical sulky expression.

"Good morning," said Agnese.

"What time does this shop open?" the other asked sternly.

"I was giving a private session, and we have just finished."

"You gave me the wrong face cream."

"Why? What happened?" asked Agnese in alarm.

"Nothing. That's the problem. I spend all this money and get nothing out of it."

She touched her cheek as if to make her point.

Mrs Lavecchia was a beautiful, rich woman, and like most of Agnese's beautiful and rich customers, she was eternally dissatisfied.

"But your skin looks perfect."

"Hah, it looks dull. I thought that buying that very expensive cream you suggested would help. But I look just the same. I wish I had not followed your advice and had gone to the supermarket to buy something cheaper instead."

"Your skin looks fine to me, but you would definitely see a decline in its glowing appearance if you were to use cheaper products. We could add a few beauty routines if you would tell me what exactly you'd like and what you're not happy with."

Mrs Lavecchia pointed to one of the images in the shop, showing a beautiful model. "Can't you see the difference? My skin looks dull. Your products aren't good enough. You promise things, but I'm no closer to looking like her." And again, she jabbed her finger at the gorgeous model on the poster.

You're a splendid woman, but you're over 50. How could you have the glow of a 20-year-old? Maybe being a little more cheerful would be your best medicine.

Agnese took a deep breath – best not to voice her thoughts. In Maratea, you could not afford the luxury of speaking your mind to a customer, no matter how impolite they were. They'd soon tell their friends, and friends of friends, and before long everyone would know. With a bad reputation, you'd risk your shop being closed down, and Agnese loved her shop too much for that. Also, it was part of shop ethics: the customer is always right. Her mother had instilled in her that she should always find alternative ways to make her point, but sticking to her ethics was so very hard with customers like Mrs Lavecchia.

She finally answered, forcing a false smile onto her face.

"But that is a picture of a professional model taken by a professional photographer for a worldwide brand. It's been Photoshopped to perfection."

Mrs Lavecchia was unmoved. "Well, you said my skin would be brighter. It isn't. I don't know why I keep coming here."

Agnese wished all her customers were like Cabiria. She got closer to the other woman, inspecting her face.

"Oh brighter, you say. Well I see that your pores are a bit enlarged, and there are quite a few dark spots. I believe you're not using the cleaning system we discussed."

"I'm doing exactly as you said."

"Not every day. Not morning and evening, for sure."

"Well at times I am too tired in the evening."

"But the evening routine is so very important! There is no sense in using a good cream if the skin beneath is not perfectly clean. That is a waste of money."

"But in the morning I always do what you say."

"You should never go to bed with your make-up on."

Mrs Lavecchia looked discomfited, at least for a second.

"Anyway, the skin on my legs is dry. I need a good cream to nourish it."

Agnese approached the shelves and took out two different products, a very expensive one and a cheaper one. She explained the differences between the two.

"Well, I guess I need that," Mrs Lavecchia pointed to the expensive one, "but it costs too much. You should really lower your prices, they are outrageously high."

"You could always buy the cheaper one if you'd like something on a different price level."

"No, I want that one, but I can't pay all that money. What kind of discount do you apply for a loyal customer like me?"

"It's around ten percent." Agnese's weak point was bargaining.

"Ten percent? That's all? I knew I should have gone to Naples, there I receive at least thirty percent. I wonder how you can steal money from people and get away with it."

Agnese wished Mrs Lavecchia would go to Naples instead of visiting her. "I simply can't give you a larger discount, if I want to keep this shop open," she said as graciously as she could, wrapping the cream with another forced smile.

"It's a disgrace the way you work here. You should go to Naples or Rome and learn about customer care. Oh no, I'm not buying this product from you. It would not work anyway. Goodbye."

And Mrs Lavecchia left in a fury, slamming the door behind her.

Agnese sighed. She knew in the next few days, Mr Lavecchia would call into her perfumery to buy the product for his wife – the expensive one. At times, she wished she'd decided to work with her sister, somewhere – anywhere – else on the globe.

4

WE'RE ALL WITNESSES

The carabinieri phoned Giò before lunch. They needed to question her further early that afternoon at the carabinieri station in Fiumicello, one of the seven small villages that made up the municipality of Maratea. Nando and Agnese decided to accompany her.

"Nando, you don't need to come along," said Giò. "I can go with Agnese."

"I'm sure you two can handle an army of carabinieri, but a poor husband might prove useful, if only to drive and park the car."

They were asked to wait in a room next to the reception, where a man in a blue suit and bright paisley silk scarf and a nervous young woman were already sitting. Nando and Agnese greeted the man, and Nando introduced him to Giò.

"Carlo Capello, my sister-in-law, Giò."

"Are you here about poor Elena too?" Carlo asked.

"Giò found her this morning and raised the alarm," Agnese explained.

"Oh, I see. It must have been dreadful." He had a slight Frenchness about the way he pronounced his Rs and a pompous manner – he was obviously rather fond of himself.

"Not as dreadful as it was for Elena, poor thing," Giò replied.

"Have you heard? She was only there by chance." They all nodded. "I guess it's a reminder of how spiteful life can be. Any single moment could be our last. We should never take anything for granted."

Giò wasn't particularly impressed by

Carlo's pearls of wisdom. "And why are you here, Mr Capello?" she asked.

"Please call me Carlo. I parked my car in the vicinity of the accident, early this morning. Elena had not arrived then."

"What time was that?"

"I arrived around 7.15. Sara here," he turned to the girl, who sheepishly greeted them all, "was telling me she arrived 15 to 20 minutes earlier and there were no other cars parked there then. Andrea Aiello parked there a few minutes after me. And then there was you, Giò. What time did you arrive?"

"Much later," Giò said. "Around 9.20ish."

"I wonder if, had you arrived earlier, you could have saved her life. You know I'm a poet and a writer, and circumstances like these stimulate my creativity."

"I confess, I fail to understand how a person's death can enhance creativity," Giò replied drily. Carlo ignored her sceptical tone.

"Death and art have always been deeply linked together."

At that moment, the door opened and Mr and Mrs Rivello emerged, accompanied by Paolo, the young brigadiere. Recognising the two sisters, he nodded lightly at them both, then invited Mr Capello in politely – maybe he was one of Carlo's devoted readers – and asked Giò and Sara to wait.

"Hello, Nando, hello, ladies," Mr Rivello said, shaking their hands and ignoring Sara. "I've heard it was Giò who found poor Elena. And you have just arrived back in Italy – not a good welcome home, I'm afraid."

Mrs Rivello did the same as her husband, greeting Giò and Agnese, and not even acknowledging Sara's presence. Sara took a seat as far from the Rivellos as she could, while Mrs Rivello said to Giò, "I'm not sure you will remember us, but we have known you since you were a child. We see more of Agnese, I guess, but I heard you're back to stay."

Giò needed to get used to people she could hardly remember knowing all about her past, present and future life.

"I've not decided yet, but I will certainly spend a few months here."

"You'll be working with your sister, I guess. That's the good thing about a family business."

"I doubt it. I don't have Agnese's patience, plus I want to carry on with my own work."

"Oh, you're a writer too, if I remember rightly. So you just met our novelist and poet, Carlo."

"I'm not a novelist, I'm afraid." Giò always felt less worthy than other authors, not to mention poets. "I just write travel books."

"Will you be writing a guide about Maratea, then?"

"I don't exactly like writing travel guides." She actually loathed them and avoided them whenever she could, which wasn't as often as she would have liked. "I want to write travel books."

"You will have to explain the difference to me, then. Why don't you come over for a coffee tomorrow afternoon?"

"I'm waiting for my boxes to be delivered; I'm in the busy process of settling in. Maybe in the next few days?" Giò doubted she would want to socialise with this inquisitive woman at all.

"Whenever you want, dear, Agnese has my phone number. Give me a call or just drop in. Well, Raimondo, we should go now."

A few minutes later, the door opened. Carlo came out looking as proud as a peacock, and Paolo asked Giò to come in.

Maresciallo Mangiaboschi was standing up in front of his desk. While asking the same questions he had asked in Acquafredda, he kept walking up and down the room. He looked like a mastiff claiming his territory, with his frowning face and muscular body. The only new question, which the brigadiere managed to squeeze in, was whether she had seen a mobile phone lying around anywhere near the crushed car when she got there.

"No, I did not see a mobile. Why are you asking me that?"

"We're not obliged to explain our questions, Miss Brando," snapped the maresciallo. "Understand that *we* are in charge of the investigation."

A few more questions later she was allowed to leave, by which time it was clear to her the maresciallo did not like her. But then, she did not like him in the least either. Sara was still in the room, as white as a sheet, and her hands were visibly shaking when she took up her bag to follow Paolo. Agnese told Giò that the girl had refused any attempt to engage in conversation, and she and Nando had left her in peace.

When they got into the car, Giò noticed a tall, tanned man walking towards the carabinieri station. He wore no uniform.

"Is that Andrea Aiello?" she asked Agnese.

"Yes, that's him. Isn't he good-looking?"

"Definitely!" Giò concurred as the athletic figure disappeared inside.

"He's OK, I guess," said Nando sulkily, looking at his own belly. The two women just laughed at him.

5

NOT AN ACCIDENT

The following morning, Giò overslept. She'd obviously needed it. To her surprise, she hadn't dreamed of accidents or women crushed under falling rocks; or at least if she had, she couldn't remember.

She opened the balcony door onto her terrace. The sun was shining; the deep blue sea was glittering in the distance. The morning was warm and pleasant; after the erratic British weather, it would take her some time to get used to the fact that good weather was the norm here. She smiled at the thought.

Giò was ready for her latte macchiato

and cornetto when her doorbell rang. Who could it be? She answered the intercom and a harsh voice shouted something she could not understand, so she opened the door and rushed down the stairs.

"Six boxes," a young man, all muscles and sweat, grumbled. "Sign here, please."

"Aren't you taking them upstairs?"

"Nope, we're paid to deliver them to the door."

She looked at the large, heavy boxes in despair.

"I'll tip you for it."

"I don't have much time." The courier put away the papers she had signed, but he was still looking at her.

"Please." She smiled her sweetest smile and wished she could be as alluring as her sister. "My purse is upstairs," she added. Better to use that temptation rather than relying on her feminine charms.

He followed her upstairs with the first box, but instead of going back downstairs, he stayed where he was, his big arms folded over his chest, and stared at her. He obviously wanted to see the money before he decided if it was worth bringing the other five boxes upstairs.

Will five Euros do? she wondered. *Or will the guy leave me to get on with it alone? Better make it 10. Gosh!* Agnese wouldn't approve, but Giò would not take the risk. The courier took the banknote with evident satisfaction, and in fewer than five minutes, the other five boxes were upstairs.

Should she open them now? They would fill the house with UK memories, even though she had had the good sense not to throw in pictures or souvenirs that would evoke painful recollections. She decided she would take out her books and clothes. Picking up a pair of scissors, she made a start.

In the first box were a few files and documents. She needed these for work as they included her contract for her next book, her notes and part of the research she had done. She was fond of her laptop and digital files, but she still printed out the most important documents. She loved underlining text with coloured pencils and jotting down her notes in ink.

As she'd suspected, most of her clothes were too warm for Maratea's weather. She put them in the wardrobe and would consider which ones to give up and which to keep later. Then it was the turn of her CDs. Each of them held a memory of her past life: the soundtrack from a French movie she had watched with Dorian; the Coldplay CD they had listened to during their holiday in the Azores islands, when she had felt like she was living a romantic dream and nurtured hopes of a life together; the Albert Hall Christmas concert, when she had been missing home so badly, but had kept smiling at him. She shook her head. No, she would not look at each one, just find them a place somewhere in the living room.

The bookshelves filled up quickly. Then she moved on to a few framed pictures. Not a single one with Dorian – thank God, she had got rid of those – just her nephew and niece when they were babies, a portrait of Granny, and a few shots of her parents. Then it was the turn of the larger prints she'd have to frame: landscapes, especially from Scotland, a country she loved deeply.

When she had finished with the second box, she decided she deserved a reward. She summoned up enough courage to go to the main square and enjoy a cup of cappuccino as she used to, although she took a book with her to hide herself from prying eyes. In the second half of September, tourists were few, but there was still the chitchat of the locals, as garrulous as the cicadas during the summer months.

She took a seat at a table in the sun. Since she was back in Maratea, she wanted to catch all the rays of sunshine she could. Here, where everyone around her was tanned by the summer sun, her pale complexion was out of place. Even at home, she'd look for a place on her terrace where the sun would reach her, and as soon as things were back to normal, she would go to the beach for some proper sunbathing.

She ordered a cappuccino and cornetto, opened up her book and pretended to read while studying the few people sitting at the tables around her. A couple of Germans were eating gelato and looking around with dreamy eyes, repeating, "*Wunderbar!*" to each other. Giò could not tell if the compliment was meant for the ice-cream, the weather, the landscape, or the surroundings. Maratea was a simple village with no exceptional monuments, but it had a charm of its own: the greenery; the statue of Christ the Redeemer above the all-embracing mountains; and the amazing view of the Gulf of Policastro. The small central square; the little streets full of shops; the two- and three-storey houses, built one on top of the other as was common in towns of the Middle Ages. And the 44 churches. An overwhelming level of spirituality for such a small place, counting just over 5,000 inhabitants.

Beyond the German couple, Giò spotted Carlo Capello talking to another man she recognised as Andrea Aiello. They were both dark-haired and broad-shouldered, but Carlo's slightly sallow, round face contrasted with the tanned and chiselled features of the other man, not to mention their dress sense: a beige suit with a pink silk scarf for Carlo; jeans and a tight blue t-shirt for Andrea. Dandy elegance versus casual.

Giò was eavesdropping on the two men, who were commenting on the newspaper which was open in front of them when they were joined by the bar owner, Leonardo, whom Giò had known since she was a child. He was a short, fat man with a plump face and a deep velvety voice that enchanted listeners. He must have whispered amazing news to them, because Carlo dropped the newspaper and was looking at him open-mouthed, for once totally unaware of how comic his expression was. Andrea was speechless too and Leonardo was clearly enjoying the moment. He prided himself on being the most informed person in town, which in all honesty, with gossips around every corner, was not an easy title to win in Maratea.

Leonardo raised his eyes, probably to see if his staff were attending to the customers sitting at the bar tables properly. Spotting Giò, he came over.

"Hello, Giò, how are you doing?"

"I'm fine, Leo, happy to be back," she replied, putting the book down.

"I haven't seen you around…"

"I've only just arrived, and it's been a busy two days."

"To think of it – you come back home only to be involved in this terrible affair. Have you heard the news?"

"What news?"

"Elena's accident – it wasn't an accident after all."

"Not an accident? What does that mean?" Her expression was similar to

Carlo's a minute earlier, her mouth open, her eyes popping out from their sockets.

"Hey, gentlemen, come over. After all, you all shared the same adventure." Leo made space around Giò's little table and drew up a few extra chairs. She closed her novel with a defeated look; no way could she go to cafés in Maratea and enjoy the same anonymity she'd had in London.

Don't even think about it, she said to herself.

Carlo greeted her with a kiss on her hand. *"Enchanté!"* he said. She could not help laughing, and he glanced at her resentfully. Andrea laughed too, showing his perfectly white teeth, and stretched out his hand.

"I'm Andrea," he said, then turned to Carlo. "She's a woman of the world, yet you stick to old provincial customs…"

"These are refined French manners, young folk," Carlo replied sulkily.

"I'm sorry," said Giò, wondering how a complete stranger such as Andrea knew about her. Did he know about her failed wedding too? No doubt. She went on, "I've been living in the UK, where the customs couldn't be further from the French ones."

"I agree," Carlo said, pushing his square red glasses back up his nose with his index finger. "English gentlemen should learn from their French cousins in matters of refinement, especially when it comes to relationships with ladies. They did a better job with literature and poetry, though they never produced anybody as decadent and deep as Baudelaire..."

"Well, Carlo," Leo said, "it seems you've been served with a rather decadent murder, haven't you?"

"A murder?" Giò wondered if she'd misunderstood something.

"Breaking news today," Leo replied, swelling with pride. "It wasn't an accident – it was murder!"

Giò stared back at him, unable to comprehend what Leo was saying. "How is that possible?"

"It seems somebody ambushed Elena, levering the rock from its resting place and pushing it down onto her when she parked."

"Oh my goodness!" Giò pulled her arms back in shock and her book fell on the floor. Andrea picked it up and returned it to her with a smile.

"*Wuthering Heights*, you are a romantic soul."

"I'm reading it for its descriptive narrative," she replied drily without returning his smile.

But my goodness, it's a killer smile. Killer? Oh no!

"If this is true, it would be the first case of murder here in Maratea, ever," said Carlo. "As an artist, I was there, where the action occurred, amid human passions, love, greed, hatred."

Giò looked at him incredulously. "You're pulling my leg."

"We're not," Leo said.

"But how could they know somebody pushed the rock down?"

"Well," Leo lowered his voice, "you've met the engineer, haven't you?"

"Mr Faraco, you mean?" Giò replied, wondering how many people had been at the accident – or rather, the murder scene – if Leo already had all the details. "Yes, he was the first one to get there after I called 112."

"Well, you know, it was his responsibility after the rockfall to decide where the road had to be closed. He wrote and signed the official report. When the carabinieri arrived, he risked being charged with manslaughter..."

Andrea interrupted. "Well, Faraco might not be the nicest person on earth, but he certainly knows his job. He is a scrupulous technician."

"He is," Leo agreed, "and he was so certain about the inspection he and his men had carried out that he asked Maresciallo Mangiaboschi to have a look at where the rock had come from. It seems they found the exact spot from which the rock fell and there were clear signs somebody had used a lever of some sort to dislodge it. There were metal scratches on the rock beneath, and traces in the dry grass that showed somebody had struggled to keep a foothold up there. Also, the natural trajectory of the rock's fall would have been different if somebody had not deliberately pushed it in that precise direction. Faraco knew his business; he actually remembered having noticed the rock, and that it was pretty stable."

A long silence fell on the four of them. Giò was bewildered, Carlo was satisfied to have been in on the action, Leonardo was already savouring the pleasure of repeating the breaking news to all his customers as the day marched on, and Andrea was a mere spectator, whose focused expression Giò could not decipher.

"This is the most incredible story." Giò broke the silence. "How could the murderer know where Elena would park?"

"That's easy," Andrea said. "Mrs Rivello in effect has a reserved space. She goes to Sapri every morning, and she is the only one allowed to park next to the barrier."

Carlo confirmed Andrea's words. "Of course, when I arrived, I knew not to park there, but imagine if I had forgotten. I would have been flattened." From his expression, Giò was certain he was thrilled by the thought, but Andrea cut his gratification short.

"The murderer would have recognised your car and changed his plans."

"Unless it was a stupid game," Leo replied. "You know, like kids throwing rocks from highway bridges, not caring who may be inside the cars below them."

"In which case, my muse saved me," Carlo thought aloud, as complacent as ever.

"We've never had anything like that happen here before," said Andrea in response to what Leo had said. "Not even common vandals. If the carabinieri confirm it was not an accident, then we have to assume somebody wanted to kill Elena deliberately."

Despite the warm sun, a shiver went down Giò's spine. She was still unable to believe a real murder had been committed in her peaceful Maratea. They were all speechless for a while, then Carlo broke the silence.

"A murder case. One human being hated another so much they decided to kill him.... ahem, her. Or maybe it was an insane passion that led to the crime. Elena wasn't married, was she?"

"She had a boyfriend, Tommaso. The guy seems OK to me. I've even been for a beer with him a few times…"

"But Elena was a strong-willed woman, Andy. Mr Rivello trusted her because she knew how to run things, how to manage people. On some occasions, he complained she could be too harsh on the staff."

"Are you suggesting revenge, Carlo?" asked Andrea, absently raking his tousled hair back from his forehead.

"I'm just examining all the possibilities. The first suspect is always someone close to the victim – a husband or boyfriend is a prime suspect to the carabinieri."

"And statistics have proven them right: I believe in most cases they are the murderers. But before we continue our investigation, we'd better order an aperitivo."

The waitress removed Giò's glass and the coloured dish with the last crumbs of cornetto.

"I'd like a Crodino. I don't think I can drink wine after a cappuccino."

Carlo and Andrea ordered a prosecco each and soon the table was covered with bowl of green and black olives, crisps, tiny pieces of pizza, peanuts, and small panzerotti. Made with the same dough as pizza, the round panzerotti were filled with mozzarella, tomato and fresh basil leaves, closed up and deep fried, and were Giò's favourites. Granny would grumble they were nothing like the homemade ones, but to Giò they were still delicious. Despite having thought there was something not quite right about eating while discussing a murder, she changed her mind as soon as the familiar appetising aroma reached her nostrils.

"Assuming the boyfriend had nothing to do with the murder, who else might have wanted her dead?" she asked almost cheerfully, biting her panzerotto.

Andrea gave her a searching look. "You're starting to enjoy this investigation, aren't you?"

"Well, I found her, after all. It's only natural I would want to know all about her and who committed the murder." She must have seemed more aggressive than she'd intended to be because Andrea raised his arms in surrender, laughing. He was a funny chap with the most delicious single dimple on his right cheek.

"It won't take long to discover who was so annoyed with Elena, they resorted to such extremes," Carlo said. "In Maratea you can't keep a secret for long." He drank a sip from his wine glass and added, "Unless it was a politician hiding his nasty actions from the public."

"Which would not concern Elena, I

daresay." Andrea took a shiny green olive with a toothpick.

"You think so?" Carlo stared at Andrea.

"Well, Elena was just a simple, albeit talented, secretary."

"But she was Mr Rivello's secretary, and we know how close he is to plenty of politicians. And he is a powerful man in his own right."

"But that is Mr Rivello, not Elena." Andrea was following the logical route, while Carlo resorted to flights of fancy.

"But she must have known a lot," Carlo replied with a meaningful look. "I guess after her boyfriend, the next suspects would be Mr Rivello and his posse."

Andrea shook his head. "Carlo, you've evidently been reading too many thrillers and crime stories. We're dealing with a real murder. It will be because of some silly jealousy or grudge, something much simpler and more mundane than the conspiracy theory you're creating."

Carlo smiled. "We'll see. The

investigation has started, anyway. And we'll soon be called in by the carabinieri."

"Again?" Giò was startled. "Why?"

"We were at the crime scene."

"But I've already been interrogated twice. I don't think I can add anything more to what I've said." She didn't add that she dreaded the thought of speaking to the maresciallo again.

"But there's a big difference: the first time you were asked if you'd witnessed an accident, this time they'll need to question you about a murder. Did you see anybody? Did you notice if the other cars were really empty? Any suspicious noises, shadows, movements from above the mountains? Are you sure you were alone?"

Giò had enjoyed their sleuthing so far, but Carlo's avalanche of potential questions almost frightened her. The killer might have been around when she reached Mrs Rivello's car – she hadn't thought of that. Had he watched her? It was disconcerting to think he – it could also have been a she – could have been observing all that happened after the killing.

Carlo, of course, had kept talking all the while she was lost in her own thoughts. She caught up with him just in time for the last piece of his three-act tragedy.

"...and most of all, did you know the victim?"

"I did," said Andrea.

"Of course not," said Giò at the same time. Only then did she realise the implication of the question. "Are we suspects?" Her voice trembled. It was almost surreal.

Carlo and Andrea both nodded silently.

6

THE ROMANTIC ROAD

When Giò looked at her watch, it was almost 1pm. She hurriedly said her farewells to Carlo and Andrea, the latter of whom asked where she was heading.

"To the primary school," she said. "I want to surprise my niece."

"If you don't mind, I'll come along with you. I've parked close to Piazza Europa, and I can give you a lift home. It's not as pleasant a walk going back up as it is on the way down." He flashed her a warm smile.

"Thank you, but I think Agnese will be

there with her own car. But we can certainly walk down together." Then she stiffened – was he being too nice? He was a very handsome man, and at his age, living in Maratea, he should certainly have been married with two, three kids. And she did not like the idea of flirting with married men, not to mention the fact that she didn't want anything to do with men for the next couple of years at least. Most likely for the rest of her life. But to be brutally honest, he probably wasn't flirting at all. In Maratea people were generally kind and considerate – at times so kind and considerate that they crossed the boundary into nosiness.

"So what do you do for a living?" she asked, deciding they had spoken of murders and suspects for long enough now.

"I'm an architect, an independent one."

"Is there enough work for you here in Maratea?"

"Thanks to the market for second houses, I can't complain. My area includes

Praia a Mare down south, and Sapri and beyond in the north. Certainly, I must maintain a good reputation with as many folks as I can, but that's true for any independent trader. You're freelance yourself, aren't you?"

They turned right onto the so-called 'Romantic Alley La Torre'. When she read the sign on the ivy walls, Gio's cheeks flamed, but she managed to keep her voice steady and reply without looking at Andrea.

"Correct, though I'm not too good at networking," she confessed. "I mean, I love to network with kindred spirits. That is, other authors, although we are a rather introverted lot, and travellers, but I'm not so good with publishers, PR, press – all necessary in my line of business."

"That is... writing travel guides?" he asked uncertainly.

"Well, I don't really enjoy writing travel guides. They are so insipid: just a list of monuments and tourist attractions. And there's so much more to travelling than sightseeing. Mind you, I need to write them at the moment – they pay the bills, but one day, I'd love to be able to leave them behind."

"So what do you like writing?"

"Travel memoirs, travel diaries, short stories that catch the spirit of a place and..." She was going to add that she might start to write novels, but that was her secret. And she would rather speak of her hopes and dreams once she had accomplished them than beforehand. Also, hadn't she been intending to ask questions of Andrea? How come he was the one doing all the questioning?

They were interrupted by her phone ringing: an unknown Maratea number.

"Hello?" she answered.

"Is this Miss Giovanna Brando?" a stammering voice asked.

"Speaking."

"It's the carabinieri here. We need to speak to you – would you come to the station in Fiumicello this afternoon?"

"OK." She swallowed hard. "At what time?"

"Half past three will be fine. Please do not let anyone else know we have asked you here."

"I will have to tell my family. I need to borrow their car or have them accompany me."

"Family is fine, just do not spread the word to the general public."

"OK."

"See you at half three, then."

"Bye."

Andrea's smile had gone. "What do you have to tell your family?"

She did not reply. Did she really need to keep it a secret from him? His face cleared – he'd guessed anyway.

"Was it the carabinieri summoning you?"

"And they told me not to tell anybody. Though, from what I've seen this morning, I'm sure people will know soon, anyway."

A telephone rang again. This time it

was Andrea's. He listened, then replied, "Four-thirty and I will not tell anybody."

He ended the call and the two of them looked at each other and burst out laughing. It felt good, because Giò had sensed her tension rising. Being summoned by the carabinieri investigating a murder case was not the most pleasant of things.

Andrea shared her train of thought. "This time it will be tougher."

Giò panicked. As a passionate mystery reader, she had always thought that if she were ever questioned in a murder case, she would somehow 'look guilty'. As simple a question as, "What were you doing yesterday?" would alarm her. She lived in her own little world and could hardly remember what she had eaten for lunch today, never mind what she was doing the day before. The more she thought she might look guilty, the guiltier she'd feel.

The small path opened onto Piazza Europa and Agnese waved at them from the front of the school on the other side of the road. Andrea shook hands with her, then said he'd better go.

"He is a nice chap. At times *too* nice," Agnese said cryptically. Giò, her mind still on her forthcoming interrogation, was too preoccupied to notice.

"The carabinieri are going to question me again," she told her sister. "They summoned me for three-thirty this afternoon. It was a murder, not an accident. They're looking for a murderer."

"What are you talking about?" Agnese gasped.

"Nobody told you in the shop?"

"It has been a quiet morning, just a few tourists. Except for Carmela who made me a coffee first thing this morning, I've not seen anyone local."

Giò told her the story, as far as she knew it. Agnese was completely taken aback.

"A murder? Here in Maratea? And such a brutal one! I can't believe it."

"It wasn't that brutal," Giò replied.

"I wouldn't call flattening someone with a rock a gentle murder."

"And what's your idea of a gentle murder?"

"Well, I've never really thought about it. Poison, maybe?"

"Some poisons cause a very painful death. You get struck down by awful convulsions, your entire body hurts – far more than if it had been crushed under a rock – and then you can no longer breathe, the agony of suffocation..."

Agnese shivered. "There might be... gentler kinds of poisons."

"Gentle poisons, fiddlesticks! Well if somebody is killed in a bathtub full of honey or chocolate cream, I will know my sister is the culprit."

At that moment, they heard Lilia announcing with extreme pride, "That's my auntie!" as she pointed Giò out to a group of five other children. "She's the one who found Elena's dead body in the car." The kids looked at Lilia with admiration as she walked away from them to join her mother and aunt.

Just before Lilia came within earshot, Giò murmured to Agnese, "My goodness, imagine tomorrow when the whole village knows that Elena was murdered and I was first on the scene."

"And they will know that you've been questioned by the carabinieri," added Agnese, gloomily.

"From there, it won't take much of a stretch of the imagination before they're all suspecting me of the murder."

"But knowing the multiplying effect of Maratea gossip, you will not be alone. There will be more suspects than inhabitants!"

They laughed at that, but when Lilia reached them, Giò rebuked her.

"Was it necessary to introduce me to your friends as the one who found poor Elena?"

Lilia wasn't in the least bit put out. "Yes it was, because Bianca told me that Rossella said her uncle found Elena first.

But that was not true since he drives the ambulance, and you said they arrived 15 minutes after you. Rossella is always pretending she knows everything, so I had to clarify the matter for the whole class. It taught her a lesson, I hope!"

"My goodness, Agnese, you've created a monster!"

"But I'm still your favourite niece, am I not?"

"And the most irresistible too!"

AFTER LUNCH, THE TWO SISTERS hurried out again, Agnese accompanying Giò to Fiumicello despite her protesting that she could go alone. When they arrived, they were asked to wait by themselves in a small room. Five minutes later, they saw the Rivellos come out of the interview room, but the carabinieri waited for the couple to leave the station before asking Giò in. They were evidently trying to ensure that the witnesses (suspects?)

wouldn't have a chance to exchange information.

Paolo, the brigadiere, smiled shyly at Giò and invited her to take a seat. Maresciallo Mangiaboschi stared silently at the wall behind her without replying to her greeting. Everything appeared to be the same as it had been the last time they'd questioned her, but Giò sensed a new tension in the room.

Then the maresciallo stood up, walked in front of his desk and spoke as if reading from a book.

"Miss Brando, I'm sure you know, as does everybody else in Maratea, that the death of Elena Errico was not a simple accident. We have reason to believe it was a case of murder. We'd be grateful if you could tell us what you did that morning, from the very moment you woke up. Possibly indicating the time of all your actions."

Giò swallowed a few times before she could speak. Then she told them all that had happened the previous morning: the visit to her family home in Acquafredda; her lingering for too long in the house; how she decided to postpone her visit to the graveyard and catch the bus to Sapri instead.

"Did you speak to anybody when you arrived in Acquafredda?" the maresciallo asked.

"No, I parked at my parents' house, so I didn't have a chance to see anybody."

"Maybe while you were driving you waved at someone from the car?"

"Not that I can remember, but it could be that someone saw me, or at least the car, from a balcony or a window."

"What did you do at your parents' house?" He walked up and down while Giò was speaking, but stopped to look at her when he was asking questions.

"I opened the windows in the living room to let a little fresh air in, went through my parents' books and photographs. When I looked at my watch again, I realised I was just in time to catch the bus."

"So what did you do?" Despite his attempts to sound encouraging, the maresciallo's cold eyes contrasted with his voice. Apparently interested in everything, he was looking for hard facts, ready to note any potential lie or inconsistency. Giò described all her actions as well as she could; it was good she had rehearsed everything at home before the interrogation.

The carabiniere who had shown Giò into the room knocked on the door to deliver a message to the maresciallo. While he was reading the note, the brigadiere sneaked in his first question.

"I know you've answered these questions before," he did not have the same fierce look as the maresciallo, but he was much more formal than last time, "but we need to go over them again. From the moment you left the house and headed for the parking spaces, tell us everything you did, noticed, thought. Even trivial things might be essential to our investigation."

Giò, as if an automaton, repeated what

she had done. Had she seen a car leaving the parking spaces? No, she hadn't. Was she completely sure? Yes, she was.

"You know, it is so normal to pass another car, you might not have noticed it."

"I've thought about it, Brigadiere, and I'm sure I did not pass any other vehicle, car or motorbike."

Had she noticed anything unusual while parking? No, because Mrs Rivello's car had been just a little ahead of where she parked. She could see its back end, but not the rock that had fallen on the front part. It was only when she had gone towards the car that she'd seen what had happened.

Did she see/hear anything? No.

"Could someone have been hiding there?"

"They could have been," she admitted. She had not been looking for anyone. And if somebody had been hiding in the vegetation, she doubted she would have realised it. All her thoughts had been concentrated on the dead body, trapped inside the car.

Just when she thought she couldn't handle any more questions, the maresciallo started up a whole new chapter.

"Miss Brando, what's your job?"

"I'm a travel writer."

An avalanche of questions followed: what brought you back to Maratea? What's your financial position? Who were you in touch with here in Maratea apart from your family? How often did you speak to them? What's your relationship with your sister like?

Giò replied to all his questions, wondering if she should have asked for her lawyer to be present. Not that she had ever had a lawyer.

Half an hour later they let her go, reiterating their request that she keep this second interview secret.

BRIGADIERE ROSSI KNEW HIS superior quite well. He guessed that Maresciallo Mangiaboschi's excessive harshness towards Giò could mean he suspected something. So, once the woman had left, he asked the maresciallo a question.

"Do you think she could have done Elena in? She arrived on the scene rather late, given Dr Siringa's hypothesis on the time of death."

"We should check her alibi carefully. Maybe she was there much earlier than she declared. She said nobody saw her." The maresciallo added meditatively, "Which is rather strange…"

"Is she our main suspect?" The brigadiere cut him short, but the maresciallo would not be tricked into revealing his inner thoughts, nor his wishful thinking.

"Firstly, we're not sure yet it was murder. Secondly, we suspect anybody who had an opportunity to commit the crime. Then, we will move from opportunity to

motive. And finally, from motive to proof."
He spoke as if he was reading from a
manual, but Paolo suspected his boss had
already made up his mind to accuse Giò.
And that made no sense to the brigadiere
at all.

"If she's lived in the UK for 15 years,
surely she wouldn't have had any reason to
harm Elena," he insisted.

"She is very close to her sister. She
looks like the kind who would do anything
for her family."

"Murder included?"

"Murder included."

"But why would her family want Elena
dead?"

"We don't know... yet. That's why we
need to check her alibi, but also dig for
more information about the relationship
between Elena and Agnese, and Elena and
Nando. Who knows, we may uncover a
disagreement or an affair." The
maresciallo did not like having to explain
his train of thought to his subordinate
and decided it was time to end the

conversation. "Let us have Mr Capello in."

While they were waiting for Carlo Capello, Paolo wondered if the maresciallo simply found it convenient to view Giovanna Brando as the killer rather than anybody else in the local community. Having lived away from town for so long, she was no longer a local; she was more of a stranger.

When Capello entered the room, one thing was evident to Paolo: if Giò had been worried and anxious, so was Carlo. He was nowhere near as bold as he'd been during his first interview, when he had looked extremely satisfied to be there. Now, despite his intricate theories about passion, distorted love and power, he became rather nervous when they questioned him about his movements. He reiterated that he had arrived at 7.20, confirming that at the time, only Sara's car had been parked in the spaces, and no, he had not seen her, nor anybody else. He had simply taken the scooter he had parked on the other side of the road and ridden to Sapri. While he was speaking, he kept pausing as if expecting approval from the carabinieri.

Strange, Paolo thought, *he never considered our reactions last time.*

7

TURNING TABLES

"Had they kept me 10 minutes longer, I would have confessed to the murder," said Giò as soon as she and Agnese were out of the carabinieri station. "My, I feel tired. It's been dreadful!"

"Carlo arrived while you were in there, but they asked him to wait in another room. They were extremely careful to make sure we didn't exchange so much as a look," Agnese informed her. "How about a cup of coffee? At the harbour, maybe?"

The journey from Fiumicello to Maratea passed the road that led down to the harbour. Moreover, Agnese knew it was one of Giò's favourite spots in Maratea.

"Don't you have to open the perfumery?"

"I asked Nando to stand in for me this afternoon."

Giò flashed her a smile of gratitude; she loved the idea of having her sister's company for longer.

"OK, let's go."

They parked the car on the hillside that led onto the harbour road. It was a little far from where they wanted to be, but they could enjoy the view of the small fishing and tourist harbour during the walk down. No large ferries, no cruise ships; just family boats, a few posh motor yachts, a handful of sailing ships. But to Giò, it was the white and pink houses nestling on the rocks above the water and enclosing the harbour, with the massive mountains all around, that made it a little corner of wild beauty.

The sisters walked in silence, taking a little path across the rocks facing the restaurant terraces, looking out to sea. They sat at the very end of the path, where there were a few benches, smelling the Mediterranean air and letting the view sink in, the harbour on their right, the infinite horizon on their left. This was the time of the year when the sun seemed to go to sleep in the middle of the water. The oranges and reds of the sky promised one of the spectacular sunsets that Maratea people became accustomed to during the autumn.

"How I have missed all this," Giò said. Then suddenly, for the first time since she broke up with Dorian, the tears came. Agnese gently caressed her back, but she did not say anything, waiting for her sister's soul to open up. After a few minutes, still sobbing and trembling, Giò finally told her story.

"We'd had another argument about my travel arrangements, so I decided to come home a few days early. I didn't call him; it was meant to be a surprise, so I arrived unexpectedly very early in the morning.

And I found a blonde sleeping with him. In my own bed! I screamed and screamed; I'd never thought I would have to deal with anything like this.

"The blonde was young – maybe 20, maybe younger – and she repeatedly told me to calm down. Calm down? I could have killed her! Dorian came over and told me it wasn't what it looked like. He kept saying that the forthcoming wedding had put so much pressure on him and the commitment was taking its toll, and I should try to understand it from a man's point of view. The blonde meant nothing to him, and she even backed him up.

"'You can have him,' she said while she was putting her clothes on. 'I've had enough of him.' I couldn't believe the two of them were real."

"Oh my goodness!" was all Agnese managed to say. She'd had no idea things were that bad.

"How could I have been with such a disgusting man for 10 years? I begged him to marry me, to share his life with me, never realising he was a cheat and a liar. Have I been blind?" Giò stopped, blowing her nose on a tissue Agnese handed to her, and waited for an answer.

"When you're in love, you can't always be objective, I'm afraid."

"He lied to me! Maybe he had girlfriends over every time I was away. Actually, I'm pretty sure he did. 'Only a few times,' he said, 'but you were away so often.' Would you ever have expected him to stoop so low?"

As a matter of fact, Agnese would have expected exactly that from Dorian. She had tried to alert her sister, as gently as she could, that he seemed to be an unfeeling man who did little to fulfil Giò's need for genuine love and friendship. But how can you tell someone who is deeply in love that they're making a big mistake?

Granny had simply hated the stupid fop. After meeting him for the first time, she had commented, "He doesn't want anything to do with us. Now, if you don't love her family, how can you pretend to love our dear Giò?" Agnese was not convinced about the family part – plenty of people hated their partners' families, but loved their partners all the same. But from what Giò had told her, she suspected Dorian's failings extended much further. He had been dismissive of Maratea – "Such a boring village, I can hardly bear to spend a couple of hours here" – and was scathing about everything and everyone Giò cared for.

"You know, Giò, my words may be inadequate, but the truth is I don't think he was the right man for you. It's not about his disliking us, or Maratea; it's not about the differences between him and you; it is simply that I never saw you joyful and serene with him. You were sometimes proud of the things you had done together, momentarily satisfied, but once he came into your life, I never saw you simply happy. I mean happy for no reason; happy to be alive. There was always a reservation, a shadow."

Giò looked at Agnese, taken aback. She

had expected her sister to launch a scathing verbal attack on Dorian, but not this. And, Giò realised, Agnese was right. She had always had to search for a reason to qualify her happiness, to convince herself it was true; never had she woken up and smiled because her heart was singing, as it used to do when she was a child.

"You might be right. But in that case I, and only I, have been stupid for the past 10 years."

"You know, Giò, I feel very tired at times. There's so much to do with the shop, the kids. Nando is the best of men, but sometimes I wish I still had my independence and freedom. But when I wake up in the morning, I feel curious about what the day will bring. What will Lilia and Luca say or do? Will Nando remember to make a cup of coffee for me before leaving for work? Will Granny deliver one of her unforgettable statements? Will one of my customers find a little happiness thanks to my advice?

Will I learn something new? I just can't wait to get out of bed and see what life is gonna bring."

She looked Giò straight in the eyes, and said in a murmured rush what she had wanted to tell her sister for a long time.

"I'd rather you were single, but surrounded by real friends, free to call your family whenever you want, than lonely and trapped in a bad relationship like you were."

"Oh my goodness, was it so bad?" Giò asked.

"Frankly, yes, it was. I shouldn't say this, but I detested Dorian. Not because he disliked us, not because he was so conceited, but because he tried to destroy who you were. Your work, your family, your home, you. I could never forgive him for that"

"Bless the stupid blonde, then," Giò sniffled, her nose still red, her eyes still wet.

"Bless her and the pressure of the forthcoming wedding."

Their eyes met. They laughed, they cried, they laughed again, then Giò wiped the tears from her cheeks.

"Shall we go for a coffee, or something stronger?"

"Something stronger. Today we celebrate your rebirth."

They retraced their steps to the main square in front of the harbour, where the bars and cafés had their tables out, and ordered an aperitivo with prosecco and olives.

"Salute!" They clinked glasses. "To my sister, that she might have all she deserves!" Agnese added with a huge smile on her face.

"Hello, Agnese. Hello, Giò." Paolo, the brigadiere, looked even chubbier than normal in civilian clothing. Realising he had interrupted something, he tried to slope away, but Agnese stopped him.

"Hello, Paolo, please take a seat. Are you off duty? Can we offer you something to drink?"

He was slightly embarrassed, but took

a seat nonetheless. "We've had a long night and a long day, so when we finished the interrogations, the maresciallo gave us a break. I badly need something to drink." Paolo took one look at the prosecco the women were drinking and ordered one for himself too.

"Anything new?" Agnese asked.

He reddened. "I can't really say…"

"I beg your pardon, I didn't mean to pry. It is so incredible to think a thing like that should happen here in Maratea, I still hope it will turn out to be a natural death after all."

"That's what the maresciallo hopes too. But I expect forensics will confirm that a metal lever was used to dislodge the rock from the mountain, and fragments of the same metal will be on the boulder that smashed into the car. Somebody had already noticed the rock and knew that Elena was going to park there."

"How about Elena? Did you interrogate her family too?"

"Yes, we did." Paolo took a large sip of wine, sighing with obvious relief.

"Is the victim's partner not usually the first suspect in a murder case?" prompted Giò as if she discussed such cases every day. Paolo picked up an olive and watched the crimson sunset for a while before replying.

"He has a perfect alibi since he was working on a building site down south in Praia a Mare. His boss and colleagues said he was there by 7.30am, and he'd picked up a colleague in Marina di Maratea at 7am. Elena's death, according to Dr Siringa, occurred between 7am and 8am, no earlier and no later. No, we can rule him out."

"By the way, do you know if she suffered?" asked Giò awkwardly.

"The doctor says she died instantly. She must have realised what was about to happen because she opened the car door, but no, she did not suffer."

"It might be stupid, but I feel better for that. I found it unbearable to think she might have been lying there in agony, and if I had arrived earlier..."

"No, there was nothing you or anybody else could have done for her."

Agnese coughed. "People say... well, maybe I should not repeat this... but it seems Elena was not what you'd call a gentle soul."

Paolo waited for Agnese to finish what she wanted to say. She continued, stumbling over her words.

"One should never speak ill of the dead, I know, but it seems she took advantage of her position. Working for Mr Rivello gave her status, but she used it to make her workers' lives a misery."

"Wouldn't Mr Rivello have complained?" Giò asked.

"I don't think so," Paolo said meditatively. "He's the kind of man who likes to foster animosity and competition between his staff in order to make sure their first loyalty will be to him, not each other."

"In any case," said Agnese, "Elena was

not well liked. She knew things about Mr Rivello's staff because essentially, she was one of them. She knew if a worker drank too much, or if they were taking sick leave when they weren't really ill. She certainly used her position to her own advantage."

"Do you think she did something so bad that someone would kill her, though?" Giò asked.

"I know of a few times when she was spiteful, but none was a motive for a murder," Agnese replied.

"I think we should investigate a bit and find out!" Giò uttered the very words Agnese had been fearing. Paolo frowned, too.

"May I remind you that it's the carabinieri's job to run a murder investigation?"

"May I remind you that the maresciallo doesn't believe it's a murder at all? You just said so yourself. I will be conducting my personal investigations in Agnese's perfumery."

"I'd rather you didn't do anything of

the kind," Paolo said seriously. "Agnese, please explain to your sister that this is not a joke. If it is a case of murder, a real killer is currently at large in Maratea."

The river has already burst its banks, thought Agnese. *We can only try to contain its waters.* Now her sister had got the idea of investigating into her head, she would only become all the more determined if anyone tried to stop her.

"Perhaps it's not such a bad idea. You know, in a shop like mine, people make all kinds of comments – things they would never freely admit to the carabinieri."

"What are you suggesting?"

"That we carry out secret investigations while the carabinieri carry on with the official investigations. We'll be the ones digging up the dark secrets."

Giò looked at Agnese, full of gratitude.

"So you're determined to play the sleuths?"

"I found the body," said Giò. "She might not have been the nicest woman on earth, but I found her dead. Somebody killed her. And I cannot bear to allow a murderer to run free here in Maratea just because a short-sighted maresciallo wants an easy life. I have just come back home after what seems like a lifetime away and a gruesome death is the first thing I stumble on. I believe that I was meant to witness all of this, and it's my duty to help to resolve it whether you want me to or not. I need to know the truth!"

Agnese suspected that Giò might be looking for a way to rediscover the meaning in her life, as if those 10 years she'd spent with Dorian had been pointless, or worse, the called-off wedding had somehow been her fault. Or maybe she simply needed to channel her energy into something other than brooding over him. Whatever the case, before Paolo could answer, Agnese spoke up.

"I'm not going to leave her to do this alone, Paolo. And since we're going to investigate anyway, wouldn't it be better to cooperate? We will be able to alert you to the gossip we hear, anything that may be relevant to your inquiries. You can use the information as you wish."

Paolo scratched his head. "Agnese, this is not like someone stealing a jar of olives. There is a killer around who's shown no mercy, and you two may be putting yourselves in real danger. How could I ever face Nando if anything happened to you? Do I need to remind you that you've got two kids?"

"Paolo, I would never put my family in danger, you know that. But in a perfumery, people are talking all the time. All we need to do is listen out for hints and clues, perhaps leading conversations in the direction we want them to go. There will be no danger; we will just be gossiping, so nobody will even realise what we're doing."

Paolo thought it over.

"I might say yes, but I need you to abide by my conditions. One, you're not going to put yourself in any kind of danger. Two, you will do exactly what I ask you to do – no acting on your own initiative, please, unless it's approved by me. Three, you will stop your investigations completely if I feel you might be in danger."

"I agree," said Agnese solemnly.

"So do I," said Giò. But, with the experience of an entire childhood spent together behind them, they both had their fingers firmly crossed under the table.

"I just hope I'm not making the biggest mistake of my career," said Paolo.

"OK, I declare the Maratea Amateur Sleuths officially founded." As Agnese raised her glass, the sun slipped behind the horizon, its last pink lights reflecting on the sea.

"Why did you ask me about Elena's mobile?" Giò asked, turning to Paolo.

"Because we found her bag but not her mobile, which was strange. Even after a thorough search, it was nowhere to be found."

"Did you ask Tommaso whether she left it at home by mistake?"

"No, no mobile at home, either. It

looks as if the killer took it. He didn't take anything else, though."

"Let's reconstruct the murder scene. Who got there and when?"

Paolo looked at her, amused. "You'd make a good cop, you know." He then told them the movements of Elena, Sara, Carlo and Andrea as he'd recorded them during the interrogations, confirming the exact times with the help of his scrappy notebook. The first to arrive was Sara Salino, who parked at 7am and took the 7.15 bus. Carlo Capello arrived between 7.15 and 7.20, and reached Sapri using a scooter he'd kept parked on the other side of the road since the closure. Andrea got there around 7.25. He saw the two cars already parked up, and travelled to Sapri on a bike that he also kept on the other side of the road. According to him, Mrs Rivello's car had not arrived at that time. But any of them could have hidden and waited, killed Elena and then gone on their way. The carabinieri still needed to check each one's alibi carefully.

Strangely, Giò looked rather absentminded. She had been silent for a while, but now she put down her wine glass and looked at the other two.

"You know, I get the impression we're looking at the whole story from the wrong end."

"What do you mean?"

"We're concentrating on people's movements on the morning of the murder. But our story starts earlier on – we should be looking at what happened the day before. Originally, it was Mrs Rivello who had to go to Sapri. Then in the evening, she does not feel well. I imagine she would have spoken to her husband first, to check whether he could spare Elena to run an errand for her the next morning."

"Correct, but I can't see where you're heading," Paolo said.

"Her husband said he could spare Elena. What time would that have been? 9, maybe 10 in the evening?"

Paolo nodded.

"So what?" asked Agnese, starting to feel a little impatient.

"Then Mrs Rivello phoned Elena to ask her to go to Sapri in the morning. As it would have been late by then, who would have known the next morning that it would be Elena in the car and not Mrs Rivello? Most likely just four people: the two women, Mr Rivello and Tommaso. Now, if the killer was not any of the above..."

She let the words linger in the air.

"He would have thought it was Mrs Rivello in the car!" Paolo jumped up from his chair, the wine splashing from his glass onto the table. "Of course, from his position amongst the rocks, he would have recognised the car, but not who was driving. So it's looking likely that the killer was after Mrs Rivello rather than Elena."

Agnese gasped. "But if that is the case, it means..."

"That Mrs Rivello might still be in danger," Giò confirmed. "But actually, it's worse than that."

"What do you mean?"

"Paolo said that Tommaso has a solid alibi, so only the Rivellos could have known that Elena was in the car. Either Mrs Rivello was the intended victim, or one of them is the murderer."

As night descended on Maratea harbour, a cold wind rose and Agnese shivered. Taking a woollen shawl out of her brown bag, she wrapped it around her shoulders.

Finally, Giò broke the silence.

"Paolo, what do we know about the Rivellos? What were their movements that morning?"

"Mrs Rivello says she stayed at home. Mariella, the house cleaner, confirmed that Elena went to pick up the car keys at 7am. They actually arrived together at the Rivellos'. Mr Rivello was already out, and Mrs Rivello was in her bed. She handed the car keys to Elena and asked Mariella for a hot tea. The doctor went to visit her at around 8am, so there's enough to provide her with a good alibi."

"How about Mr Rivello?"

"He said he left home at around 5.45 as he does every day and went to his office in the warehouse. At 6am, he held his usual morning meeting with the whole staff on the shop floor, foreman and technicians included, to give out instructions for the day. He then returned to his office. Apparently, his staff know not to disturb him once his office door is closed, so no one spoke to him until 10am when we informed him of the accident. He immediately phoned his wife at home, who reassured him she was in bed, and that it was Elena who had taken the car."

"So it's looking like the murderer wanted to kill Mrs Rivello, not Elena."

"Do you have any clues? Any possible motive?"

"We've been concentrating on who may have murdered Elena, so we will now have to start investigating who might want Mrs Rivello dead. The maresciallo will have to decide whether to warn her she may be in danger."

"But it is only a theory at the moment?"

"Yes, but it's a good one. And we don't want the theory to turn into reality."

"Giò and I will listen out for gossip about Mrs Rivello, then."

"And I will question the Rivellos, and Tommaso too. We need to find out if anybody else knew who was driving the car that morning. I will also question a few more of Mr Rivello's employees, especially those who work in the warehouse, to make sure he was there that morning between 6.30 and 9.45." Paolo browsed through his notes. "We sort of assumed he stayed in the office, but I want to be sure. By the way, will I see you at Elena's funeral tomorrow?"

"Yes, we will be there."

"Please, not a word to anybody about our theory. I will discuss it with the maresciallo and we will decide whether to let the public know the course of the investigation has changed."

"Wouldn't it be better to let the

murderer believe he is safe and nobody suspects anything?" Agnese asked.

"If he feels safe, he might strike again. My priority is to avoid a second murder."

"Oh my goodness, I didn't think of that."

"But of course, it is the maresciallo who has the final decision, and he does not like complications."

"I just hope he will be as wise as you are," Agnese concluded gravely.

8

FUNERALS AND GERANIUMS

"Granny, why are you dressing up?" Agnese asked.

"Are you forgetting there's a funeral at 11 o'clock this morning?" Granny replied with a hint of impatience, adjusting a pearl necklace over her perfectly ironed white shirt.

"No, but I didn't think you would be coming."

"Of course I am. I never miss a funeral. I might not like weddings and christenings, but I definitely love funerals."

"The weather is so poor, wouldn't you

be better staying at home?"

"Silly girl! A murder in Maratea, and you want me to stay at home?"

Agnese tried to keep herself from smiling, but failed abysmally.

"Are you expecting drama?"

"Well, you never know."

"What, like the killer standing up and confessing all his sins?"

"I frankly doubt that will happen. Not with Don Eustachio preaching, anyway."

"He'll probably keep us there for hours," Agnese agreed. "The church will be filled up with old gossips of the worst kind," she glanced meaningfully towards Granny, but the old lady didn't even blink, "and he won't be able to resist one of his dreadful sermons about people not attending mass on Sundays."

"We may be able to turn that to our advantage. It will give us more time to observe how people react – I mean the murderer in particular. So I will endure all he has to say this time," Granny said, adjusting the white fringe on her forehead.

"He puts folks off going to his church. Some people would rather drive all the way to Sapri or Praia."

"I'm not surprised. On Sundays, he gets angrier and angrier with the 30 poor faithful who still attend his Mass, blaming them for all those who are absent. So, shall we call Giò and go?"

"Isn't it a bit too early?" Agnese looked her watch. It was still only 10.30, and even Granny wouldn't take more than 10 minutes to get to the church.

"We must make sure we secure good seats and get to talk to people. It's always interesting to hear what they say before and after a funeral."

Agnese wondered whether she should include Granny in the Maratea Amateur Sleuths; she had a certain natural talent for nosing around. Instead, she called Giò and the three of them left for the church under a continuous light rain. Once they had arrived, Granny took her favourite seat and gossiped with everyone who came over to greet her.

When Mass started, the church was as full as Granny could ever remember. It was crammed with people right to the back, and some were standing up as there were no seats left for them. A few even had to stay outside, watching through the open church doors and sheltering from the rain under a sea of umbrellas.

When he appeared, Don Eustachio's face was red with rage, his eyes shining with fanaticism. He started with a little sarcasm.

"There are a few of you I haven't seen in a while."

He had possibly planned to be cold and detached, but he soon succumbed to his usual tantrum about the duty of a good Christian to attend Mass every Sunday, not only for weddings and funerals. Sweat droplets formed on his forehead, his face went purple, and the veins on his temples were pulsing so violently, he looked as though he might have a stroke at any moment. The congregation almost feared they'd end up observing a double funeral if he didn't calm down. He was shrieking about the devil possessing the whole village, promising hellfire and damnation more gory than anything even Quentin Tarantino could have imagined.

At the apotheosis of his rant, a mobile phone rang. Silence fell as priest and congregation tracked the culprit. Carlo Capello, without any trace of embarrassment, spoke coolly.

"Don Eustachio, your speech was so passionate, I forgot to turn it off." He then answered his phone, saying to whoever was calling, "Sorry, I'm attending Mass and Don Eustachio is giving us a lesson about Christian love and compassion. I'll call you later." Giò and Agnese had to try their hardest not to burst out laughing, as did most other people present. Amazingly, Don Eustachio remained silent. Perhaps he felt he was powerless to do anything as Carlo's family was one of the most important in Maratea. Or maybe the priest had finally realised he'd gone too far. There was a family in pain in his congregation because a young woman had died far too young.

When he spoke again, he didn't deliver the most brilliant homily, but at least he opted for more moderate and consolatory tones. Only when he approached the coffin for benediction did he stare long and hard at the congregation, scanning each group as if he knew the murderer was amongst them, ready to confess his sins.

When Mass was finally over Giò noticed, with a certain degree of amusement, that most people, once they had offered their condolences to the Errico family, went over to Carlo to pat him on the back. Maybe in future Don Eustachio would think twice before delivering a fire and brimstone sermon. Overall, Granny had been right – it had been a most satisfactory funeral, definitely not to be missed.

Outside the church the rain had got heavier, but even so, most people lingered to gossip. Some were convinced it must have been an accident, just a falling rock.

A murder in Maratea was simply out of the question.

Giò found herself standing next to Mrs Rivello. "Hello, dear," the older woman said. "I'm so sorry you had to witness that scene today. Don Eustachio is getting too old and set in his ways, but I can't condone Carlo's lack of respect."

"It seems to me that in Don Eustachio's view, not going to Mass is a worse sin than killing a young woman."

Agnese kicked Giò's leg. It was not a good idea to contradict Mrs Rivello, but the woman herself seemed unruffled.

"I'm sure that's not what he meant. By the way, how are you settling in?"

"I've received my boxes from London and I'm still arranging all my stuff," Giò replied, remembering Mrs Rivello had invited her for a coffee. "With all the carabinieri interviews, I've hardly had any free time."

"Why not come over for a cup of coffee this afternoon?" said Mrs Rivello with a smile. "It will be a pleasure to talk to you."

"I certainly will. How about four?" Giò replied, thinking what a stroke of luck it was to have been invited again. The visit could turn up some very useful information for their sleuthing.

Granny finally emerged from the church, where she must have been gossiping with almost every single member of the congregation, and joined her granddaughters.

"Granny, be careful. Hold on to my arm, the stones are rather slippery," Agnese said, covering Granny with her umbrella. The alley that led back to their home consisted of cobblestoned steps, which were treacherous in wet weather.

A few metres ahead of them, the Rivellos had stopped in front of their home. Mr Rivello was looking for his keys in his pocket and his wife stepped backwards to give him room to manoeuvre. He had just pressed the intercom – maybe he couldn't find his keys – when all of a sudden, he pulled his wife towards him. With a tremendous crash, a heavy terracotta pot, planted with geraniums, fell from a window ledge above them and broke into pieces on the ground.

Mrs Rivello cried out, but she was unhurt thanks to the sharp reflexes of her husband. He held on to her with one hand, alternately banging on the door and pressing the intercom buzzer with the other. Giò, Agnese and Granny approached and they all looked up.

There were plenty of geraniums growing in pots on the Rivellos' balconies and ledges, but there were also a few on the windowsills of the unoccupied building on their right, the placing of which would be more consistent with the trajectory of the falling pot. And it looked as if one was missing.

The Rivellos' door finally opened and Mariella, the housemaid, let them in. Mr Rivello stopped on the threshold, then asked Giò to take care of his wife. As if struck by a sudden idea, he knelt down to examine the broken pot, then got up and rushed around the corner of the abandoned building.

Agnese followed him. "What is it?" she asked, approaching him from behind.

"Please make sure nobody leaves from here." He indicated the door of the abandoned building, then ran through the tight alley. The wet surface put him at risk of a bad fall, but he managed to keep his feet.

Watching him, Agnese put two and two together. Obviously Mr Rivello did not think the geranium pot had fallen because of a gust of wind. Had he seen someone, or was it just a suspicion? Should she enter the building and check if anybody was inside? Maybe not a good idea. What if someone was hiding in there, waiting for her? What if they decided to attack her too?

A few minutes later, Mr Rivello joined her. "Have you seen anybody?" he asked.

"Nobody came out of here," she replied, indicating the door. "And you? Did you see anybody?"

"I spotted someone at the end of the alley, but he reached the main street and mingled with the crowd leaving the church. Mind you, it could have just been a passer-by. Still, I need to go upstairs and check nobody is hiding inside." He took his mobile and switched the torch on – there was no electricity in the empty building and the day was rather dark.

"Shall I come along?" Agnese said.

"No, you'd better stay here and make sure nobody comes out of the building once I've gone up."

"It might be dangerous, though."

"I'm almost certain the guy left through the alleyway. I just need to be sure."

Inside he went, and Agnese waited nervously. A few minutes later, Giò joined her.

"What are you doing here?"

Agnese told her.

"I'm going in too," said Giò.

"It's too dangerous. Wait here with me."

"No, I'd better help Mr Rivello. I will just scream if I see something."

Before Agnese could stop her, Giò was inside. Moments later, someone called out.

"Who's there?"

"Mr Rivello, it's just me, Giò. I'm double checking to make sure nobody is hiding in here."

Mr Rivello was on the second floor, close to one of the glassless arched windows.

"Look here, there's no protection for the vase. It was stupid to have flowers up here at all."

"It looks as if a border was removed," Giò said, pointing at the mark it had left all around the windowsill.

"Correct. Look at this other one." He pointed to the vase next to the empty space. All around it was a 10cm high concrete border, protecting it from falling.

"Did you go all the way to the top?" Giò asked, indicating the stairs to the third floor.

"I did, but why don't you look too?

Much better to have another set of eyes checking."

They climbed the stairs. On the windows of the top floor there were more geranium pots, but they were all safely surrounded.

"The man you saw must have been the culprit."

"I wish I had thought to give chase faster, but at first I believed it was an accident."

"Let's go and check on your wife. There's nothing more we can do here."

Agnese was downstairs, visibly relieved to see they were both OK. Mr Rivello looked gravely at the two sisters.

"What do you think of what's happened?"

Giò replied without any hesitation, "It was not an accident, Mr Rivello, nor someone playing around. This was our murderer's second attempt to kill your wife."

Mr Rivello seemed both relieved and surprised. "I wasn't sure if you would see it as I do. I've thought from the beginning that my wife was the intended victim, not Elena."

Agnese nodded. "This latest development seems to prove it beyond any doubt."

"Who else knew Elena was due to go to Sapri the day she was killed?" Giò asked.

Mr Rivello slowly massaged his ample forehead. "I don't know if Elena spoke to anybody the night before – apart from her boyfriend, obviously. On our side, only my wife and I. It was already late when we made the arrangement, so we didn't have much chance to tell anyone else."

The sisters looked at each other. Yet again, their theory had been confirmed.

"Before we go in to see my wife, there is one thing I want to ask you." He lowered his voice. "My wife does not suspect any of this. I wonder if I should tell her..."

Giò interrupted without hesitation. "Of course, you must tell her. She needs to know someone is threatening her life. The next time, you may be not around to save her."

Agnese nodded in agreement.

"I know, but first I want to inform the carabinieri. Afterwards, I will tell my wife her life is in danger."

"That's a good idea," said Agnese. "She doesn't need to know right now; she will already be in shock because of her narrow escape."

They left the old building, then Mr Rivello opened the door to his home and invited the sisters to stay with his wife while he went to call the carabinieri.

Mrs Rivello was sitting on her sofa. Mariella had already given her a glass of water, and Mrs Rivello had asked for a glass of brandy too.

"Please take a seat. I really cannot get up, I do apologise."

"Don't you worry. Are you feeling any better?" Agnese asked.

"A sip of brandy does wonders, no matter what. What can I offer you?" She already seemed to be in command of her emotions. Maybe Mr Rivello needn't be so concerned about telling the truth to his wife.

"Just a glass of water," Agnese said.

"The same for me," Giò added.

"Not a glass of prosecco or brandy?"

Agnese replied she had had such a fright, her stomach was likely to protest whatever she drank.

Mr Rivello arrived back.

"Raimondo, why did you run like that?" his wife asked. "Did you see anybody, or was it just the wind?"

"I'm not sure, dear. I believe I saw somebody running away through the alley, but it could just have been a coincidence. In any case, I have called up the carabinieri. They are coming round now."

"We'd better go, then," Giò said, dreading the thought of a third meeting with the maresciallo.

"I will have to tell them that you were here and saw what happened."

"Of course, you have to," Agnese replied.

"They may visit you after they've spoken to us."

"This is why we'd better go straight home. I want the children fed before they arrive."

"Well, Giò and Agnese, today is looking like being a rather busy day. Shall we put off that famous cup of coffee till tomorrow?" Mrs Rivello asked.

"Certainly. We'll check you're OK tomorrow afternoon."

"You take care and have a good rest," Agnese added softly as Mr Rivello accompanied the two of them out.

AT 4PM, THE CARABINIERI KNOCKED on Agnese's door. Paolo had had the decency to call her beforehand to announce their plans. The maresciallo asked them to tell him what they had seen, turning to Giò with a sneer.

"So, you were there this time too."

"I hope that is not causing you any inconvenience," Giò replied drily.

"It's not a matter of convenience, rather of opportunity. It seems since you arrived back in Maratea, you have always been in the thick of the action."

"It's not a pleasure, I can assure you, but it's better than being the one under a falling rock or vase. If you don't mind, of course."

Agnese interrupted her sister. She feared nobody more than people who, like the maresciallo, totally lacked a sense of humour. Without the safety net of irony, they could easily become obsessive, even when they were on the side of justice.

"Please, Giò, let the maresciallo speak. I'm sure he wants to know what we saw and if we can contribute in any way to the investigations."

As much as the maresciallo disliked Giò, he was starting to like Agnese, who acknowledged his authority instead of challenging it.

The two women described what they

had seen and done, from the falling vase just missing Mrs Rivello, to Mr Rivello's fruitless pursuit of the mysterious runner in the alleyway, to the inspection of the empty house.

"So it was probably the same murderer, wasn't it?"

"We don't know yet if this was an attempt to kill Mrs Rivello," the maresciallo replied huskily.

"Well it wasn't an attempt to romance her with a bunch of flowers..."

Paolo intervened to smooth the atmosphere. "We can't jump to conclusions. We don't know if this was an accident or not."

"Accident fiddlesticks! Same style of killing, same victim."

Giò's sister kicked her to tell her to keep her mouth shut, but it was too late.

"What do you mean, the same victim?" the maresciallo asked, while Paolo and Agnese both glared at Giò.

"Well, Maresciallo, you know how small Maratea is, and how fast gossip travels. Nobody believes the victim was meant to be Elena – we all thought it was Mrs Rivello in the car when we first arrived on the scene, so in all probability, the murderer did too. Since he didn't get it right the first time, he's tried again, using a falling vase instead of a falling rock. Maybe we can't jump to conclusions, but you'd better protect Mrs Rivello just in case."

The Maresciallo shrugged. "You can be sure, Miss Brando, that we know what we are doing. As much as you enjoy playing the amateur detective, you'd better leave it to the professionals."

Red in the face, the maresciallo signalled to Paolo that it was time to go, leaving without a thank you or goodbye. Unnoticed by his boss, Paolo silently indicated to the two sisters that they'd speak again soon.

9

IT'S A SMALL WORLD

"Can I try the other one too?" asked the short woman, pointing at a green enamelled necklace in a display window.

"Of course you can," Agnese replied, freeing the trinket from the pins that were holding it in the right position. "It's gorgeous, and this shade of green should suit you splendidly."

But when Mrs Tristizia, the estate agent's wife, tried it on, the necklace did not look half as gorgeous as Agnese had hoped. Mrs Tristizia was in her fifties but looked older, probably because she had neglected herself since her second son had been born. Truth was, she had never been a beauty, but self-neglect had taken its toll.

"Oh, it doesn't suit me," Mrs Tristizia said, disappointed. "Could you show me something else?"

"Mrs Tristizia," said Agnese sweetly, "I believe this piece of jewellery is right for you. I can show you others, of course, but may I suggest that a little make-up would highlight the green of your eyes?"

She looked at the older woman with a knowing smile. Mrs Tristizia had always refused similar suggestions from Agnese in the past, but this time she seemed more interested.

"Do you think make-up can help me?"

"I'm sure it can!"

"Will you show me something simple that I can do on my own that reflects who I am and won't turn me into someone else?"

"That's exactly the idea of make-up. I won't turn you into a rock star, I promise," Agnese replied.

For the first time since she had entered the shop, a faint smile dawned on Mrs

Tristizia's face. Agnese felt exultant, as she always did when she knew she was going to be useful to one of her customers. She had dreamed of helping Mrs Tristizia, as everybody in town knew her story far too well.

"Please take a seat. We need to start by taking care of your skin. I will clean it first, and then apply a gentle red clay mask to brighten it up and eliminate a few impurities."

"I didn't know this was a beauty salon."

"It is not a beauty salon. I will just show you which products to use and how they should become part of your beauty routine. You will see, it only takes a few minutes. It is a shame not to take care of your skin properly. As Granny says, we can change clothes whenever we want, but we're only given one skin to accompany us for our entire lives. Still, we use more care when we wash our shirts than when we rinse our face."

As she spoke, Agnese applied the clay

mask, staying away from Mrs Tristizia's eyes.

"It will take just three minutes. Use this mask once or twice per week."

The woman nodded.

Agnese removed the mask with a cotton wool ball and lotion, massaged hydrating cream into Mrs Tristizia's face, and with a few swift movements, applied eye corrector and a light foundation. Mrs Tristizia's skin was glowing. Agnese went on to add a gentle touch of eyeshadow, abundant mascara, a few strokes of peach blusher, and a natural gloss with a hint of peach.

"I'm done!" Agnese said, still holding the lip brush in her hand.

"Is that me?" cried Mrs Tristizia, staring at the mirror and hardly recognising herself. Of course, she was still not a beauty, but she looked fresh, neat and tidy. Then Agnese took the necklace and placed it around her neck. It made her green eyes sparkle vividly.

"My goodness!" the woman exclaimed.

"You've convinced me. Would you show me all the products I should use, and the make-up too?"

Agnese pulled down from the shelves a day and night cream, a smaller tub of eye cream, and everything Mrs Tristizia needed to use to clean her skin daily. She piled the products up on the counter and added a face scrub, a mask, a hand cream, some make-up, and finally the necklace.

"Shall I add it all to your husband's account?" asked Agnese, barely hiding a smug smile.

"Please do," Mrs Tristizia replied with gratitude as she signed the receipt Agnese had handed her. "I will pass by tomorrow, if you don't mind, so that you can see if I have applied the foundation properly."

"I will look forward to seeing you. Just call in any time you need my advice."

The two women smiled at each other, then Mrs Tristizia left the shop. As she walked out the door, Giò came in.

"No way could I stay at home

unpacking today. Was that Mrs Tristizia I just saw leaving?"

"Yes, it was."

"She looked different; she usually looks so tired and defeated. What has happened to her?"

"Nothing good, I'm afraid."

"Is Mr Tristizia still enjoying the good life while she works hard at home?"

"It might be worse than that. He's been seen around with the same young woman for a while now. They shop together, go to restaurants and the cinema together. Basically, they act as if they are the perfect couple."

"He used to be more discreet," said Giò.

"Yes, he's betrayed his wife since the day of their wedding, but he was at least secretive about it. Since he started to go out with Eleonora, he has done nothing to hide his infidelity."

"How long have they been together?"

"A year or so, I believe."

"That's a long time for Mr Tristizia."

"That's what I'm worried about. She's got him wrapped around her finger. When they come in here together, it is almost comical the way he looks at her when she tries a lipstick. It's as if he's never seen a woman before in his life." Agnese let her labeller fall on the counter with a crash.

"These pathetic 60-year-old men falling for 20-year-old girls. It's all the rage at the moment, but it is so unfair. Poor Mrs Tristizia – she gave up her career for her family, not so he could have a string of love affairs. And now do you think he will ask her for a divorce?"

"I do." Agnese nodded sadly as the shop door opened again.

"Good evening," a woman called, coming in.

Giò was shocked. She immediately squatted down, hiding behind the counter and leaving Agnese dumbfounded.

"Good evening, Mrs Di Bello, what a pleasure to see you," Agnese managed to say as her sister signalled frantically from beneath the counter not to give her away. "How are you?"

"I'm doing fine, dear, thank you."

"Has your daughter got married yet?"

"Not yet, but she will in a week's time. I need your advice on a lipstick to wear on the day."

For once, the woman didn't launch into a monologue about her daughter's wedding, much to Agnese's surprise. Instead, they went through a number of lipsticks until she found the one she liked.

Andrea walked into the perfumery and Agnese greeted him without taking her attention from Mrs Di Bello.

"Hello, Andy, we're choosing a lipstick, but I will be with you in a minute."

"Hello, Agnese, take your time. I will have a look around in the meantime." He browsed a cabinet filled with perfumes while Agnese picked the shade of lipstick Mrs Di Bello had chosen from a drawer and put the tester back in its place. The woman looked at her lips once again in one of the mirrors.

"It is perfect. Thanks, Agnese."

"Best wishes to your daughter, and if you pass by, I'd love to see the pictures from the wedding."

"I will certainly bring them in, you are such a dear. Bye bye."

As Mrs Di Bello left, Agnese gave her sister a quizzical look. "Why did you hide?"

"It was her!" Giò gasped, slowly rising up, making sure Mrs Di Bello was no longer in view.

"Her who?" Agnese asked.

"The woman I met on the train from Naples."

"Oh my goodness, you mean it was Mrs Di Bello you upset? You will be the death of this shop if you don't learn how to behave around people."

"But she was awful to me!"

Andrea was witnessing the whole scene with a mixture of surprise and amusement. "Do you usually squat behind the counter? I would have joined you, if I'd known you were there."

Giò flushed. "Of course I don't, but this was a special case."

Agnese nodded. "Now I see why she was so silent about her daughter's wedding. Usually once she's started, she keeps going for hours. You must have really scared her, but maybe you've cured her… at least for the moment."

"What are you talking about?" asked Andrea.

Giò gave her sister a pleading look.

"Mrs Di Bello and Giò had a difference of opinion about weddings. Ever since, Mrs Di Bello has kept her family tales to herself."

"Are you against weddings?" he asked Giò, half-mockingly.

"Totally!"

"It shows you're a foreigner," he said, admiration in his voice. "Weddings are the only things girls around here think about."

"Andy, it's not only like that in Maratea, I can assure you," Agnese said.

"Anyway, it will be a pleasure to speak

to someone who has a broader view on the topic," he replied.

Giò looked at him with a certain amount of suspicion. Was he teasing her, or was he flirting?

"I'm extremely sorry to disappoint you, Mr Aiello, but I don't agree with men's tendency to live in the moment and avoid any kind of commitment, either. This is folly. I think human beings need to create, to build relationships as well as things. Nothing can fulfil them as much as working on 'a project', and that includes a long-lasting friendship and/or relationship."

"So you're looking for a husband too?" Andrea tried to sound disappointed.

"No, I'm not. But I believe most men are blind: they mistake frivolity for freedom. It is not for me to cure them, but I don't want to be a victim either."

"Yours is a strong opinion, no doubt about it."

Agnese took advantage of the temporary truce in their conversation to ask, "Andy, did you come in for a reason? Any way I can help you?"

"Actually, I wanted to ask you about your sister. Is she OK? It can't be easy to arrive home and find herself in the middle of a murder inquiry with the carabinieri questioning her every day."

"She is made of stern stuff," Agnese laughed, "so I guess she is coping alright. Or at least, that's what she pretends."

"I was wondering if she'd like a little fresh air. Perhaps a short trip out on my boat, to help her relax."

Giò's eyes shone; she loved going out on the sea.

"Agnese, you can tell Mr Aiello that his offer is most welcome, as long as it's not an attempt to flirt. I believe I have explained my position thoroughly on that matter."

Agnese turned towards Andy. "Do you want me to repeat the conditions on which my sister will accept your thoughtful offer?"

"No need for that. And you can

reassure her that no flirting will be permitted on board."

"In that case, I'm glad to accept your invitation," Giò said, speaking directly to him this time.

"Shall we meet tomorrow, 9am at the City Hall fountain?"

"I'll be there. Should I bring something to eat?"

"No need for that, I will have everything on board."

"Fantastic!"

"See you tomorrow, then, and Agnese, thank you for your mediation."

"You're very welcome." As he left the shop, Agnese looked at her sister. "That was thoughtful of him."

"Indeed."

"I hate to say it, but beware... he knows how to handle women."

"What do you mean?"

"Despite what he might say, he is a flirt. He knows what women want, and he's ready to play the perfect guy."

"Perfect? But he's in his early 40s and

still unmarried, which is rare for such a handsome man in Maratea." Giò spoke as if she was an authority on Maratea's bachelors.

"He got married maybe 10 years ago, but it didn't last and they got divorced."

"No kids?"

"A girl, who's stayed in Rome with her mum."

"Anyway, I think I will enjoy a boat trip with him."

"Yes, I hope so, too. You've hardly had a break since you arrived."

"This is my settling-in week before I start work, and I've still got three boxes to sort, plus all the papers…"

They were interrupted by the sound of the door opening up as a new customer came in.

"Hem… good evening. Hem… would you mind if… er… I had a look around?"

"Not at all, you're most welcome," Agnese replied, smiling. "And should you need any advice, just ask. I'll be very happy to help."

"Hem, I will, thank you." The man was a giant, bigger than Nando. Not fat, but tall with broad shoulders, his size contrasting with his evident shyness. He moved through the cabinets, not touching a single object. Perhaps he didn't trust his big hands to handle the delicate items in the perfumery without damaging them.

Ten minutes later, he looked as lost as he had when he'd arrived, and Agnese felt it was time for her to intervene.

"Are you looking for a present, maybe?"

The man was evidently relieved by this offer of help.

"Yes, hem, in fact I am."

"For a lady, I guess?"

"Correct."

Agnese realised there would be no point in asking him if he would prefer a perfume, a trinket, a body cream; the question would only have made it even harder for him to decide.

"I have a very nice necklace here," she said, and she showed him a long piece made up of laces of different metals, each with a few fancy charms. The longest lace had no frills, but it carried a big heart in gilded metal, the top of which could be unscrewed to fill it with perfume. "It's a beautiful piece," Agnese continued, trying on the jewel to show the man what it looked like.

"Indeed," said the man.

Agnese removed the necklace and handed it to him so that he could have a better look. He barely touched it with the tips of his clumsy fingers.

"It's gorgeous, please could you... hem... wrap it nicely for me? Hem, I mean for her."

"I would be delighted, but don't you want to see anything else before deciding?"

The man looked around as if to evaluate the dazzling number of possibilities in the shop. Then he shook his head and said, "No... hem... I think this one should do. Don't you think so?"

Agnese wore her most sympathetic expression. "It will certainly do!" She took a turquoise box with the perfumery logo on and packed the necklace nicely, using a navy blue satin ribbon to seal the box. Her expert hands tied it in a bow on top, then she thought for a second. Choosing one of the bottles from behind the counter, she sprayed two jets of perfume into the carrier bag before sliding the box in and handing it to the man.

Curious as a child, he smelled the bag. "That is a beautiful perfume," he commented. "Should I buy a bottle of this too?"

"Let us wait and see if the lucky woman appreciates the perfume when you give her the present." Then Agnese opened one of the counter's drawers and took out a sample of a male fragrance. "This is for you. It's a nice musky scent." This man was clearly prone to giving away more than he asked for himself. Musk was also the scent of confidence, so it should give him a much needed boost.

"Thank you, I will... hem... definitely

try it. Not that I use perfumes much, but... hem... I like your shop. Thank you."

"Agnese, you certainly did well there. He was so worried when he came in," Giò commented as the man left.

"I wish I had more customers like that, just following my advice. I'm used to struggles and conflicts." She chuckled, then indicating a couple of boxes on the floor, she added, "How about we get a little work done? I have a new line of toiletries waiting to go on display."

"I'd be glad to help, and I'm curious to see them."

"I thought you would have had enough of boxes waiting to be opened."

"But that only applies to my own boxes. I already know what's inside, so there's no surprise, and in one of them I will find all my folders, invoices, bills and documents. Nothing as nice as a new toiletry line."

"First we need to make some room for the new stock. I think the cabinet next to the window should do. We only need to rearrange the old line to make space for the new one." She looked critically at the products on the shelf and decided, "I will put a few of these old items on discount here on the desk."

They moved the old stock around, then checked and priced the new line and tried the different testers. Agnese read the information cards so that they would know the properties of each product while they were smelling the Chinotto Bodywash or trying the Chestnut Hand Lotion.

"Oh, this Fico d'India scrub is absolutely phenomenal," Giò cried when she opened the tester bottle and smelled it. Not only did it have a delicious scent, but it was a delicate pink colour with Kiwi grains and Fico d'India seeds.

"Take it home with you. They sent two testers, so you can have one if you wish."

"Thank you, I will."

"Once you have tried something yourself, it's so much easier to sell it."

"Is that an attempt to hire me?"

"First you've been offered a date, now a

job. You're definitely enjoying your fair share of popularity since you arrived."

"I should decide what to do... for a living, I mean. I don't think that I will be able to maintain the same volume of travel writing here as I did when I was in London. Maybe I don't want to, either."

"Are you fed up with writing?" Agnese asked in wonder. Since childhood, Giò had loved two things above all others: writing and travelling, not necessarily in that order.

"I simply love writing, I'd just like to have more freedom about it. I hate writing travel guides, they're so predictable. And most of my time doesn't go into writing or travelling, but into searching for practical information. When does the museum open? What days, times, prices? The info on the website, is it correct? Will part of the building be under restoration for the next two, three years?"

"But you get to see places..."

"That is exactly why I keep accepting guide-writing projects. But even when I'm travelling, it is hardly heaven. Publishers only pay for a very short stay, which means I have to see an incredible amount of things one after the other. I need to find local guides to help me make the most of my time, and I try to add a few days of my own to develop 'a feel' for the place. But in a guide, that feeling is not allowed to emerge... My goodness, it sounds like I'm complaining. I'm not; I feel very grateful to be able to do what I do for a living."

"When I started this perfumery business, I had to sell all sorts of cheap perfumes and cosmetics. But I've evolved over time. You can't compare this shop to what it was 10 years ago, and I think it's the same with you. Now you've had your fill of your former dream, travel guides, what's your inner voice asking for? What's your next challenge?"

Giò hugged her sister and planted a big kiss on her cheek. "As usual, you have put my nebulous thoughts into words. I don't know what my next challenge will be yet, but you're right: I long for a new direction, a new purpose. I want to use more of my creativity, travel at my own pace. And maybe mend my broken heart at the same time. But don't feel sorry for me, I am already so different from the woman who left London."

"Oh, Giò, I'm so glad to hear that. If you need to make a big change, you might need time to prepare for it. Stay here for a few months, even a year. Why not? Don't rush into decisions. You can keep going with your work and decide later if you want to stay or go. Just allow yourself a little time."

"As usual, I will take my sister's advice, just like the Shy Man, and follow it thoroughly." Giò raised her hand to her temple. "O Captain! My Captain!"

10

A BOAT TRIP

The following morning, when Giò got up, the sun was shining in the clear sky with no trace of haze. She had her breakfast on the terrace, relaxing with a book while the sun caressed her back, but when she next looked at the clock, she almost shrieked in horror. It was a quarter to nine. As usual, she had mysteriously gone from being too early to being too late.

She brushed her teeth quickly, dressing in a hurry in jeans, white t-shirt and cardigan. No time even for a light touch of make-up, as Agnese had suggested.

Blessing the UK for ensuring she always had her waterproof jacket to hand, she grabbed her small rucksack, throwing in a towel and a pair of goggles.

On the way out, she stopped by at Granny's. When she told her about Andrea, Granny replied, "Oh, he is certainly a handsome man," and stared at Giò meaningfully.

"Granny, in a month's time I should have been marrying Dorian. I'm not running into another man's arms this soon, and maybe not ever."

"I was just making conversation. No hidden agenda."

"I don't trust you," said Giò, shaking her head vigorously.

"Well, you are almost 40, I have a right to be a little concerned."

"No you haven't. At 38," and she emphasised 38, "the best decision I can make is to stay single."

"Single?" Granny seemed to meditate upon the unusual word. "A spinster, you mean?"

"Oh, these southern Italian pressures to marry, all these subtleties and subterfuges," Giò burst out.

Granny put on her most innocent expression, but Giò was not to be fooled. "Gran, you use PCs better than I do. I almost suspect you are a hacker – you're more up to date than CNN news on what goes on in Maratea and the whole world. And you want me to believe you're not familiar with the word 'single'?"

"Well I might have heard it every now and then, I just wanted to make sure I knew what it meant..."

"Make sure, fiddlesticks! Please, Granny..."

"You know, he is an architect. He must be earning good money."

Giò rolled her eyes. "Gran, I'd better go before I say something I'll regret. No matchmaking, please, or I might flee back to London tomorrow."

"Oh dear me, I will stay as quiet as a mouse, but don't tell Agnese. She might get mad at me."

"And you fear her more than you do me?"

"You're the barking dog…"

"And she's the biting one. Poor Agnese, if only she knew what you thought of her."

"Better to keep it secret!"

When Giò left, Granny looked rather satisfied.

That worked well. Telling her how eligible he is was a stroke of genius. It provoked the Miss Contrary in Giò. I don't like that chap and I don't want her getting serious about him – I'd rather she stayed single. For a while, at least.

THE CHURCH CLOCK STRUCK 9 AS Giò reached the Town Hall Square. From a sleek black sports car, Andrea waved at her, then got out to greet her.

"You arrived on the dot – British punctuality?" he teased her. Goodness, Agnese and Granny were definitely right. Handsome? Oh yes, he was handsome, and he knew it. Tanned, sparkling dark eyes, a winning smile with perfect white teeth…

"I guess so," she said, getting in the car and pretending that she hadn't rushed. "Any breaking news this morning?"

"Do you mean about the murder?"

"That or anything else. Since I arrived, Maratea has been anything but the nothing-ever-happens-here kind of place it used to be."

"No, since the flowerpot episode, I haven't heard anything else. Maybe it's too early in the morning. We'll find out what's new on our way back."

"By the way, I'm due to visit Mrs Rivello at 4pm. She invited me for a cup of coffee when I first came back home and I haven't managed to take her up on it yet."

"We'll be back on time, don't worry."

"So, you've heard about Mrs Rivello and the flowerpot?"

"Of course, I have. As has everybody else in town." But Andrea wasn't as loquacious on the subject as she would have hoped.

"What do you think?" she prompted.

"About the accident?"

Is he playing for time? "Yes."

"Mr Rivello is worried. It seems the vase didn't simply fall off because of a gust of wind. It may have been that someone pushed it deliberately."

"But who would want Mrs Rivello dead?"

"The Rivellos have a number of enemies. They are notorious around here. Though, you know, I wouldn't expect them to be victims of a murder attempt."

"What do you mean?" Giò asked, grasping the door handle on her right. Andrea was a fast driver.

"Mr Rivello is involved in a number of political issues – lobbies and such like. And he has his business to promote. But in the sort of circles he moves in, an adversary wouldn't be likely to make an attempt on his life, or his wife's. It's more of a political tug of war, you know, to obtain public money, project funding, invitations to tender, etc. Blackmailing maybe, threats, but killing? I can't believe that. What I'm trying to say is that it seems there was more of a personal reason behind these attempts on Mrs Rivello's life, if they were murder attempts at all."

"Maybe she knows something she shouldn't?"

"If she knew something business related, she would inform her husband. No, I believe it has to be something personal."

"Like what?"

"A grudge, revenge. She is a strong-willed woman who speaks her mind far too openly. She might have wronged someone... I mean, in the eyes of the killer."

They'd arrived at the harbour. Andrea parked the car as close to the dock as possible, since they had quite a few things to transport onto the boat. He owned a powerful motor yacht, which was not exactly what Giò had expected as she preferred sailing.

Andrea took out a cool bag and grinned.

"Our lunch!"

"I'm impressed with your organisation."

"What else would you expect from an architect?"

Once they were on board the boat, Andrea gently manoeuvred it out of the little harbour. Giò could not take her eyes off the view. From land, Maratea harbour was beautiful, but from the water it was stunning, maybe because she could now appreciate the backdrop of the huge mountains surrounding it, the prettily coloured houses reflecting on the surface of water. Maybe she could only embrace it all from the sea.

"Please, Andy, do not go full speed till we reach Sapri. It's been too long since I last saw the coast."

Andrea nodded, and she was grateful to him for not speaking, letting the bays, the beaches, the forests pass by silently. She had a memory for every landmark. As a child, she had kayaked, swum and snorkelled in all these bays, and she had fancy names for each inlet, cave and rock, both above and under the water.

"Have you finished daydreaming? Are you back on board?" Andrea waved at Giò, who had drifted off into her own little world.

She walked over to join him in the cockpit. "I'm on board, and so very grateful. You can't imagine how many memories are coming back. I've been around the world and seen many memorable places, and I am so proud Maratea is one of the most beautiful. I wonder if you, living here all the time, are aware of it."

"I've not always lived here; I studied in Florence and lived in Rome for a while. But large cities are not for me. I like to visit them every now and then, but I love it here, despite all the limitations of living in a small place, pretty far from anywhere else."

"I know what you mean. I have to

make up my mind what to do, where to live my life. But today is too glorious a day to think about it. Where are we going?"

"How about a cup of coffee at the Cala di Mezzanotte and a dip in the water at Punta Infreschi?"

"Sounds like a perfect plan to me."

Andrea gently accelerated. They passed the closed road, but from beneath, with the dramatic mountains dropping down into the expanse of green and blue sea, Giò could hardly believe anything as evil as a murder could have happened there. But soon after they'd passed the closed road, they came to what was left of the landscape after the summer fires. Hectares and hectares of burned pine forest faced them, the black area standing out on the side of the mountains like a dark cemetery, a few skeletal trunks standing like gravestones with their bare branches reaching towards the sky.

"Oh my goodness, I didn't realise it was this bad. It's such a terrible sight!

Each summer, the same story. Why do people start fires?"

"They say it's the shepherds," Andrea replied casually.

"Shepherds? Why?"

"To gain land for new pastures."

"Come on, Andy, it is just solid rock. I can't imagine sheep grazing here."

"There are plenty of animals on the highlands."

"Yes, I know, but the fires are always started at road level or on the rock walls. They're hardly ever started where animals could be put out to pasture." Andrea looked up too, but didn't reply. Giò didn't like discussing the fires with the locals: they always replied as Andrea had, blaming the shepherds.

They stopped at a deep bay. On their left was the entrance to a tall cave, sunny reflections glimmering on the water. Andrea anchored the boat at a safe distance from the cave and poured two espressos.

"Sugar?" he asked.

"Two and a half, please."

He laughed. "You're definitely not on a diet."

"I can never get used to how strong it is." She smiled, wondering at how well the sea air and the aroma of coffee blended together. Andrea offered her some butter and lemon biscuits he had picked up at Iannini's.

"Delicious! Lemons from Maratea have an amazing flavour."

They stood in silence for a while.

"I think I should look to go kayaking soon. I thought I would wait till next spring, but I'd forgotten how beautiful the bay is in autumn."

"You'll get plenty of good days in October and November too. But we've got the boat, you don't really need a kayak."

"It's so different on a kayak. I can't go as far or as fast, but I have time to notice small things... and I just love the feeling of my arms paddling. There must be something fundamentally natural in it."

Andrea looked at her intensely, as if she

had said something he couldn't quite understand.

"Well, if you plan to go kayaking soon, we'd better take advantage of the fast boat today." With a gesture, he asked for her empty coffee cup, but she kept hold of it.

"No," she said, laughing. "The only thing I can do to help is to wash the dishes. You concentrate on the boat."

Andrea launched the yacht at full speed, keeping further from the coast and aiming for Punta Infreschi. The wind was exhilarating, and the temperature warmer than Giò had expected. They passed Sapri, Villamare, and the little village of Scario that Giò simply adored.

She looked up at Andrea.

"Next time, we could go to Scario for an aperitivo," he said, as if reading her thoughts.

"I'd love that."

After Scario, the landscape became dreamy again, with the rocks creating an infinite number of inlets, bays and coves. No villas; no buildings at all. When

Andrea slowed the boat down, Giò recognised a little tongue of rock that stretched out into the water to protect the inner bay. He turned to the right and they entered Infreschi Bay, the colour of the water going from deep blue to a crystal-clear green. On the sea bed, she could distinguish stones, rocks and the occasional fish swimming by.

Giò cried in wonder, "Oh, Andy, thanks so much. I've not been here for ages."

He smiled. "There's not a boat in sight, we have the place to ourselves. In August, you'd think it was the only place worth exploring, you have to fight so hard for space." He dropped anchor about 15 metres from a small beach. "How about a swim?"

"Impossible to resist."

They could see the blue shadow of the boat on the green sea bed, as if they were on a tropical island. In under two minutes, they were splashing in the water. Giò couldn't help but notice Andy's perfectly formed body. He was surely a gym fanatic:

broad shoulders, muscular arms, well-defined abs. Then she thought about her skinny figure.

All the better, she thought. She did not want him to be attracted to her... did she?

They raced towards the beach, and despite Giò being a fast swimmer, Andrea got there before she did.

"You're a good swimmer," he acknowledged, sounding surprised.

"But you won!"

"I had to fight tooth and nail for it."

"Give me a few weeks in Maratea and you won't stand a chance."

He laughed, and then he came closer. A bit too close. She dipped under water and appeared a good few metres away from him.

"A school of sardines!" she cried in wonder. The fish created a dark cloud, but as she dipped into them, the school opened up to let her in. Their thin bodies sent silver reflections all over the water. She followed them until she was tired and realised she had ended up on the other side of the bay, quite far from the boat where Andrea was already on the deck.

She swam back slowly and Andrea helped her on board.

"You can have a shower, if you want."

"But what are you doing?" she asked, watching him busy himself in the galley. "Are those clams?"

"Somebody has to prepare lunch. You don't want to fast, I hope."

"I was expecting a sandwich of some sort, not a real lunch."

"A sandwich? No way!"

"It wasn't a complaint."

"I hope not! It won't be a full lunch, though, just some spaghetti with clams and a fruit salad."

"It sounds wonderful to me," Giò replied, heading for the shower in the aft cabin.

When she came back, Andrea was already testing the spaghetti to make sure they were al dente. Two glasses of slightly sparkling white wine were ready for their toast.

"To your return to Maratea!"

"To my return!"

"Please, take a seat," Andrea said, serving a dish of delicious smelling pasta. "Garlic, olive oil, and just a couple of tomatoes. Very fresh clams. A sprinkle of finely chopped parsley, and we're done."

"I didn't know you were such an amazing chef."

"Come on, it is the simplest of dishes. But yes, I love cooking."

"Not typical for an Italian man."

"I'm afraid I'm divorced, so I have had to learn a few things to survive."

"Are you telling me you'd be a better husband now?" Giò could not help joking while twirling a mouthful of spaghetti around her fork.

"Just as bad, only now I can cook a few more things than I could."

They laughed.

"Agnese told me you have a child."

"Valeria. She is an eight-year-old beauty." He handed her his mobile phone to show her a few pictures of his daughter.

"She's gorgeous. And is that her mother?"

He nodded.

"She's a beautiful woman. Is it wrong to ask you why you broke up?"

"I could no longer bear to stay in Rome. Here, I knew I could get the same amount of work, but without all the stress."

"In Maratea? You can work as much as you did in Rome?"

"Yes, thanks to Mr Rivello. He has always liked the way I work. And here if you are in the right network, you can land quite a number of jobs. Enough for a more than decent living. In Rome, it's much more competitive. You need to work harder to get your name known, and life in general is so stressful."

"And your wife didn't like the idea of bringing up her child in a quiet and peaceful place?"

"She's always lived in Rome. It was OK for her to spend her holidays in Maratea, but she couldn't bear the thought of staying here all year round, particularly in the off season."

"Well, you were luckier than I was. Dorian, my former fiancé, wouldn't even come here for holidays. A weekend every couple of years was more than he could bear."

"Now, don't you think he was a fool?" said Andrea, looking around at the heavenly bay.

"To be honest, I think I was the foolish one." Giò chuckled. "Do you manage to see your daughter much?"

"Some weekends and during school holidays. She loves it in Maratea." He passed her a bowl containing a colourful fruit salad.

"I'm glad to hear that." Giò ate a spoonful of the salad meditatively, then asked him, "So, have you known Mr Rivello long?"

"In Maratea, everybody knows everybody as soon as they're born."

"But you've been working with him. Did he hire you?"

"No, I'm an independent architect. Mr Rivello hired a young architect for his building firm, but he often needs extra help. He also passes my name on to friends and friends of friends. He's usually working on large projects, but if friends contact him for advice on smaller jobs, he refers them to little companies and independent architects like me."

"If he only takes on large projects, is there enough work for him in Maratea?"

"Of course not, but remember we're close to Sapri and all the Cilento towns, and down south you have Calabria with its larger towns. Also, Mr Rivello's line of business goes beyond construction. You know, those political circles in which he moves mean all kinds of jobs passing through his hands: reforestation, assessments and intervention on risky areas, like the Acquafredda road. He has a share in these lines of business."

"Do you mean that Mr Rivello's company won the contract for the road security works in Maratea?"

"It's actually his brother-in-law's company that deals with that kind of work, but maybe Mr Rivello has a share in it. I'm not sure. You're questioning me harder than the carabinieri!"

"I'm sorry." Giò smiled guiltily. "I'm just so curious. I wonder if there's a connection between the fires, the tender for the contract and the attempt to murder Mrs Rivello. Maybe someone from a competing firm who didn't get the job is unhappy?"

"There's not a 'competing firm'; not in Maratea, at least. And killing your competitor's wife just for the sake of a contract doesn't make sense to me. It would make more sense to set fire to your rival's premises and machinery and put them out of business for a while."

"Hmm, you're right, it doesn't make any sense," Giò acknowledged, deciding to bring the conversation to an end, "I will do the dishes," and she crossed over to the sink.

He followed her inside with the cutlery.

"If you want to play the sleuth, I'd look at whether she has fired anybody, or flirted with someone's husband, or disappointed a lover…"

"Do you think Mrs Rivello is having an extramarital affair?"

"That's the word in the village, but according to the local gossips, there's no such thing as a happy marriage. You can never tell fact from fiction."

"And you? Have you ever heard anything about her that could be a motive for murder?"

He gave her a strange look. "No, I don't think so." But Giò didn't feel he was being completely honest with her this time.

"We'd better go if you want to get back in time to visit Mrs Rivello," he said, moving back to the steering wheel in the cockpit. "And then you can ask your questions directly of the individual concerned."

"It's still warm – you don't mind if I stay outside, do you? I can never get enough sun."

"Not at all, but only if you promise me you'll think about something other than the murder."

~

AN HOUR OR SO LATER, ANDREA dropped Giò off at the Town Hall Square where they had met that morning.

"I'm going to Rome this weekend. I actually had to ask the carabinieri for permission, which sounds ridiculous. They finally said yes, though the maresciallo complained a little."

"He's so stupid!"

"Maybe, but he's in command."

"That's exactly what frightens me the most: stupid people having power over others."

"I will call you when I get back... or maybe sooner."

Giò smiled at him. "It's been a wonderful day, Andy. I badly needed some fresh air."

"Don't I deserve a kiss?" He closed his

eyes, leaning his face towards hers. Giò was taken aback for a moment, then she kissed him on the cheek, laughing.

"Thank you for the day out, but don't forget my golden rule."

He pretended to be disappointed. "Next time we're going to Sorrento."

"Next time, we're hiking on Mount Coccovello."

"Hiking?"

"You look fit enough."

"I am, but in my free time I prefer to drive my boat. Wasn't it beautiful?"

"It was, but I love to conquer places with my legs and feet."

He shook his head, as if to say *I don't understand.*

"I'd better go. Have fun with your daughter."

11

DON'T SPEAK ILL OF
THE DEAD

Giò had texted Agnese from the harbour, so when she reached home, her sister was ready to go.

"How was it?" Agnese asked.

"It was fine, although he started flirting a little at the end, so I'm not sure I will see him on a one-to-one basis again. I believe he's a good chap, but he's not my type."

Agnese didn't say anything, but Giò was sure she was relieved.

"As for the murder, Andy believes there'll be a personal motive rather than something related to Mr Rivello's work."

"I think so too, mostly because it

wasn't intended as a warning: 'If you keep doing whatever you're doing, we will kill you'; it was two plain attempts to murder her."

Approaching the Rivellos' house, Giò raised her eyes to the empty building next door. The geranium pots were all gone, the empty windows looking sad and neglected.

Agnese rang the doorbell and Mariella opened the door. She was excited, they could tell. Here was another person, it seemed, happy to be involved in the case, even if only marginally. Giò imagined how the housemaid must have been the centre of attention in Maratea for the last few days, and how important she must have felt.

"Please come in, Mr and Mrs Rivello are waiting for you," she said in a solemn tone.

"How is she?" Giò asked.

"She is fine, though the carabinieri have asked her to stay home for the next few days. And I'm afraid she doesn't like that." Mariella stopped to answer Giò's question before leading them into a large living room. A rich sofa, finely crafted tapestries, antique paintings and dark ebony furniture created a luxurious, if rather formal, atmosphere. This was the 'public' living room, as compared to the smaller but more homely room they had seen the previous day.

Rising from an armchair where he had been reading a newspaper, Mr Rivello greeted them.

"I'm glad you came to visit Camilla. She will be happy to see you; she's not used to spending this much time at home. But we agreed with the brigadiere that it's better to avoid unnecessary risks. Today, I stayed home too."

Agnese enquired in a low voice, "Have you told her about her life being threatened?"

"I had to. The carabinieri suspect, as we do, that she might have been the intended victim in the car accident. They convinced me I could not protect her from the truth."

At that moment, the living room door opened and Mrs Rivello walked in. After she had greeted the sisters warmly, there was a momentary pause in the conversation. It seemed unnatural to discuss anything other than the murder, but at the same time it seemed indelicate to broach the subject with the victim herself. In the end, it was Mrs Rivello who restarted the conversation, and she wanted to talk about that very thing.

"I'm sure you've heard the news, that I should have died instead of Elena."

"Oh yes, we have heard," replied Agnese, adding, "The poor girl."

"She was not a poor girl!" Camilla Rivello replied drily. The two sisters were shocked by the hardness in her voice as they looked at her, waiting for an explanation.

"I know one should not speak ill of the dead, but I'm not a hypocrite. I didn't like the woman when she was alive," she glanced defiantly at her disapproving husband, "and I'm not going to pretend to like her now she is dead."

That wasn't what Giò and Agnese had been expecting at all. Both sisters had imagined finding the woman feeling guilty because another human being had died instead of her. Of course, they knew it had not been her fault, but still, that's how they imagined they would have felt in Mrs Rivello's place.

"I certainly wouldn't have asked her to run an errand for me if I'd had the slightest idea of what would happen. I didn't like her, but I certainly didn't wish her dead."

"I heard she'd been working for you for a long while, Mr Rivello, and that you trusted her."

Mr Rivello was evidently annoyed by the turn of the conversation. "Elena was a great help to me," he snapped. "She was a good secretary, an efficient employee, and I'm sure my wife appreciated her services too, since she used them on a number of occasions."

Mrs Rivello waved a dismissive hand at his words. "I realise that she was good at her work. If you told her to do something, you could trust her to carry it out on time and with due diligence – a rare talent here in Maratea. What I'm referring to is more a gut feeling. I never liked her and will never pretend I did."

"Women are rarely appreciative of other women," was Mr Rivello's stern reply.

"Did you appreciate her?" Agnese asked him.

"Of course. As Camilla acknowledged, it's not easy nowadays to find someone so efficient and reliable," he said, looking at his wife meaningfully.

"Was she dealing with confidential issues? At your company, I mean."

"Of course, she knew almost everything that passed through the business. A secretary becomes a sort of diary in a company."

It was obvious that Mr Rivello trusted Elena completely, but had their relationship gone beyond business? Mrs Rivello seemed jealous of her husband's absolute confidence in the young woman, but that didn't necessarily mean there was more to it. It was a typical reaction, to be expected. Or was it?

Mariella knocked on the door and came in with a silver tray and porcelain cups for the coffee, a jug of water and a few homemade biscuits. The Rivellos and their visitors moved to a larger table to drink their coffee.

"Do the carabinieri have any theories about who the murderer could be?" Agnese asked, holding the thin porcelain cup to her lips.

"No, not really," Mrs Rivello replied. "It seems they have no idea."

"But maybe you have some suspects?" *I certainly would have,* Giò thought, *if somebody wanted to do me in.*

"I really can't think of anybody."

"I don't understand it myself," said Mr Rivello. "He must be a psychopath. I can't imagine why someone would make an attempt on my wife's life."

Giò and Agnese exchanged a glance, having heard about the controversial character of Mrs Rivello only too often. So far they had only elicited obvious answers, so they had to dig deeper.

"Maybe somebody held a grudge against you, Mrs Rivello. Did you sack somebody, perhaps?" Giò asked boldly.

"Sack? I don't work at my husband's company, I work in a school office in Sapri. I can't sack anybody. In any case, if every dismissed worker was to kill his former boss, we would have a massacre on our hands."

"But I imagine you have strong views on... ahem... discipline, and you might have encouraged your husband to sack someone."

"Only once, years ago. I heard that a new employee was dealing drugs. The carabinieri never found anything, but yes, that time I encouraged my husband to get rid of that awful guy."

"Yes, Camilla opened my eyes in that case, and all my employees were grateful to be rid of him."

"Then what happened?" Agnese asked.

"He was not from Maratea. Salerno, I believe. But after we sacked him, he stuck around for a few months. He clearly didn't appreciate his treatment, but he didn't dare confront me or my husband. After that, he was seen in somewhat dubious company, and for a couple of months, there were quite a few robberies in the nearby villas. And you know, that's unusual – we can normally leave the doors unlocked as we feel so safe here. Anyway, I'm sure it was him and his friends, though the carabinieri never caught them. Finally, when things got too tense for them, they scooted off."

"Could it be that he has returned?"

"But that was almost three years ago. I can't imagine him coming back simply to kill me. After all, I didn't manage to send him to prison as I'd hoped. Nor would he have alerted me with threatening letters."

"Threatening letters?" Giò and Agnese asked at the same time.

"Camilla received a couple of threatening messages before this business started," Mr Rivello explained reluctantly.

"Oh my gosh!" Agnese said, putting her cup down in surprise. "It is worse than I thought. I kept hoping it might all be a mistake, that it was an accident that just looked like a murder attempt. But this changes everything."

"What kind of messages were they and when did you receive them?"

"I'm not sure we're allowed to share this with you," Mr Rivello said. "The carabinieri might want to keep this information private during their investigations."

If the Rivellos aren't talking, Paolo will tell us even less, Giò thought miserably. But Camilla Rivello unexpectedly came to her rescue.

"Sure, we can tell them. After all, poor Giò was involved from the first moment. She deserves to know."

This time, Mr Rivello did not seem as annoyed as when they had been talking about Elena. Maybe he was just used to giving in to his wife. Whatever the case, he explained without any further reservations.

"The first letter arrived two weeks ago. It was slid under the door and made out of newspaper cuttings, and it read, 'You will pay for it'. On the envelope, my wife's name was written in capital letters."

"Do you still have it?"

"No. At the time, I just thought it was a joke in poor taste. The cut-out letters made it seem to be nothing more than a kid's prank. I read it by mistake, thinking it was for me, then destroyed it and didn't mention it to my wife. I only told her to be careful."

"And the second one?"

"The second message arrived on the day of Elena's funeral. This time it was in the letterbox – it had been sent with the rest of the post from Maratea. It arrived in the morning when we were at the funeral, but with all that happened, I didn't open the mail till the evening. I had to call the carabinieri back."

"What did it say?"

"'You will not escape for a second time!'"

"Oh my goodness! Have you got this second message?"

"We gave it to the carabinieri this morning. I may have thought the first one was a joke, but this time I knew it was something far more sinister, and I'd have to tell Camilla about both notes."

"And neither of you have the slightest idea who the author could be?"

"Absolutely not."

After that, Mrs Rivello made it clear she was no longer interested in talking about the murder. She asked about Granny, then asked Giò a whole load of questions about her cancelled wedding and plans for the future. She asked Giò if she was sure she could make a living writing, insisting – much more than Giò could tolerate – that the arts should be left to the financially independent, or to those women who have a rich husband to pay the bills. Eventually Agnese, sensing an imminent reaction from Giò, said it was time for them to leave.

~

MARIELLA ACCOMPANIED THE TWO sisters to the door. She was wearing a light jacket as she was ready to go herself. Once they were downstairs, Agnese stopped and patted her pockets.

"Oh, silly me, I've left my sunglasses upstairs."

"I will go to fetch them..."

Agnese smiled. "Thanks, Mariella, but I'm not sure where I put them. I'd better go and look myself – you've already had a long day anyway."

"Oh, it has been a long day," Mariella replied, clearly grateful that someone had finally realised how hard she had to work.

Agnese went back upstairs, where she

could hear Raimondo Rivello speaking in the living room.

"Was it necessary to put Elena down like that? Couldn't you just have said you felt sorry for her?"

"That's exactly how I don't feel. I can't see why I should pretend."

"Because this is a case of murder!"

"So what?"

"Murder means 'suspects', and you should stay clear of suspicion."

"Clear of suspicion? I was meant to be the victim!"

"And that is exactly why you shouldn't give people other ideas."

There was a pause. Agnese, feeling she couldn't eavesdrop any longer, knocked on the door and entered the room, pretending to be slightly out of breath as if she had just climbed the stairs.

"I'm sorry, I forgot my sunglasses."

Mr Rivello was startled. Mrs Rivello spoke first.

"Come on in, dear, I can't see them,"

she said, looking at the sofa where Agnese had been sitting.

"Here they are," Agnese said triumphantly, crossing over to the table where they'd had their coffee and showing the Rivellos the glasses. "I'm so sorry, I'm always forgetting things."

"Don't worry. Just try to persuade your sister to find a serious job."

Agnese decided she'd better ignore Mrs Rivello's last remark – it would take the patience of a saint to deal with that woman more than once a year.

Mr Rivello accompanied her to the top of stairs.

"No need to come down with me," she told him, aware of him watching her till she reached the ground floor and shut the front door behind her.

WHILE AGNESE WAS UPSTAIRS, GIÒ had a short chat with Mariella.

"Mrs Rivello is a dear, but she must be

a very demanding person to work for."

Mariella looked up, as if to check that all the balcony doors were shut.

"She really is. I mean, it's a well-paid job – the Rivellos are amongst the few people who give a housemaid a decent salary – but I can tell you, I earn every single cent. Mrs Rivello wants her home to sparkle. She notices every detail, saying the ironing isn't good enough, the carpets aren't hoovered well enough."

"But you must know things about them, too..."

"I shouldn't say it, but..." she paused, "I do know a lot about them."

"So do you have any idea who might have tried to kill Mrs Rivello?"

Mariella looked around again to make sure nobody was listening, then nodded mysteriously.

"I have my suspicions."

Giò gasped. "Have you told the carabinieri?"

Mariella raised and dropped her

shoulders. "They never asked me," she said, sounding a little resentful.

At that moment, Agnese rejoined them. "I found my sunglasses – I'd left them on the coffee table."

"I'm glad." Mariella looked at her watch. "I need to rush, I'm very late."

"I hope to speak to you again," was the only thing Giò managed to say before Mariella left.

"I have to open the perfumery," said Agnese, also looking at her watch, "but I've got things I want to discuss with you."

"I've got a few errands, and Granny asked me to buy something for dinner."

"Shall we talk after dinner? Nando will be watching football in the bar with his friends, and Lilia and Luca will almost certainly be playing computer games."

"Sounds good," Giò said.

12

GOSSIP IS THE GLUE

"Auntie, can I sleep at yours on Saturday? There's no school on Sunday," asked Lilia, the second part mainly for her mother's benefit.

"Of course you can. Actually, I have a better plan: Luca and you could come over for dinner, we'll watch a ghost movie on TV, and then you can be my guests for the night."

Lilia screamed with joy, but Luca looked rather worried.

"Are you going to cook? For real?" he asked.

"No, we will get pizza and chips."

"That sounds better," said Luca with obvious relief.

"You don't trust me to cook?"

"Not at all!"

"Agnese, you remember when I said you'd created a monster?"

Agnese nodded.

"Well, I was wrong: you created two!"

To Lilia, sleeping at her auntie's and watching a ghost movie sounded so grown-up. It didn't matter that Giò only lived one floor above her home, it was the treat of a lifetime. Luca was just as happy, but being 12 years old, he couldn't show it as plainly as his younger sister.

Agnese looked at her watch and said, "I'm afraid it is not Saturday yet, so it's time for kids to go to sleep."

"Are we allowed 30 minutes on the internet first?" Luca asked.

"Only 15."

"Mum! At least 20 – please?"

"OK, but come the 19th minute, I will warn you that I'm going to shut down the

Wi-Fi in a minute, and there will be no arguments."

They knew their mum meant business.

Once the children had run to their bedrooms, Agnese and Giò sat around the kitchen table to tell Granny what had happened that day, including their visit to the Rivellos.

Granny, pulling two trays of dried tomatoes out of the now cold oven, commented casually, "This proves that woman has no idea how tactless she is. For my part, I can think of at least three people who might wish her dead."

Agnese and Giò's mouths dropped open. It was a good minute before Giò finally babbled, "You mean they just wish her dead, or they might do something about it?"

"The difference between the two is not as big as you might think," Granny said. She was preparing preserves of dried tomatoes in olive oil, and all her attention seemed to be on putting the tomatoes into the sterilised jars.

"Come on, Granny, there's a lot of people I wish dead, but I wouldn't kill any of them myself."

"Do you wish Dorian dead?" Granny asked, raising her eyes from her work.

Giò was taken aback. She was thinking of him, yes, but she couldn't believe it was so obvious.

"I'd think about it for a second before replying," Granny said, layering the tomatoes with oregano, garlic and chilli.

"Well, maybe not dead, but... almost!" In truth, had she received news that he had died, accidentally or otherwise, she would have felt it – badly. She hated him for all she'd suffered, but it was not enough for her to enjoy the idea of his death.

"So who are the three suspects?"

"Wait one moment," said Agnese. "It's curfew time for the children."

When Agnese had returned from ending Luca and Lilia's internet time and chasing them off to their beds, she looked expectantly at Granny. Granny glanced at her first jar, which was only a third full.

"I see this discussion is going to take longer than I thought. I'll tell you just one story. This happened last year, and the person involved moved away from Maratea. Agostino Atena, the son of a lawyer, was to marry Valeria, a beautiful young local woman. But we all knew Agostino was an unrepentant philander, and marriage wouldn't inhibit him from carrying on with his libertine ways.

"It so happened that one evening, Camilla Rivello found him in a backstreet, kissing a girl passionately, and made such a scene, you would have been forgiven for believing Valeria was her daughter. It was no good the young lawyer telling Camilla to mind her own business; she went into one of her tantrums and threw all his past affairs back in his face while a few passers-by stopped to listen. Of course, by the next day, the whole village knew about the incident. Agostino was furious, but even madder was young Valeria."

"She was mad at Mrs Rivello? Why?"

"Because she'd wanted to marry Agostino, regardless of his reputation. She knew all about it, but it was one thing for people to believe she didn't, quite another for them to know that she knew, if you see what I mean."

"No!"

"It was one thing to have people pity her because she loved an unworthy man, another to put up with their insinuations if she were to marry him, knowing full well that he'd betrayed her."

"So did they split up?"

Granny kept silent. She was filling one of the jars with olive oil, but to make sure no air got trapped in between the tomato layers, she had to keep gently swirling it around till the layers were completely submerged. Only then did she reply.

"They did, and Valeria left Maratea and went to live in Marina di Camerota, swearing she'd never set foot here again. And she never has done since."

"Oh my goodness," said Agnese.

"So what's the moral of this story?" Giò asked, both sisters looking at the jar Granny was scanning against the light to make sure no bubbles of air were coming up.

"There's not a moral. But I'm convinced that given the opportunity, Valeria would kill Mrs Rivello if she were sure she would get away with it."

"I thought Agostino would be the likely killer. After all, he was the one who was found out."

"Not at all. For Agostino, the risk of being found out was all part of the game. It's like gambling: you accept the risks. He knew he could get caught anytime. But for Valeria, it was altogether different. I guess it also depends on the personality. Agostino is an epicurean – he loves the good life, and would never risk ending up in prison. Valeria, on the other hand, is a more vengeful type."

"But you said she never came back, so she can't be among the suspects."

"No, of course she can't. I only told you

this story to show you what kind of person Camilla is, not because I suspect Valeria. Camilla thinks no one could possibly want her dead, not realising her superiority complex and lack of tact have made her lots of enemies. She is totally unaware of the consequences of what she says. In fact, she is rather proud of being such an outspoken person."

"Shouldn't you tell us who the other people you suspect are?" Giò protested.

"I do not suspect anybody – yet! All I said was that there are at least three people I know of who would be very glad to kill Camilla, if they knew they could get away with it."

"I don't understand your point of view, Granny. Are you protecting them?"

"Of course not. But if there's no reason to believe they had occasion to murder her, there's no point in me drawing attention to them. You should try to find who the carabinieri suspect. And of course, if any one of my suspects is also on their list, I will give you the full story."

"Granny, let me help you," said Giò, reaching for one of the jars of tomatoes, exasperated by how slowly the old woman's answers were coming.

"No!" Granny replied, snatching the jar from Giò's hands. "I'm sure you'd press the tomatoes to death, or let too much air in, or lose track of the layers of chilli and garlic, putting in too much of one and too little of the other."

"Can't see what difference it'd make."

"That's exactly why I won't let you do it."

Before the conversation could descend into a quarrel, Agnese asked, "And what do you think of what I overheard, Granny? Mr Rivello was mad at his wife."

"That woman is an absolute disaster. Raimondo is afraid she might cause even more trouble."

"Don't you think it's a little suspicious? His reaction, I mean."

"Most natural, I'd say. She might put the idea in the carabinieri's heads that she had a reason to kill Elena. And now this second jar is done."

"Couldn't that be the case?" Agnese asked, ignoring the remark about the tomatoes.

"If it were the case, even Camilla wouldn't be so outspoken about it. Also, she's not the type who would ever kill anybody. She doesn't need to inflict a physical death on anyone, her tongue is sharp enough."

"I'm not convinced, there's something fishy going on," Giò grumbled, looking at the perfectly filled jars.

"This is exactly what Raimondo fears. If she keeps speaking her mind about how much she disliked Elena, who died in her place, people won't know how to feel about her. From being the victim, she might end up suspected of being the culprit."

"How about their marriage? Is Mr Rivello a faithful husband? Does he really care about his wife?"

"Raimondo is an ambitious and

sometimes cruel man. He loves his position of authority here in Maratea, and has always had few scruples in pursuing his objectives. But I've never heard any convincing stories about him betraying his wife. It looks as if he simply adores her, and his daughters, and wants them to be as successful as he is."

"Talking about suspects, while Agnese went upstairs to fetch her sunglasses, Mariella told me she could think of someone, but she left before I could question her further."

"Speak to her again, but she's probably just read too many mysteries. Mariella loves to be the centre of attention and will make up any story in order to get there. So, Giò, how was your day on the boat?"

Giò told them what she had discussed with Andy, but didn't say anything to Granny about his little flirt. For a moment, she remembered his body in his swimming shorts – *my gosh!* – but after Granny's unsubtle attempt at matchmaking that morning, she wanted to keep her report as impersonal as she could.

"So I can't see him having any reason to want Mrs Rivello dead," she concluded.

"I frankly doubt he would tell you if he did. Don't be so naïve!" Granny grinned, tilting her head.

"Granny, may I remind you that you're not an expert detective either?" replied Giò resentfully. She was trying her best.

"But I'm an expert gossip."

"So what?"

"If you want to hear the gossip about Andrea, you don't ask Andrea, you ask Carlo. If you want gossip about Mrs Rivello, you ask her closest friends. My impression is that you went barging in there with the wrong questions. You want people to talk in confidence without reserve, which of course they will only do when they are talking about someone else. Certainly not when they're speaking about themselves."

"But gossips rarely tell the truth," Agnese said.

"Of course they do. Certainly, you have to do some homework – you need to ignore all the embellishments and the fluff, and seek out the juicy bones."

"How can you tell the difference between what is true and what's not?"

"Look for patterns. If something keeps cropping up over and over again, that's where the truth generally lies. There's no smoke without fire." And she looked at the transparent oil in her jar.

"You are an expert, aren't you," Giò teased.

"I've lived in Maratea for a lifetime, not in London." Granny smiled meaningfully.

"Oh, I'm sure you would set up a Secret Gossip Club in London if you lived there," Agnese said, laughing.

"You're right. After all, Shakespeare was from England, and he certainly knew the importance of gossip in any society."

"I thought love, charity and respect were the worthy things in society, not gossip," Giò said.

"Love, charity and respect are

important values, but gossip is the glue that holds small communities together. It controls social behaviour. Of course, too much gossip can lead to bigotry and negativity, but overall, here in Maratea we generally enjoy the healthy side of it, and only a pinch of the poisonous flip-side." Granny looked extremely pleased with herself, but it was hard to tell if that was because of what she had just said or because of the six jars of tomato preserve that were finally sealed and ready to be stored.

"And on this pearl of wisdom, I'd say it's time we all got some sleep," Agnese concluded pragmatically.

13

AN UNEXPECTED WARMONGER

Agnese was putting out the few pieces of outdoor furniture she stored in the perfumery overnight, including bulky rattan armchairs and a little table. She loved to sit outside and read a good book, although this didn't happen very often. Only on the rare occasions when she felt she had done all she needed to do in the shop. Sometimes, she also enjoyed sitting at the table and chatting with some of her customers while testing a selection of perfumes.

As she placed the table in its usual

spot, a firm masculine voice spoke behind her.

"Good morning, Agnese."

"Good morning, Mr Lavecchia."

"Am I disturbing you?"

"Of course not. What can I do for you?"

"My wife said she came over and really enjoyed trying a body cream you sell."

He was such a perfect gentleman. Agnese was positive Mrs Lavecchia would have expressed herself in very different terms.

"Yes, I remember. In fact, she was deliberating between two. Please come in," she said, and inside they went. Agnese showed Mr Lavecchia the two products; he enquired about their prices, and chose the more expensive one. She was slightly concerned that the woman might come back in a fury, claiming Agnese had tricked her husband, a solid engineer over whom she certainly had no influence, into buying the more costly product.

"Please, keep the receipt. Should your wife decide she would prefer the other one, she can come back and exchange it in the next seven days."

"I'm sure this is the product she wants, but I will keep the receipt, just in case. Thank you." He smiled at her before leaving.

Let's hope for the best. I'd rather not have any more scenes this week, she thought as the door opened to admit another customer.

"Good morning," said a woman wearing heavy, almost theatrical make-up. It took a whole minute before Agnese recognised her. Behind tonnes of foundation and lashes burdened by too much mascara, staggering on exceedingly high heels that she was not used to, squeezed into an incredibly tight electric blue dress, was Mrs Tristizia.

Agnese was too shocked to hide her surprise.

"Mrs Tristizia, is that you?"

"Of course it's me, dear. Your advice was precious." Then she added in a conspiratorial tone, "But I need more!"

"More of what?" cried Agnese, feeling more bewildered by the second.

"You see, I've heard that you give advice on perfumes." She lowered her voice and got closer to Agnese, leaning her elbows on the counter. "Not just in choosing one, as we've always done, but that you actually offer a consultation. I'd love to do that."

Something had clearly gone badly wrong since Mrs Tristizia last visited the perfumery, but the woman's imploring eyes begged Agnese for a positive reply. "*At least,*" Mrs Tristizia's expression seemed to say, "*let someone be on my side.*"

"Yes, I do, but perfumes are not magic potions. They only help us to understand what is going on inside ourselves."

Mrs Tristizia nodded. "I understand. So will you give me a session?"

"Let's move to the larger table," Agnese replied, but she wasn't convinced any good would come out of the consultation.

Agnese handed her the candles. Mrs

Tristizia discarded all the fresh, simple scents, and chose an enveloping and sensual jasmin. Agnese had the feeling that the older woman had not been totally honest with herself, as if she had chosen to appeal to a certain idea hovering in her mind rather than her senses. As for the accord, first she chose a sophisticated aldehydic one, then a pungent if sensual chypre. Agnese did not like the direction the process was taking.

When they used the perfume table, the spinning top indicated Chanel No.5. Agnese could hardly imagine anything more unsuitable for Mrs Tristizia, who not only bought the 200ml bottle, but also asked for the whole toiletry line: shower gel, body cream, hair perfume and body powder. Then, wobbling on her high heels, she left with a cheerful, hopeful grin.

Agnese was extremely disturbed. *Never, ever have I been cheated in this way. Why did I allow myself to be complicit in that?*

In the hope she would see no more demanding customers that day, Agnese took the monthly credit card receipts, checked them against the bank balance sheet and registered them in her account file. It was a boring task, but she needed some sensible numbers to deal with. There were times when bookkeeping provided her with a much needed sense of stability.

Two hours later, the door opened and Agnese smiled when she recognised young Cabiria. But the girl's face was completely different from the sweet one of their first meeting. In fact, without returning her smile or greeting, Cabiria faced Agnese.

"What kind of perfumes did you give me?" she demanded.

"I gave you a sample of Dzongkha! and one of Io, Myself."

"That's not what I mean," Cabiria snapped. "They are not normal perfumes, they are doing things to me. What are they really?"

"What do you mean?"

"I started to wear them as you..." she stumbled over her words "...as you prescribed, but since then I have had strange dreams. I see places I've never been to. What kind of spell have you cast? What are you trying to do to me?"

"Perfumes do not cast spells." It was so hard to find the right words under the young woman's accusing glare. Cabiria's eyes were deep black, and more penetrating than you would ever suspect from such an apparently fragile little person. "Of course, they can connect you with your inner feelings, remind you of who you are and where you come from. The sense of smell is the least rational of the five senses..."

"I did not come here for a lesson in the art of perfumery. I want to know what else you put in those two vials."

"I just filled the vials with the perfumes we chose. Could you please explain to me what's happening?"

"I don't understand. I'm sure you put

something else in those perfumes which is causing hallucinations..." She shook her head vigorously.

This time, it was Agnese who lost her temper. "This is a perfume shop, no more than that. It's been in my family for three generations, and I'm certainly not playing tricks on my customers. You are making some serious accusations. But I have the impression you're blaming other people while it is obvious that what you are afraid of is looking into yourself."

Cabiria looked at Agnese in dismay. Agnese calmed down a bit and repeated, "So what's been happening, exactly?"

"From the very first night I wore Dzongkha! I started to see things I do not like and that have nothing to do with me: foreign countries I've never even thought of visiting, rural villages in faraway places, faces of people I don't know. I don't want any more of that." Cabiria's face went red. Agnese didn't know if it was in anger or if she had simply blushed.

"You're an adult, and you are free to do

what you please. Just make sure you don't neglect yourself while playing the perfect daughter. Later on in life, it might become more difficult, if not impossible to make a free choice."

"Thanks for your help, but I don't need an advisor. I don't even know why I came here in the first place. Bye!"

"Courage be on your side, Cabiria," Agnese added just before the young woman left, slamming the door behind her.

"Who was that?" Giò had stopped by the shop on her way home and seen Cabiria leaving in a fury.

"That was young Cabiria."

"She didn't look much like the sweetheart you described."

"She's fighting her demons, and nobody looks nice during that struggle."

"How's she coping, then?"

"She is running away from herself just now, which seems like the easy path to take. But I hope she will stop and accept the fight."

"I didn't realise you were such a warmonger."

"I'm a pacifist when it comes to wars with other people, but a fighter when it comes to inner battles."

There was a beep from Giò's phone.

"It's time for the Maratea Amateur Sleuths to get together!" she cried, reading an SMS from Paolo. "Should we meet at home?"

"Better in your flat," Agnese thought aloud. "There will be no family eavesdropping there."

"He says early this afternoon. That should be fine."

She messaged him back. And at 3 that afternoon, Paolo arrived in Giò's flat.

14

UNDER SUSPICION

Paolo listened to what the two women had to report, asking them precise questions and scribbling down notes of what they told him. He wasn't happy to hear that Mariella had spoken to Giò, but tried to roll with the punches nonetheless.

"When I spoke to her, she didn't say a thing. Giò, could you find a way to get more out of her? She will probably open up to you rather than us."

"I will find a way to speak to her. But what have you discovered so far?"

"I'm sorry, I'm not allowed to share the details of ongoing investigations with anybody." Paolo at least had the decency to look embarrassed. Giò put down her coffee cup to express her disappointment, but Agnese cut her short before any words could come out of her mouth.

"Come on, Paolo," she said amiably, "the maresciallo gossips at the bar, so the whole village knows where you are with your inquiries. He said he isn't convinced it's a murder case at all. And even the least observant people think all he really wants is an easy life."

"It's true. The maresciallo doesn't like any kind of inconvenience." Paolo gulped down a huge bite of cake. "He is in denial and would like the whole thing to come to an end right now. He keeps repeating that it was an accident, and Faraco made up the story about the rock being levered from its spot to cover up for his mistakes."

"I never thought of that!" Giò banged her forehead with her hand. "This case is like a kaleidoscope – the picture keeps changing, taking on an altogether different form according to who is looking at it.

Each time we turn round, there's a new scenario to consider. First, we thought it was Mrs Rivello who had died, then no, it's poor Elena. Then we thought it was an accident, but no, it's a murder. We believed the murderer wanted to kill Elena, but it was Mrs Rivello they really wanted to do in. It's so confusing!"

"Might it have been an accident after all?" asked Agnese, ignoring her sister's comments.

"There's a vague possibility, but the maresciallo is excluding any other. And we might have a killer out there who has not yet accomplished his mission."

"But how does the maresciallo explain the threatening letters?" Giò asked.

"He thinks they were a kids' game," Paolo replied, clearly unconvinced.

"How about the flowerpot incident, then?" Agnese asked.

"A gust of wind. It came down because it was the only one with no protection around to stop it from falling." Again, his words lacked the ring of truth.

"What a coincidence, though! A vase falls, just missing the woman who's already had one attempt made on her life and who has received two threatening letters."

"Exactly. As a carabiniere, I don't believe in coincidences, and in this case there are just too many."

"So how are you going to proceed?" Agnese asked as Paolo refilled his coffee cup.

"I'm looking at both motive and opportunity. Who was or might have been at the murder scene? The first thing we did was to reconstruct the movements of all the people we know who passed the scene on their way from Maratea to Sapri."

"Wait a second, Paolo, Nando has just got me a magnetic blackboard from Praia a Mare." Giò disappeared into the adjacent bedroom, continuing to talk as she went. "I normally use one for planning my travel books, creating a mind map, remembering the locations and facts I want to share, adding a few photos or images from papers, that kind of thing." Giò reappeared with a large box containing a 70 by 100cm board. "It's perfect for our investigations, isn't it?" she asked, looking very pleased with herself.

"I'm impressed! You look like a real... ahem... British detective from a novel," Paolo joked. "But won't you need it for your work?"

"I will just use pen and paper for that. The blackboard will be entirely devoted to the case till we come up with the solution."

"But your nephew and niece will know everything about the case!"

"Nope." Giò flipped the board around and on the other side was a map of the world.

"Again, I'm dazzled," Paolo admitted.

With the help of the other two, Giò hung the board on the only free wall space. A hammer and nails were already to hand – she had been intending to do the job soon anyway.

"Ta dah!" she cried with satisfaction,

adjusting the coloured chalks on the pen tray. "Let's start."

"Our story begins the night before Elena's murder. At around 9pm, Mrs Rivello starts to feel unwell. She speaks to her husband, and then she rings Elena to ask her to go to Sapri the next morning to deliver some documents on her behalf. Elena agrees to pick up the keys to Mrs Rivello's car from Mariella at 7am, which is when she usually starts work. After Elena has gone, Mariella finds Mrs Rivello in bed and prepares a lemon tea for her sickness while waiting for the doctor to arrive at 8am.

"Mr Rivello had left home at 5.50 in the morning, when his wife was still sleeping after a difficult night. He went first to his office in the warehouse, then chaired the morning meeting on the shop floor from 6 to 6.30 with all his staff. Afterwards, he retired to his office. His car stayed on the premises in full view until 10am when two carabinieri went to the warehouse to inform him of the accident.

He immediately phoned his wife, worried, but she confirmed that it was Elena who had taken her car. At that point, he left the warehouse and drove home."

"If we ever suspected the Rivellos, they both have pretty good alibis," Giò said.

"It would make no sense to suspect them after the flowerpot incident, but I'd rather clear them without a doubt. We will get back to them. For now, let's start with the crime scene.

"The first person that we know of who arrived at the road block was Sara Salino. She parked her car a few minutes before 7am. At 7.15 she took the bus to Sapri. We're still waiting for confirmation from the carabinieri in Sapri, but we hope to be allowed to question the bus driver tomorrow. If he confirms that Sara took the 7.15 bus, she is pretty much in the clear because we're sure the death occurred at 7.30, but I will get to that later.

"The thing about Sara Salino is that she seemed very worried when she was first questioned, and even more so when it was declared a murder. It's like she has something to hide. So I wouldn't be surprised if we were to discover she didn't take the 7.15 bus after all. Maybe she took the next one, but she was not seen by either Carlo or Andrea. We will need to check her entire alibi, move by move. In any case, she declared she didn't see or hear anything unusual. No other car was parked there, nor did she suspect anybody else was around.

"At 7.15, Carlo Capello arrived. Like Sara, he says he didn't see or hear anything unusual. After he parked, he walked through the road block and took an old scooter to Sapri. He said he was enjoying the perfect morning and took the journey very slowly, finally arriving at Sapri harbour where he didn't meet anybody. His first trackable movement was at the newsstand in Sapri at 8am, which leaves him with enough time unaccounted for to kill Elena, get on the scooter and ride to Sapri. Unless we find a witness who saw him at the harbour, he is still a suspect. It takes fewer than 15 minutes to reach Sapri harbour from the scene of the murder, and another five minutes to get to the newsstand in the town centre."

"My goodness, it's so weird to think of people we know of as 'suspects'," Agnese said in dismay. "But please carry on."

"Not yet," said Giò. "Give me a second to catch up with my notes." At the top of the blackboard, she had written 'Murder Scene', followed by the list of suspects and the timing of their movements. Under Carlo's name, she added a last line: 'Where was he between 7.15 and 8am? Does the newsstand man confirm his timing?'

"At the time of the first interview, Carlo was very cool and relaxed, but when we summoned him the second time, he didn't seem as bold. Which is normal... partly. I don't know, I'm used to people being nervous when they talk to the carabinieri, but Carlo is the type of person who always feels a bit superior when dealing with a mere maresciallo or brigadiere, so I was surprised. And I have a feeling he might be hiding something. Was he the murderer, or did he just notice something unusual?"

"Maybe it was something he didn't think was important during the first interview," Agnese speculated, "but it became significant once he knew it was a murder case. But why would he decide not to tell the carabinieri?"

"Exactly!" Paolo stared at Agnese in admiration. Both sisters had a certain cop's hunch. "Then at around 7.20ish, Andrea arrived. He saw the other two cars, then rode to Sapri on his bike. Like Carlo, he was in no hurry and paused a few times to get some shots with his camera. The first public place he entered was a bar on the Sapri coastal road where he bought a coffee and exchanged a few words with the bartender at around 8.30."

"So Andrea also had time to commit the murder," Agnese concluded.

Giò couldn't help feeling a pang inside. She had avoided, she believed, making an emotional connection with this man, but still…

Agnese sent a worried look in her direction. Paolo continued undaunted.

"From what Tommaso, Elena's boyfriend, said, Elena left home at 6.45 to get the car keys from the Rivellos' house at 7, and she arrived in Acquafredda at 7.30 in time to catch the 7.45 bus. According to Doctor Siringa, this fits in perfectly with the estimated time of death: 7am to 8am, but likely around 7.30. We checked Tommaso's alibi and spoke to his employer, who confirmed he arrived at work on time at 7.30. He works in Tortora. We will double check with his colleagues, but it seems as if he's got a cast-iron alibi."

"Tortora is 35 minutes south of Maratea, while Acquafredda is 20 minutes to the north. It sounds as if we can easily rule him out, despite the theory that murderers are usually the victim's nearest and dearest." Giò couldn't hide her disappointment.

"Giò, he's not having an easy time. His

girlfriend has been brutally killed, but at least he can be spared the agony of being accused as her murderer. Also, he phoned us the other night to tell us the house he shared with Elena was ransacked and a few things were stolen. It seems he's not going to be allowed any peace to grieve."

"What did the thieves take?" asked Agnese.

"Nothing much, just Elena's laptop, a little money she'd left in a drawer. There was nothing particularly precious in their home, but the laptop contained memories, I guess."

"It never rains, but it pours." Agnese shook her head in sympathy. "But let's go back to her movements."

"Well you know the next part, I guess. Elena arrived at 7.30, parked her car, and before she knew what was happening, the rock had crashed onto the car, killing her on the spot. Then we have you, Giò. You stayed at your parents' house till 9.20, and arrived on the murder scene a few minutes later, but by then it was too late to save

Elena, if what the doctor says is correct. So you're not on the red list..."

"I might have lied to you and been there earlier..."

"The thing is, we have witnesses who saw you leaving Maratea at 8.30," Paolo smiled, "and witnesses who saw you parking at your parents' house. Finally, you were seen passing the graveyard a few minutes before 9.30. Sorry, but you're not under suspicion. I can see this is a disappointment to you."

"You really checked all my movements?" Giò cried.

"I had to," Paolo replied apologetically, slightly red in the face. "After all, you found the body. And there's one more thing. I can be precise about when people arrived on the crime scene because we have a witness."

"A witness?"

"Yes. Gerardina lives in the last group of houses in Acquafredda, just a few hundred metres from the road closure. She was on her balcony, preparing lines of chillis to sun dry, and she confirmed everyone's arrival time. It's a pity the bend in the road obscured her view of the murder scene, otherwise our killer would have been found out. In any case, Gerardina recognised the cars passing by. She saw Sara, Andrea, Elena and you."

"How about Carlo?"

"Apparently she didn't see him. Actually, she insists he never passed by that morning."

"But that's impossible. Andy and I both saw his car, so he must have passed by after Sara arrived, but before Andy."

"Exactly, but Gerardina is sure he didn't."

"Maybe she wasn't looking. She may have left the balcony to get a glass of water or go to the toilet."

"It seems she did not."

"Maybe she is not as reliable a witness as she pretends to be."

"But she was very precise about all the others, including you, Giò."

"I didn't even notice her."

"She was on her balcony. She could see people arriving, but it was unlikely they could see her, especially from a car."

"So she saw Elena too?" Agnese asked.

"Well, she recognised Mrs Rivello's car, and like the rest of us, she assumed it was her. She said it was a couple of minutes before the Acquafredda bells rang at 7.30."

"No other passers-by?"

"None according to her."

"But since it seems that Carlo was able to sneak past unobserved, anyone else could have done so too." Giò preferred to think that someone else had been there – a stranger who was not Andy or Carlo or Sara. It was hard to think that someone she knew, even someone like Sara Salino who she'd only met at the carabinieri station, could be a killer.

"It's a possibility, but he would have had to have passed by twice unobserved, or gone on to Sapri. But then, there were no other bikes or scooters there. So did he take the bus? We don't know yet, but I'll be questioning the bus drivers on duty that morning. Did they pick anybody up from the Acquafredda bus stop? Did they notice anyone cycling, walking or riding a scooter?"

"But, for now, these are our suspects. Do they have a motive?" Agnese asked.

"Apparently not. But that is exactly why we need to do some digging. And when I say digging, I don't mean I want you to interview the suspects. That is for the carabinieri to do; you just need to listen out for local gossip. And don't hang around any of the suspects on your own. Almost certainly, one of those three is the culprit. We know they were all present at the funeral; what we don't know is where they were when the flowerpot fell. Any one of them had the opportunity to get into that building after the Mass, push the vase and attempt once again to murder Mrs Rivello. Also, we need to protect Gerardina, so please don't mention her to anybody. That's strictly confidential information."

"So you don't think anybody but one of those three could be the murderer?"

"They are the ones under suspicion at the moment. We're not excluding the theory that someone else could have passed by unnoticed, but Gerardina's testimony seems trustworthy."

"But she didn't see Carlo passing by," Giò protested again, feeling a surge of hostility towards the old bat who could send an innocent person to prison.

"We need to investigate further. We're interrogating people in Maratea and Acquafredda, and we've asked the carabinieri in Sapri for support. We're following all leads, but I need to know if we can exclude any of the three current suspects. If any of them has a good alibi, then the net will inevitably close in.

"As for Mrs Rivello, when we questioned her, she didn't even try to conceal her dislike for Elena, so I had to check her alibi. But Mariella said she found her in bed at 7am, while the doctor confirms she was still in bed at 8 with a bad attack of gastric reflux. In any case, Mariella's statement is the perfect alibi for Mrs Rivello."

"Really? She could have got in a car after 7, killed Elena and been back by 8."

"I don't think so. Firstly, it would have been very difficult for her to reach the murder spot, climb all the way up to the rock and be waiting for the victim before Elena arrived, then drive back home in time for the doctor at 8am."

"She's a very organised woman, and there was just enough time…"

"And secondly, Mariella said that Mrs Rivello kept calling for her all morning to adjust her pillows, open the window, draw the curtains. I asked her how many times Mrs Rivello called between 7 and 8, and the answer was too many to count."

Paolo smiled. Giò resented him for sweeping away all her theories, but nonetheless she wrote on her board, 'Mrs Rivello – watertight alibi. She's the victim. Who might want to murder her? For what reasons?'

"How about Mr Rivello?"

"His car was in full view of his employees all morning, and it was typical for him to return to his office after the meeting. Nothing unusual in that. And he wouldn't have saved his wife from the falling flowerpot if he wanted to do her in."

Agnese added, "He also knew it was Elena in the car and not his wife."

"I'd say we should concentrate on the three main suspects. I'll check their movements, but you can help me with the rest. Who would want Mrs Rivello dead?"

"I CAN'T BELIEVE WE'RE surrounded by murderers!" Giò grumbled as Paolo left. "What a weird story. Maybe I should move from travel writing to mysteries. They sell better than guide books, and I will have plenty of material after this adventure."

Agnese had to contain her sister.

"We're not surrounded by murderers. There's only one, but he has to be dangerous as he's twice tried to kill Mrs Rivello."

"You think it's a man?"

"Mr Rivello said he saw a man in the streets after the flowerpot incident. And we have two men under suspicion versus one woman. And Sara... well, she doesn't seem at all like a cold-blooded murderer." Agnese then added, "I need to go and open the perfumery. Are you staying at home this afternoon?"

"No, I think I will take my laptop down to Leonardo's and see if I can catch any gossip there. I might even try to put in some work as well. Give me a moment and we can walk down together – I'll be quick." While packing her stuff, Giò continued talking. "As for Sara, she looked as scared as a mouse that morning the carabinieri called us all in. And Mrs Rivello never even looked at her."

"And Paolo says she was even worse

during the second interview, almost panicking."

"If she's that nervous, how could she be a murderer?" Giò was standing with the laptop wires in her hands, not sure if she'd need them or not. "I mean, how could such a nervous person be brave enough to make a second attempt to kill Mrs Rivello?"

"That's true. You need a certain amount of bravado to push the vase and run away before anyone suspects it may have been more than an accident."

"Bravado indeed. We can exclude Sara." Giò put her laptop and wires down and reached for her blackboard, but Agnese stopped her.

"Oh please! What if she's just pretending to be fragile? No, as Paolo said, we shouldn't jump to conclusions. Let's stick to facts; let's assume she's as culpable as the others until we can prove otherwise with facts, not psychology."

Giò murmured, unconvinced, the red

chalk still in her hand ready to cross Sara's name from the board.

"But for Hercule Poirot, psychology was such a big part of an investigation…"

Agnese was merciless. "I have at least three objections. One, none of us is a psychology expert. Two, Poirot was blending psychology and observation…"

She stopped as if thinking hard.

"And three?" Giò encouraged.

"And three, this is by no means an Agatha Christie mystery, just in case you have forgotten. This is real and it's scary."

"Such a pity. I would have loved to be involved in an old-fashioned mystery."

"You'll have to be happy with what you've got: a modern murder and three suspects. By the way, how are you going to handle Andy?"

"What do you mean?" Giò replied defensively, pulling her bag onto her shoulder and gesturing to her sister to leave the flat before her.

Agnese knew she was moving into dangerous waters. "You were out at sea with him only a few days ago. You're not going to spend any more time alone with him until he is cleared, are you? If he is..."

"When you talk like that, it doesn't sound real. I don't think Andy has anything to do with this murder." Giò tried to stay cool, but slammed the door far harder than she needed to. Agnese jumped at the noise, carrying on more hysterically than she would have liked.

"How can you say that? You don't even know him that well!"

"Come on! Andy repeatedly told me that he can only work here in Maratea, where he wants to live, thanks to Mr Rivello. So why would he want to kill his wife?" As they were out on the street, Giò had to keep her voice down, as much as she felt like shouting.

"I have no idea, but please don't get too involved with him."

"I am not. I'm just reasoning."

"We said we would stick to facts! And that means we need to dig for information about Andrea and the Rivellos. Is their relationship as friendly as he made out? Has anything happened between him and Mrs Rivello that we are not aware of? You can't exclude anybody just because they're nice. And please, promise me you will refuse to go on his boat, or on any other trip with him, until the murderer is found."

"You don't like him, do you?" Giò retorted.

"I've got nothing against Andy, it is the same with Carlo. Don't go anywhere with him either, until he is in the clear." Agnese could only hope she was convincing her sister.

"OK, I promise. I will speak to the two of them, though, if I happen to see them. But I will say no to going out, except in public places..."

"Giò!"

"What's wrong with that? I've been fine with them so far, so it would only look suspicious if I were to snub them now. And if it wasn't for an old gossip, I would be on the list of suspects too, remember? I wouldn't have appreciated being ostracised by the whole community for being a potential suspect."

"You're right," Agnese was forced to admit. "I'm just so afraid you will get yourself into some sort of trouble."

Giò softened a little. "I will tell you everything I plan to do so you can let me know beforehand if you're concerned."

When they arrived in the town square, Giò stopped at Leonardo's while Agnese continued on to her shop with an unusually worried look on her face. They had to find the murderer as soon as possible, not only to stop him (or her) before he succeeded in his attempt to kill Mrs Rivello, but also before her sister ended up in trouble.

15

DIGGING DEEPER

"Speak of the devil!" Agnese murmured to herself, arriving at her shop only to find Mariella peering through the windows with dreamy eyes. "Hello, Mariella, how are you doing?"

"Fine, I've just finished work. Your shop has some lovely trinkets, and your perfumes are delightful."

"I'm glad you think so. Why don't you come in?"

Mariella looked embarrassed. "Your prices are probably out of my reach," she said. "Especially now I have to save for my wedding next June. It's not far away now, as my fiancé keeps reminding me."

"I've just received a box of interesting perfume samples. Come on in. I'm sure I can give you a few, and you may find the right one for a bride-to-be among them." Agnese unlocked the turquoise shutters, and when she turned back to the other woman, Mariella's face was glowing. She was more than happy to stay.

When they entered the shop, Agnese switched on the lights and invited Mariella to browse while she prepared a bag of samples. Mariella was enchanted simply to be there – the same perfumery her employer used. She sampled a few perfumes, but mainly stared at the variety of beautiful objects inside.

"You told me the other day how demanding Mrs Rivello can be," Agnese said, wearing her most sympathetic expression.

"Indeed she is," Mariella said cautiously, moving closer to the counter. But when she saw the bag Agnese had prepared for her, filled with a whole collection of samples, all her resistance and doubts melted away. "She is extremely demanding, and at times she really pushes me to the limits. Well, maybe I shouldn't say that..."

"Why not? That's exactly how things are. And that is probably why somebody tried to kill her."

"I'm not a detective," Mariella replied, "but I know things Maresciallo Mangiaboschi doesn't even suspect."

Agnese tried hard not to show her surprise. Instead, she faked admiration for the young woman in front of her.

"Well, you've been with the family for a long time now."

"Not that long," Mariella explained, pleased to have Agnese's undivided attention. "Three years ago, Anna worked for them, and when she left, it was Sara's turn. But she lasted less than two months. She acted very stupidly."

"Sara who?"

"Sara Salino, of course."

"Ah!" A million questions suddenly popped into Agnese's head, but she kept them to herself for now. *Mild encouragement, that's all it'll take.*

"How did she act stupidly?"

"You know the story, don't you?"

"I may have heard something at the time," Agnese lied, "but in a shop, I hear a lot of second-hand gossip and never know what is true and what is not."

"Well, from me you will get the story first-hand. Anna had been with the family since forever, but finally she retired. Sara is Anna's niece, so it was sort of taken for granted that she would replace her aunt. I also applied, but the Rivellos preferred Sara."

"How disappointing for you!"

"Time is a gentleman, they say, and it certainly was in this instance. Mrs Rivello noticed a few things were disappearing. In fact, she tests people. She did the same with me, leaving small banknotes in her husband's pockets or on the floor as if they had slipped from his trousers when he hung them up. I know it's a trick because they're both usually very tidy and careful, and Mr Rivello would never put money in his trouser pockets in the first place."

"You mean she tries to catch people out?"

"Yes. I'm sure most families would do the same: set little tests to see if their new employee is honest. But Sara was so stupid, she didn't realise. Mrs Rivello then prepared a trap. She told Sara that a few months earlier, she had lost a precious old brooch, which she'd actually hidden behind a chest of drawers. Later that day, Mrs Rivello discovered it in Sara's bag. A huge scene followed and Sara was dismissed on the spot. Mrs Rivello told her she would not speak to anybody about the incident, she would hold her tongue, but if she heard of anything disappearing from any of the other houses Sara worked in, then she would have a moral duty to inform the owners. And not only them, because if Sara stole again, it would be Mrs

Rivello's duty to let the whole community know she was a thief."

"Wow, that's almost blackmail, even if it was masked with good intentions."

"Sara was terror-stricken. If anything happened wherever she was working, even if she had no part in it, she would be ruined forever."

"That was cruel! Almost better to be denounced and have done with it."

"I don't know. You see, the Rivellos pay well, contributions included, which is very rare around here. So it was stupid of Sara to risk all that for a few Euros. Whenever I find money left lying around, I always put it back on the chest of drawers, or if she is at home, I hand it directly to Mrs Rivello. She also tested me with a ring, but I handed it back to her. Now she knows I'm trustworthy, she no longer plays tricks on me."

Agnese was not sure if Mariella was more proud of her honesty or being cleverer than her mistress. Possibly the latter was more important – in Mariella's eyes, at least.

"So when you mentioned to Giò that you suspected someone of the murder, you meant Sara."

"Oh no, not at all. Three years have passed. She certainly holds a grudge against Mrs Rivello, because in the end Mrs Rivello reneged on her promise and told lots of people what had happened, and Sara was obliged to find work in Sapri. But I can't see her as a murderer. No, what I meant when I spoke to your sister was a different business."

Agnese looked at her quizzically and Mariella continued.

"There was one time Mr Aiello came to visit Mr Rivello, but he had just gone out in response to an urgent call from the office. So it was Mrs Rivello who received Mr Aiello. It was the end of my working day, so I said bye, leaving them in the living room while I went to get my stuff. They were so absorbed in their conversation, they didn't wait for me to leave the house. By the time I was ready to go, their voices were raised. Mr Aiello was almost screaming that she couldn't do this to him, that he would be ruined if she told everything to her husband."

"Told him what?" Agnese gasped.

"I couldn't hear that part. I think it was something related to work."

"What did Mrs Rivello say?"

"She said she wasn't going to tell her husband, but she would watch and make sure he – Mr Aiello – did his duty."

"Do you think she was blackmailing him?"

"What, asking for money?"

"Yes."

"Oh no, she simply wanted him to do the right thing, I guess. Though by the tone of their voices, I'm not sure who was in the right. I mean... how can I explain it? I'm sure right was on Mrs Rivello's side, but when somebody is in great distress, almost in despair as Mr Aiello was at that moment, you're not so sure who is right and who is wrong, if you see what I mean."

"I see." Agnese nodded before asking, "Did you mention any of this to the carabinieri?"

"I didn't. Actually, they only asked me what time I arrived at the Rivellos' house on the day Elena died and if Mr and Mrs Rivello had been there. Do you think I should tell them? It is so vague, and..."

"And?"

"And I'm afraid it could put Mr Aiello in a compromising position."

"But you told me!"

"That's different, you're not the cops. It's just gossip. Before we were talking about Sara, now we're discussing Mr Aiello, but it's just chit-chat. Nothing is gonna happen to either of them."

"I wouldn't treat it like a game. Actually, I wouldn't repeat any of what you've told me to anyone except the carabinieri. Keep your eyes open – you might be in grave danger if you've been going around bragging that you know things."

Mariella looked worried.

"It wasn't my fault! I just happened to be there, and they were speaking so loud."

"I'm not saying it's your fault, but you work in a house that a murderer is targeting. I seriously think you should tell the carabinieri, and only the carabinieri."

"But the maresciallo wouldn't even look at me. When I was there, he waved me out as if I mattered less than nothing. I'm sure he'd say I'd been eavesdropping and give me a piece of his mind. Or he would say I'd made it all up just to be the centre of attention."

The girl's fears were completely justified: the maresciallo was as arrogant as he was stupid. In fact, Agnese herself was struck by a sudden doubt.

"You didn't make it up, did you?"

"Of course not! I swear, Agnese."

"OK, if you agree, I will speak to Brigadiere Rossi about the things you've told me. He is so much more understanding. He might want to speak to you directly, so make sure you tell him the whole truth – without embellishments."

"Naturally!"

"Remember that someone killed Elena mercilessly. This is not a game!"

Mariella nodded, but Agnese could only hope she really understood.

GRANNY HAD SPENT THE LAST 30 minutes peering out of her open window. The time was about right. She was sitting on a chair reading, feigning absorption in her book, but she was alert, waiting for someone to walk by like a spider waiting for prey to fall into her net. It wasn't long before she heard what she was listening out for: high heels tapping against the pavement. She glanced out of the window, as if casually.

"Good morning, Rosa."

"Oh, good morning, Paloma. How are you?"

Granny did her best to look surprised to see Mrs Parasole, a tall woman with a delicate, fair complexion. There was something aristocratic about her features, but when she spoke to Granny, two huge rabbit teeth rather spoiled the effect.

"I'm doing fine, and how are you? I heard your granddaughter is back."

"She is. Oh, but hers is such an awful story. It was a real tragedy the way that man treated her..."

Mrs Parasole's eyes lit up. Granny knew her weaknesses and kept spinning her web. The other woman loved gossiping as much as she loved interfering in people's lives.

"There aren't many people I can trust, but I need to talk before I go insane."

"I absolutely understand. That man has to be the worst kind of scoundrel to hurt a sweetheart like Giò."

"I knew you'd understand..."

Mrs Parasole looked at her, full of expectation.

"I'd love to invite you in for a cup of

coffee, but I believe this is your afternoon at the Pink Slippers Society in the library."

"But I'm ahead of time, and they will not mind if I arrive a bit late. It's for a good cause, to support a friend in need."

"Oh, that would be so very kind of you," Granny chirped, clasping her hands together. Giò would have seen right through her, but Mrs Parasole stepped blithely into the spider's web. "Please come in and I will prepare coffee."

Mrs Parasole sat down in one of the two comfortable armchairs Granny was so proud of. They were older than she was, but upright enough for her to be able to get up easily without the help of an ugly modern device that would push her up while massaging her until she felt like a piece of jelly. On the little table between them sat the finest porcelain cups Granny owned and a silver dish filled with her renowned vanilla and rosemary biscuits. Mrs Parasole liked them so much, she soon had her mouth too full to speak. And Granny took advantage of that to turn the conversation exactly where she wanted it to go.

"By the way, have you heard any more about the murder?"

Mrs Parasole swallowed her mouthful of biscuit, washed it down with a sip of her coffee and was finally able to reply.

"Oh, I suspected from the start it was not an accident. Mrs Rivello is such a pest. It seems her ambition in life is to drive people insane."

"Are you referring to the case of Valeria and Agostino?"

"Agostino got what he deserved, though it wouldn't hurt Mrs Rivello to mind her own business every once in a while. No, I meant she can be so annoying... sometimes to the wrong people."

"With you?"

"Well, she tried to preach to me about how to bring up my kids, but I told her to stop right there. My boys are two perfect young gentlemen. Certainly they're a bit lively, but at their age in a town like

Maratea, where there's nothing much for the young ones to do, they have to amuse themselves."

"Like when they painted Mrs Donadio's new door? The poor woman had just spent her savings on it."

"But the teen years are such a hard time. They feel like rebels, and I guess their hormones are going crazy."

Granny bit her tongue. The two young demons had been no better when they were kids. "But did you say something about Mrs Rivello making enemies?"

"Absolutely. The woman is spiteful, and I'm afraid she can provoke extreme reactions from respectable people."

"You are not speaking of the handsome Andrea, are you?"

"Oh no, I believe he gets along well with Mr Rivello, so he is not exposed to her barbed tongue. Though he's got his fair share of faults: it seems he enjoys gambling every now and then, and hides his vices behind that good-lad smile."

"Oh, is that true?"

"Nothing too serious, I guess. He's a man without a wife to care for him. And again, what's he supposed to do in Maratea?"

"So, who do you think Mrs Rivello annoyed so much that they'd want her dead?"

"I'm not saying... I'm sure he wouldn't try to kill her, but certainly he has good reason, and..." She stopped and looked around to make sure the window was properly closed. "You know about Mrs Capello's argument during the last Pink Slippers Society Dinner, don't you?"

"In fact, I don't," Granny admitted reluctantly. It wasn't like her not to know something.

"It was such a scene. You know, Mrs Capello has never liked Camilla. She considers her 'new money' without worthy ancestors or proper manners. 'She's all money and no style,' she'd say. For her part, Mrs Rivello hates not being of noble origin and tries to reinvent her family history, but I guess it still hurts."

"But this seems to be a good reason for Camilla to hate Mrs Capello rather than the other way round."

"Wait until you hear the rest. After the summer fires, the Pink Slippers Society organised a dinner at Za' Mariuccia to collect money and plant an oak tree for each of us present. We ended up buying almost 50 trees."

"That was admirable of you."

"Then Mrs Capello, in the role of president, thanked each of us one by one, but when she came to Mrs Rivello, she told her she'd better pay for more than one tree since her husband would be making money from the reforestation works. Mrs Rivello saw red and said her husband was doing an honest job, while the Capello family considered honesty an optional extra."

"Oh my goodness!"

"It was most embarrassing because Mrs Rivello didn't stop there. She said something about the fact she'd always been faithful to her husband, and that her daughters were without a doubt his. Her allusion to Carlo's story was clear."

Granny remembered the gossip about Carlo looking far too similar to one of the family's drivers, who was dismissed two years after he'd been born.

"And was Carlo there too?"

"He was. He smashed his glass of wine on the floor, and when he looked up, he glared at Mrs Rivello with such hatred as I have never seen in human eyes before. He recovered quickly and went to sit with his mother, feigning indifference, but it was so embarrassing for all of us there. It had been such a delightful dinner up to that point. Luckily there's no longer a Mr Capello or something bad could have happened there and then."

"Camilla has never been able to weigh up her words before she speaks them. She is so inconsiderate," Granny commented meditatively.

"But you were telling me about Giò and that awful man. What did he do to the poor one?" Mrs Parasole had finished the biscuits and was hoping Granny would offer to refill the plate.

"Oh, you know how these young folks are, don't you? They decided their lives were taking two different paths and they'd be better off apart."

Mrs Parasole was clearly disappointed. "But calling off their wedding with only one month to go. He must have done something really bad to her!"

"Better a month before the wedding than a month after, don't you think?" Granny asked with an innocent smile.

"But maybe something happened..."

"As I said, they simply realised they had different views on life. But it's getting late, I don't want the Pink Slippers ladies to miss out on your company because of me." Granny rose from her armchair. Mrs Parasole would have felt badly cheated, but fortunately Granny knew exactly how to sweeten her up. "Before you go, I must pack up a few biscuits for you to take," she chirped, heading for the kitchen.

When she came back, Mrs Parasole put

the parcel of biscuits in her bag to hide it away from her greedy Pink Slippers associates and left with a smile on her face. After all, biscuits were better than gossip.

~

THAT EVENING, AGNESE AND GIÒ discussed all their findings with Granny. This time, Granny had news to share with them, too.

"Mrs Parasole popped in for a visit..." and she told them the woman's story, being careful to omit any details about having used Giò's situation as bait.

"That's very interesting, and you were right, Granny," said Giò. "Apparently, folk are willing to share far more information about others than themselves." But it was obvious she was not in her usual enthusiastic mood. The news about Andrea had hurt her more than she liked to admit, even to herself.

"Should we tell Paolo?" asked Agnese.

"Of course," replied Giò, "I've already messaged him. We're meeting up late tomorrow morning and I'll tell him everything. Goodnight."

But she hardly slept a wink.

"AND THAT'S IT!" SAID GIÒ WHEN she'd finished the long report about Sara, Mariella, Carlo and – *gosh!* – Andrea.

"Congratulations! You have dug up more information in a couple of days than my men have done in a week. Some of them would make very good cops, but the maresciallo does all he can to undermine them."

Then Paolo drifted off, lost in the implications of all he had heard.

They had gone for a late breakfast together in a bar on the way to Marina di Maratea. As it was out of town, with outside tables and only a few customers at that time of day, it was the perfect place to chat freely.

Paolo's phone rang. He listened carefully before asking, "Have you called Dr Siringa?" He paused again, then added, "Do it now, I'm on my way to Acquafredda. Do you know where exactly the house is? OK, I understand, the small road on the left before the last group of houses. I remember now."

When he ended the call, his expression had changed. He was no longer a quiet, thoughtful man, but a carabiniere who needed to act fast.

He called the waiter for the bill and explained to Giò, "I can give you a lift to the crossroads in Maratea, then I need to go as fast as possible to Acquafredda."

"What has happened?" Giò asked.

"Antonio, a man who worked at Mr Rivello's warehouse, has been found dead in his home."

16

A BAD FALL

"Natural causes, I guess?" Giò asked Paolo once they were in the car.

"Apparently he fell and hit his head on the floor."

"Oh my goodness, he died from a fall? Look, if you're in a hurry, I can come to Acquafredda with you. I won't get in your way."

"You wouldn't mind?"

"Of course not, and you will save yourself a few minutes."

"Well, I want to get there as soon as possible, before anyone moves things around. You never know."

Paolo set off for Acquafredda so fast, Giò soon began to regret having offered to go with him.

"You knew the man?" she asked, pretending to be indifferent to the speed at which they were travelling.

"I did. He was a poor devil, used to drink too much after his wife and child passed away. He lost his job, and I think he had a hell of a time, but Mr Rivello gave him a job in his company and Antonio seemed to have found his feet again."

Despite the fact that the road was getting more winding, Paolo kept driving far too fast and Giò didn't have the courage to speak further. It was a relief when they reached Acquafredda. She noticed they were heading for the cemetery, but just before they got there, Paolo finally slowed down and took a gravel road almost hidden on the left. It led to a small country house where two women were waiting outside, gesturing to them frantically.

"The ambulance is on its way," Paolo

said to the women. "Giò, you wait here," he added as she was unfastening her seatbelt.

As the three rushed inside the house, Giò got out of the car in need of a little fresh air. No, she had no intention whatsoever of following them, but it might be a long while before Paolo could go back to Maratea. What a stupid offer she had made. She could have been home by now, maybe getting a little work done.

She was still close to the car when she heard the sirens. A few seconds later, an ambulance and a carabinieri car arrived. Maresciallo Mangiaboschi got out of the car and looked at her with disdainful surprise.

She indicated towards the house and murmured, "Brigadiere Rossi is inside."

Hearing the sirens, Paolo emerged from the front door and told the maresciallo and paramedics that nothing more could be done for the man.

"An unlucky fall. He hit the edge of the mantelpiece. I believe he died straight away since there are no signs he tried to move anywhere."

Doctor Siringa, with his happy round face and big moustache, arrived a couple of minutes later. A carabiniere younger than Paolo extracted a huge camera from a black bag with a long strap and they all disappeared inside. Only Giò was left hanging around outside.

The lawn was overgrown, but the rest of the garden was in good order. The plants were well tended, with lemon trees carrying small fruit that would get bigger during the winter season, four large olive trees, and a few roses in their second bloom, which was common in Maratea's mild climate. Behind the house, Giò found a small kitchen garden. A few tomatoes were still hanging from their branches, dancing in the sun. The mix of vegetables and herbs with hibiscus, marigolds and geraniums showed that Antonio had really enjoyed gardening.

On the far side of the kitchen garden was an opening in the stone wall surrounding the whole property and a small iron gate without a lock. Beyond, a little path that had been kept clear of wild plants led upwards through holm oaks and pine trees. Just what Giò needed: fresh air and a walk to stretch her legs and disperse the adrenaline that was running through her body from the wild drive.

She glanced at the house. Everyone was still inside, and there was no indication they would come out any time soon, so she ventured along the path. After a short while, it climbed steeply, and before long, Giò was facing a tall stone wall. She could see rows of cypresses on the other side and realised she was standing at the back of the cemetery.

She walked around the stone wall till she came to the entrance that faced the State Road, not far from the crime scene. Giò was about to walk into the cemetery and say hi to her parents, but she stopped, her hand on the tall iron gate, her heart almost jumping into her throat.

The killer might have come through

Antonio's garden rather than the State Road. If he had, even Gerardina wouldn't have seen him. Or her. My goodness, does that mean I have found out how the killer arrived?

The realisation was so sudden, she had to take a deep breath, but her heart was still beating furiously when she turned her back on the gate and ran down the path she had come up.

When she arrived at the front of the house, Paolo was outside, discussing something with the maresciallo. Giò butted in, forgetting her manners as well as her dislike for the maresciallo, who looked rather disturbed by her interruption

"There's a path!" she cried. "There's a path going up to the cemetery!"

The two carabinieri looked at her. She was red and sweaty, and evidently out of control.

"Can't you understand?" she shouted. "This could have been the path the killer used."

All contempt disappeared from the

maresciallo's face and the two men moved to follow her. She led the way to the small gate and pointed to the path.

"And from there you walk up to the cemetery. You approach the back of it."

The two carabinieri went through the gate and disappeared from sight. Giò just stood there, feeling exhausted. It hadn't been a long walk, but what a discovery! The kaleidoscope had changed the whole scenario, again.

It was a good 15 minutes before the maresciallo and Paolo came back down. To Giò's surprise, the maresciallo smiled at her.

"You might be right," he said encouragingly. "Might be right," he repeated as he and Paolo entered the house, talking excitedly. The maresciallo called one of the women in again, while the other stayed outside and joined Giò.

"You must be Giovanna Brando."

"That's me, and you are...?"

"Gerardina, I live on the other side of

the road. Your Granny and I are good friends."

"Oh... I've heard of you as well," Giò said, remembering just in time she was not supposed to know what Paolo had told her. Her brain worked quickly while the lady enquired about Granny and whether she, Giò, was back to stay.

"I will certainly stay for the winter. Can I ask you what brought you here this morning?"

"Rosaria, the other lady you saw with me, had brought round a few eggs for Antonio. He did some odd jobs for her, and she returned the favour by cooking him meals and giving him fresh eggs every now and then. When he didn't answer the door, she walked in, thinking he was at work. We don't lock our doors here, you see. But once inside, she found him on the floor, blood around his head. He was already cold, so she ran out screaming and crying for help. So I came down to see what had happened, and then we called the carabinieri."

"Poor chap," Giò said.

"Poor chap indeed. Antonio has not had an easy life. He had just recovered... he had a problem with wine, but when Mr Rivello gave him work, little by little he seemed to get it under control. If only his wife hadn't died..."

"Was she sick?"

"She had a tumour. She fought against it with all her might for two years, but the disease won in the end. And they had already lost their young daughter in a car accident years earlier..."

Giò sighed.

"Oh, I shouldn't have mentioned that," Gerardina said, remembering that Giò's parents had also died in a car accident.

"Oh, it's OK, really. I was going to the cemetery to visit their grave and I noticed there's a path there from Antonio's home."

"Well, there used to be, but now it will be overgrown."

"Actually, it's not. It looks well-trodden."

"That was it, then!" Gerardina said, looking satisfied.

"That was what?"

"I live on the State Road, and now that I'm old, I spend most of my time at the window, cleaning veggies, preparing beans for the winter, knitting or crocheting, or just waiting for a chance to talk with passers-by. In all the years since he lost his family, I've never seen Antonio going to the cemetery, but there are always fresh flowers on his wife and daughter's graves. I had completely forgotten about the path – we used to play there when we were children..."

"So on the morning of the accident, did you see Antonio at all?"

They had walked all the way to the State Road, and from there they could see a row of houses leading up to the cemetery.

"You see, the house before last is mine," Gerardina replied. "The one with all the geraniums on the balcony." Giò nodded. "That morning, I woke up early – I simply couldn't sleep, so I decided to prepare dry chillis for the winter. So I happened to be on my balcony and see all the people who passed by. Not that there were very many, mind you. Since the road has been closed, hardly anyone drives here."

"So who did you see?" Giò already knew the answer to the question, but she wanted to hear it in Gerardina's own words in case the old woman added something new.

"The first one to arrive that morning was Sara. She's always here at the same time because she catches the 7.15 bus. Then it was Andrea. I didn't see Carlo. Despite his saying that he arrived before Andrea, I'm sure he didn't pass by, unless he was earlier than 6.45."

Giò decided not to interrupt her.

"After Andrea, I saw Mrs Rivello's car arrive, just before the church bells rang at 7.30. Nobody else passed by until I saw your car. Of course, I didn't know it was you, but I noticed the car and wondered if it was someone going to Sapri or the graveyard. Next, I saw Mr Faraco and the whole kit and caboodle."

"So apart from these people, you didn't see anybody else?"

"Exactly."

"Not even Antonio?"

"I saw Antonio's car, but he didn't pass under my balcony."

"You mean you saw him leaving for work?"

"Not quite. I noticed it because it was rather unusual. He came back home at 7am, and then went out again at 8am."

"Wasn't it normal for him to go out very early?"

"Of course it was. He would normally be at the warehouse by 6.30am at the latest, but it was strange for him to come back at 7. Initially, I thought he had forgotten something, but it took more than an hour before he went out again."

"Did you inform the carabinieri?"

"Of course not. They were interested in who went up towards the closed road.

Antonio just went back home. I saw him turning here."

She indicated the crossroads where they were standing. Giò was not sure if this was an important piece of information or not.

At that moment, she saw Paolo's car approaching them. He opened the window to say goodbye to Gerardina and told Giò to jump in if she wanted to go back home.

"I'd better go. Bye, Gerardina," Giò said, kissing the old woman on the cheeks.

"Bye, dear, and do stop by if you come to visit your parents' graves."

When Giò got in the car, she couldn't help but notice Paolo's sombre face. It was so rare for him not to smile.

"Nothing new?"

"On the contrary, quite a lot of new things."

Silence fell. Wasn't he going to tell her what they were? How ungrateful! After all, she was the one who had found the hidden path, and hadn't she and Agnese given him plenty of clues between them?

"We're a team, aren't we?" she asked.

"The case is closed. The maresciallo has found the murderer. He is just waiting for a written note from the legal doctor, stating that Antonio was drunk and fell accidentally, to conclude the evidence."

"And who's the murderer? What's the evidence?"

"We found a metal bar in Antonio's storeroom beside the house. Most likely it's the one used to free the rock. We also found a number of accelerants, the kind arsonists use to ignite forest fires. He must have been setting the large fires during the summer."

"Oh my goodness!" This second piece of news shocked Giò almost more than hearing that Antonio was Elena's murderer. "How was that possible? I mean, the man tended his garden with such passion, so how could he destroy hectares of forest?"

"Maybe because somebody was paying him to do it. As for contradictions, aren't they typical in human nature? I wouldn't be surprised. It's like when you have a brutal dictator who cries over the death of his pussycat. This fire business was a surprise for me as well, but I'm more worried about the killer."

"Didn't you say Antonio was the killer?"

"The doctor told us there's a slight possibility that Antonio was hit on the head, and that the killer staged the fall to look like an accident. But the evidence is so flimsy he will not even note it in the formal report. The maresciallo told him to stop offering theories without proof and accused him of doubting what is as clear as daylight."

"So, according to the maresciallo, Antonio died accidentally, and he was Elena's killer. But how and why?"

"The discovery of the little path automatically included him in the suspects. As for why, maybe Mrs Rivello knew he was involved in the fires, or maybe he had gone back to drinking and feared she might convince her husband to sack him. Nobody would ever hire him again, and we know how important it was for Antonio to have a job."

"So why did he write the threatening letters?"

"To keep her quiet, of course. He trusted she would read them, not her husband."

When Giò looked at him, she saw an unusual tension in his face, his mouth a hard, straight line.

"But you're not convinced, are you?"

"It is not that I'm not convinced, but we have three other suspects who we will now clear without further investigation. We have a professional saying that things might not have worked out as the maresciallo thinks, but we're just embracing the most comfortable solution without finishing our job. Truth is, the maresciallo is going on holiday soon, and he wants to go with a solved case behind him."

"But if he is not around, you can keep investigating..."

"Truth is, we have no evidence whatsoever. The only thing to do would be to keep the suspects under pressure, otherwise we're telling the real killer, 'You've almost made it through. Keep quiet for a while and you'll be OK.' That's not the way to proceed."

"Also, if the real killer is not Antonio, Mrs Rivello might still be in danger."

"That depends on the killer's motives. If he stops now, he can get away with two murders. On the other hand, if killing Mrs Rivello is essential to him, he can try again because, thanks to the maresciallo, she will lower her guard."

"By the way," said Giò, "I almost forgot to share with you what Gerardina just told me."

"You mean you have more revelations?" He was looking at her incredulously. "You're a hell of a detective, you should be in my team."

It was good to feel useful, a boost to her self-esteem after years of feeling unimportant.

"Apparently, on the morning of Elena's murder, Antonio drove home at 7am and left again an hour later. If he was planning to kill Elena at 7.30, why would he go out first thing and return just in time?"

"We interrogated Gerardina thoroughly, I can't believe she didn't tell us this."

"You asked her who she saw going to the closed road. She answered your question."

"But she gave you the whole story."

Giò grinned. "Well, I prefer to use open questions."

17

WHEN THE CAT'S AWAY, THE MICE WILL PLAY

They remained silent for a long while, each immersed in their own thoughts. It was only when they rounded a sharp bend in the road and the statue of Christ the Redeemer came into view on the mountains, dominating the coastline below, that Giò broke the silence.

"When is the maresciallo leaving?"

"Tomorrow afternoon after the press conference," Paolo replied.

"And he'll be away for a week, won't he?"

"He will." This short reply was accompanied by a suspicious glance.

"We need a few good gossips to do some work for us."

"What?"

"You know how it is in Maratea, people will soon learn I was at Antonio's when you found him dead. They will ask me things. I'll be discreetly hinting that the story of Antonio being the killer is exactly that – a story to lull the murderer into a false sense of security. I'll put the word out that Dr Siringa suspects someone hit Antonio on the head and that the carabinieri are trying to catch the real murderer. And you will neither do nor say anything, but you'll keep investigating the original three suspects. Before long, the whole village will know that you smell a rat..."

"And so will our killer! He'll get nervous and make a false move, betraying himself."

"Exactly!" Giò's face was radiant with excitement, but Paolo had concerns.

"What if the maresciallo discovers what we're up to?"

"Discovers what? That you made a few phone calls to double check the evidence? All the rest will be anonymous gossip – nothing you could be held responsible for."

"You know, it makes sense." Once again, Paolo stared at her in admiration.

"Of course it does. I will speak to Agnese this afternoon. The perfumery will be the centre of our activities."

BEFORE HEADING BACK HOME, Agnese passed through Piazza Europa. It was market day, and in early autumn you could buy such an abundance of fruit and vegetables there that she never missed a chance to shop. The stalls were simple, but the market as a whole was a triumph of colours and perfumes. Tomatoes were still coming in, in all shapes and sizes, along with small green peppers, perfect for frying lightly. The stalls were festooned with lines of colourful chillies, red onions or garlic. There were jute bags of walnuts and hazelnuts, the latter still surrounded by their green leafy husks, and wicker baskets filled up with the first glossy chestnuts of the season.

From the cheese stand there came the perfume of milk and rennet, from which the softest mozzarellas were made. Agnese's stomach was growling as she approached the focaccia stall when she recognised the Shy Man in the distance. He was buying fresh eggs from an old farmer who ran one of Agnese's favourite stalls.

"Good morning," she said, approaching him while trying to silence her belly with a quick caress.

"Hem... good morning." Shy Man was just as clumsy as he had been in her shop, but the smile on his face revealed he was happy to see her.

"It's a brilliant day, and I simply adore this market," she said, trying to put him at ease.

"Yeah, a very... hem... brilliant day."

He's still smiling, but we're not getting very far, Agnese thought. *I'd better ask him something he can't repeat.*

"So, did your lady friend enjoy the necklace?"

The man flushed, his face turning such a deep red that Agnese feared his big hands might squeeze the little packet of eggs the old farmer had wrapped for him in a sheet of newspaper held by an elastic band.

"Hem... not... hem... not really."

"She didn't like it?"

"Not yet."

"She doesn't like it yet?"

"No, I mean I haven't given it to her yet. Maybe next Saturday at the library. Hem... I'm very sorry, I'm afraid it's getting late. I need to go."

Agnese had to lay her shopping bags on the ground to take in what she had just heard. The Shy Man disappeared too quickly for her to be able to question him any further.

What's wrong with him? She shook her

head and waited a good minute before lifting her bags and buying a kilo of zucchini for Granny, then going home.

AT THE CARABINIERI STATION, Paolo found the 7.15 bus driver waiting for him. The man confirmed he had picked Sara up on the day of the murder.

"You have a good memory to be so certain after a week. Some people can't even recollect who they met this morning." Apparently complimenting him, Paolo was trying to gauge how reliable the man in front of him was.

"When I heard the news of the accident, I reconstructed what had happened that morning. This is why I'm so sure Sara was on my bus."

That's a reasonable explanation, Paolo thought. "Do you remember if you met other people along the road, walking or driving?"

"No, not until we got closer to the

harbour. There, of course, were lots of people."

"Did you notice anyone on a scooter or a cyclist along the way?"

"Again, not till we reached the harbour."

Paolo sent the man on his way, thanking him.

And with this, Sara is cleared, he said to himself. God knows why the girl was so terrified. Andrea and Carlo were still on the suspects list, along with Antonio, of course.

He made another couple of phone calls to organise the press conference for the next day, working quickly since he wanted to visit Mr Rivello's warehouse as soon as possible. He wanted to know Antonio's movements on the day he was killed and on the day of Elena's murder.

He knocked on his superior's door. "Maresciallo, shouldn't we speak to Mr and Mrs Rivello about Antonio before the press conference? If Antonio wanted to kill her, they might have an idea about his motives."

Maresciallo Mangiaboschi smiled, looking self-satisfied. "I've already called them. They should be here in a few minutes."

Paolo asked if he could get Mr Rivello's permission to speak to his men about Antonio's movements on the day of Elena's murder. The maresciallo agreed to this too. For once, he was in an excellent mood.

AGNESE NODDED WHEN GIÒ SHARED her plan with her on the way to the shop.

"I thought you'd be happy to know your friends are no longer under suspicion and the case is closed."

"Of course I want them cleared, but I saw the look on Paolo's face. He clearly has his doubts, and I want to know the truth. I can't protect a murderer. Also, when I saw how well Antonio tended his garden, I couldn't believe he could be a killer, and certainly not an arsonist."

"Well, history abounds with killers who loved their pets, so I can't see why one wouldn't love their plants..."

"That's exactly the same remark Paolo made."

"Still, you're not convinced..."

"I should be. We found evidence that Antonio was involved in starting the forest fires. I can't imagine why anyone would frame him as a murderer and an arsonist, so you are right. People can be a mass of contradictions – he loved his garden, but he didn't hesitate to set fire to hectares and hectares of woodland. How sad!"

"It is. Anyway, back to our mission. If you want to spread any kind of rumour, the best person to speak to is Nennella on the newsstand. She will call in here tomorrow to deliver our magazines and newspapers, but you'd be better off visiting her tonight before she closes the shop, so that tomorrow morning she'll be all ready to pass on your gossip to her customers. By noon, the whole village will know."

"Good idea," Giò said without hesitation. "I'll see you later."

NENNELLA, A ROUND WOMAN WITH curly salt-and-pepper hair, her skin looking as fresh as a 20-year-old's, was not simply the newsstand owner, she was a talking flesh-and-blood newspaper. Her shop, at the entrance to the little village, was neat and tidy with plenty of hanging plants, both outside and inside.

"Hello, dear, how are you?" she chirped. It was clear straight away that she'd be happy to talk for hours.

"I'm doing fine, how about you?" said Giò, looking around.

Good, there's nobody else in the shop.

"Getting older! Meanwhile, you've been having plenty of adventures since you arrived."

"I never imagined life in Maratea could be this exciting."

"At least the case is closed, though I can't bring myself to think of Antonio as a killer."

Giò was speechless. It had only been a few hours since Antonio was found dead, and people in Maratea already knew the whole story. The internet could never be as fast as gossip in Maratea – maybe the folk at Google should hire somebody from this little village to improve their famous algorithm.

"How do you know?"

"Doctor Siringa's housekeeper was here, and she heard him speaking to his wife."

"Well, there's more to the story... but it's confidential!"

"I know you were there this morning. Did you see the body?"

"Oh no, I wasn't allowed in. And anyway, I'm not fond of examining corpses – I've already had my share of that with poor Elena, so I'm done for a couple of years now."

"So what do the coppers say?"

"Well, from what I overheard, they don't really buy into the idea of Antonio being the killer. Apparently, there are some anomalies. But they want the killer to feel like he's got away with it, giving them time to make further investigations."

"Really?"

"Yes, but please remember this is strictly confidential," Giò insisted, knowing full well that every person in Maratea had their own take on how large a group could be granted access to confidential information. And as Agnese had said, Nennella's group was probably the largest of them all.

"Of course, dear, of course. You wouldn't believe how many secrets I've heard doing this job of mine. But I can keep my lips sealed, which is why people keep confiding in me."

"I know, which is why I'm telling you and nobody else. At least until the carabinieri uncover the real killer," Giò lied without remorse.

"I wonder who it might be?"

"I have no idea, but I'm certain they have their suspects..."

"To think a killer might walk into my shop with a friendly smile. I can't believe I have lived to see the day murderers wander freely around Maratea."

The shop bell rang and Carlo Capello walked in. "Good evening, Nennella." He wore his usual sombre expression, as if his profound thoughts wouldn't allow him the luxury of something as inconsequential as a smile. Then he noticed Giò. "Are you here to catch up with the latest news?"

"I came over to collect my sister's magazines and newspapers for the perfumery. She might open a little later tomorrow morning and we didn't want Nennella to have to walk all the way to the shop for nothing."

"Oh, dear, you're so thoughtful!" Nennella remarked pointedly. Often Carlo's mother would call Nennella asking her to make a delivery, only to be out when she got there.

Carlo didn't show any sign of acknowledgment.

"I'd like my papers, please." He paid for the bundle of magazines, and then asked Giò if she was finished as well.

"In fact, I'm heading back to Agnese's. Are you going that way too?" When he nodded, she picked up her stuff, said her farewells to Nennella, and together they left.

"Sad news, isn't it?" he asked, then carried on without waiting for an answer. "So in the end it's the obvious culprit, nothing brilliant enough to inspire my novels."

"Obvious?"

"Yes, the poor man killing his employer's wife out of fear of being fired. Nothing new in that, I'm afraid."

"But he didn't actually kill his boss's wife, he killed someone else."

"Yes," Carlo admitted, pushing his glasses back onto his nose. "That's still the best part of it."

Giò gave him a furious look.

"From a literary point of view, I mean," he added, seeming put out that he had to justify what he clearly felt should be obvious.

"You'll be happy to know the carabinieri don't believe Antonio killed Elena, anyway," Giò announced.

"What? But that's what they are saying!"

"That's what they will say officially at the press conference tomorrow. They want the real killer to relax. As a matter of fact, they are still running their investigations, and I believe they are onto a suspect."

Carlo didn't reply. Giò was scrutinising his face and for a second his expression looked stricken. He swallowed and his eyes got larger. Was it surprise, or something more sinister?

After a rather long pause, he asked in a low voice, "How do you know?"

"I was there when they found Antonio."

"Wow!"

"Are you worried?"

"No, not all," he said, but he tried to justify himself nonetheless. "I was just figuring out the implications of this latest development for a novel. But, if Antonio is not the killer, who else might it be?"

"Well, to start with, we are the four under suspicion – you, me, Andrea and Sara." She included herself for solidarity; she didn't want to say at this stage that she was in the clear.

"Do you really think so?"

"I'm puzzled – I don't know what to believe. There's a remote possibility somebody could have passed through Antonio's property unseen."

"Unseen by whom?"

Oh no, she had made a mistake! She mustn't give Gerardina away.

"By us – the people who were on the road that morning. I didn't see anybody, and you, Andrea and Sara said the same."

"But Sara took the 7.15 bus."

"The carabinieri are going to question

the driver. If she was definitely on that bus, she will almost certainly be in the clear."

"Do the carabinieri know the exact minute Elena arrived? What if Sara killed her and still took the 7.15 bus?"

Giò realised how important Gerardina's testimony had been. Only thanks to her eyewitness account had the carabinieri been able to reconstruct the exact sequence of events and determine who was under suspicion and who wasn't. But of course, she couldn't mention any of this to Carlo.

"The carabinieri didn't share their information with me, but I overheard a few sentences when I was at Antonio's house. They suspect Antonio was framed."

Carlo wasn't concerned about the literary aspect anymore. This time, his interest seemed genuine. Did she mean interest? No, the right way to put it was that he looked worried.

By this time they'd reached Agnese's perfumery, and Carlo had a look at his watch and said he had to go. When Giò went in, her sister was serving and saying goodbye to her last customer. While helping Agnese bring in all the things that spent the day outside the shop, including the two rattan armchairs and the little table, Giò told her everything about her conversations with Nennella and Carlo. Once they'd cleaned up inside the shop ready for the next day, they went home, talking animatedly.

As they passed a backstreet, illuminated by wrought iron lamps with yellow lights typical of Maratea, Agnese spotted Carlo speaking to a woman.

"Look there," she whispered to her sister, "isn't that Sara?"

"Yes, it is!"

The sisters peeped round the corner so as to remain hidden from sight.

"It looks like an animated conversation," Agnese murmured.

"Shhhh!" Giò waved at her. If they stayed silent, the alley would channel the conversation from the other end, amplifying Carlo and Sara's words so the sisters could hear them.

"What are you worried about?" Carlo was saying. "Can't you see that in the end, I will be your alibi?"

"I wish I had told the truth from the beginning," Sara whined.

"Now it's too late. Stick to what you said in the first place and you will be OK."

"The brigadiere keeps asking questions, and he looks at me as if he suspects I did something!"

"He's a carabiniere, he loves to see that people are afraid of him. Don't you worry. You'll be OK. Just stick to your story."

"OK," Sara replied, but she sounded unconvinced.

At that moment, someone entered the alley from the opposite end and Carlo and Sara nodded to each other, going off in opposite directions.

Giò took her sister's arm and they walked into the alley in full sight of Sara. They greeted her with the falsest smiles ever, but the woman, although she responded to the greeting, said she was in a hurry and didn't even slow her pace.

"She looked worried."

"I wonder what they were talking about," Giò said.

"They're obviously hiding something."

"I am happy I didn't mention Gerardina to Carlo, I'd be seriously worried now if I had. Should I call Paolo?"

"He might be having dinner, just text him."

Giò wrote a message without going into detail. He replied almost instantly, and she read the text to her sister.

"I will be at yours tomorrow as soon as the maresciallo leaves for Rome. It will be after the press conference, I expect around midday. I've got news too."

THE NEXT DAY, IT WAS ALMOST ONE o'clock when Paolo finally rang the doorbell. An impatient Giò let him in.

"How was the press conference?" she asked him without preamble.

"Better than I could have hoped. The maresciallo only gave vague details about the case – he didn't want to expose himself to criticism by delivering his verdict before he had the official results from forensics. He highlighted the fact that Antonio was involved in the summer fires, but declared that we're still investigating his role in the murder of Elena so he couldn't disclose any more information."

"I'm amazed."

"He must have realised that if he doesn't jump to conclusions now, he can call another conference when he comes back and close the case for good. But this fits our plans perfectly."

They high-fived before sitting in front of Giò's blackboard, then Paolo continued.

"Yesterday afternoon, Mr Rivello came to the station. I told him to keep an eye on his wife until the whole thing has been settled."

"What did he say?"

"He was surprised. He asked me why, if Antonio was the killer, he and his wife should be worried."

"And what did you say?"

"That we're still investigating other options."

"Was he worried?"

"Of course he was, and he didn't try to hide it. He confided that he'd hoped the mystery had been solved, as painful as it was for him to find out that Antonio, a man he had rescued, had been trying to murder his wife."

"So he had accepted the fact that Antonio may have made an attempt on his wife's life?"

"He said Antonio had changed recently, had once again taken to the bottle. Mrs Rivello is rather strict, religion giving her rigid morals, so although she might help a person once, she is merciless if they fail again. In fact, she had threatened Antonio, saying he might lose his job."

"That woman is really awful!" Giò cried

while adding and deleting information from the board.

"Anyway, I got his permission to interrogate the employees at his warehouse. I told him that I needed to find out exactly what Antonio had done the day he died. However, I also asked his men about the day Elena died." Paolo took out his notebook. "Let's start with the first murder. Actually the day before. After work, Antonio went to a bar with other workers and drank way too much. When they left the bar, they stumbled into Mr Rivello who singled Antonio out and scolded him rather harshly. He told him to go home and stay away from alcohol."

"And did he drive home drunk?"

"Apparently so. He parted from Mr Rivello and his colleagues, and they did not see him till the next morning."

"What time?"

"I'm starting to wonder who's the carabiniere here, you or me? You're putting your questions to me in a logical sequence – well done. You have a copper's hunch." He laughed as Giò blushed. "We checked the register with the foreman, Antonio signed in at 8.20."

"So the time fits in perfectly with what Gerardina said."

Paolo nodded.

"Except we don't know where he was before 7am," Giò continued.

"He wasn't at the warehouse, that's for sure."

"What if he slept in his car overnight?"

"Apparently nobody has ever seen him sleeping in his car. He might have parked the car at the warehouse and slept there, but according to the other employees, by 6am the following day the car was no longer there."

"And if he had left the warehouse before 6am, it wouldn't have taken him an hour to reach home."

"So, he either spent the night at home and went out very early, or he slept somewhere else. In any case, he came back home at 7am, killed Elena and left again at 8am."

"A rather busy morning for someone with a hangover!"

"Apparently so."

"Are we overcomplicating things? Might the maresciallo be right?" Giò wrote under Antonio's name and previous notes, 'Where was he before 7am?' then asked Paolo, "How about the day Antonio was murdered?"

"The other workers confirmed that despite Mr Rivello's harsh reprimands, Antonio had taken to drink again. It seems that since Elena's murder, he was drunk more often than sober. Mr Rivello wouldn't allow him to take on any potentially dangerous tasks at work and asked the others to keep an eye on him. He warned Antonio that if he became a liability to the company and staff, he'd rather sack him than risk falling foul of the Inspectorate for Health and Safety at Work.

"The day he died, Antonio had gone to the bar after work and was in a mildly drunken state, but not too bad. In fact, we found his bed had been slept in, and Antonio was in his pyjamas when he died. If he had been intoxicated, we would have expected to find him still in his work clothes and sleeping on top of the bed rather than inside it."

"But in the middle of the night, he got up, fell and fatally injured himself?" Giò asked.

"We have two possibilities. Either he suffered from dizziness and fell or, as the legal doctor suggested, someone got into the house and attacked him. It must have been a person Antonio knew well if he let them in, even though it was the middle of the night. He trusted his killer, but the moment he turned his back, the killer hit him on the head with something as heavy and sharp as the edge of the mantelpiece."

"We have to act fast, we have less than a week before the maresciallo comes back," Giò grumbled. "And then, he will be determined to close the case, no matter what."

"But now is not the right time for

action," Paolo calmed her. "You have stirred the waters well – I've already overheard a few people commenting on the fact that somebody is framing Antonio."

"For once, it is a piece of luck that rumours spread so fast in Maratea."

"I should also speak to both Andrea and Carlo again; I need to put more pressure on them."

"And Sara?"

"We cleared her," he said, and told her about the bus driver.

"How weird!" Giò exclaimed, sharing the conversation between Carlo and Sara that she and Agnese had overheard the night before. "What do you think they're hiding?"

"I don't know, but if she's got nothing to do with the murder, she's stupid not to tell the truth," Paolo mumbled.

"Plus, there's that conversation between Andy and Mrs Rivello. Why don't you ask her directly what it was about?"

"That's only going to work if she's

willing to reveal it. She is not the kind who bends to pressure. I've asked her again and again if there is anybody who would wish her dead, but she's always said there's no one. Also, she would realise that it was Mariella who'd told us about the row, and I'd prefer Mariella not to be suspected of gossiping."

Her pencil held aloft, Giò asked, "So, what shall we do now?"

"Nothing, just observe and wait."

"But the days will soon pass and the maresciallo will return."

"Let's put it this way. We're like fishermen: we prepare our bait, we study the place where we're going to fish, we set our hooks. Now we need to keep still and wait." He stressed the words *keep still.*

"I've never understood the fascination for fishing. I frankly hate the very idea of staying still and waiting, especially now when we might be so close to the truth."

Paolo looked at his watch. "I'd better be on my way." When she opened the door to see him out, he reminded her once more, "We made a deal: no sleuthing, no taking the initiative without my permission, no running into danger."

She nodded. "Of course. It's hard to be patient, but I'll go back to my work. I was supposed to get started this week, but I've not done much so far."

"Good girl." But he didn't feel convinced by her words.

18

SLEUTHING AND WARDROBES

As the days passed by without any news, Giò got restless. At home she struggled to concentrate on her work. She tried reading other travel guides for inspiration, but she would soon drop them and get lost in her thoughts. Attempts at writing were even worse, as if the exotic foreign places she'd visited were now too far away to hold her interest.

Andrea had gone into the perfumery to ask her out again, but Agnese had covered for her, saying she was busy settling in and getting back to her work. Truth was, Giò didn't have the courage to meet him. At first, she thought it would be good to talk to him as she had done with Carlo. But when she saw him in the street, her heart banged in her breast with such a fury that she had ducked into a side alley unseen. No, she wouldn't allow herself to get any closer to Andrea until the case was solved.

This particular morning was worse than all the others – she didn't even switch on her computer, it looked so out of place here in Maratea. Instead, she knocked on Granny's door.

The old woman read her in seconds. "You look restless, Giò. Village life already taking its toll?"

"I don't think it has anything to do with village life. I just wish all this stuff about the murders was over."

"It's none of your business, so it shouldn't affect your life so deeply. I believe that having the whole day to yourself is bad for you."

"Granny, I've had the whole day to myself for ages. It's years since I quit my nine-to-five job."

"But you had a routine in London. Here in Maratea, things like food shopping, running an errand, visiting the library can be done in a few minutes; over there, they would take a whole day. Time expands here, and you shouldn't try to fill it with work stuff to the exclusion of everything else."

The words struck Giò – Granny was right. For the first time in years, she found her days dragging. In London, time flew past – you got up in the morning only to find it was evening again in the blink of an eye, with a long to-do list still not done. It was not even two weeks since she had returned to Maratea, but it felt like she had been back forever.

She hugged Granny tightly as only a granddaughter can hug a grandma.

"What would I do without you?"

"Exactly the same things... but having less fun," was the laconic reply.

"I'm going out, Granny. Do you need anything?"

"I need to go food shopping, but I have

to make sure Gigi gives me decent veggies. If it's you or Agnese, he will pick up the first tomatoes and onions that come to hand."

"While you'll check that each one is simply perfect."

"Of course!"

"Then you'd better go, I could never do that."

"I know," Granny answered with a sigh.

Giò stopped at Leonardo's café. No other customers were in sight. She ordered her cappuccino and took out her computer. In London, she loved working in cafés. They filled her with inspiration; she never connected to the Wi-Fi, so she could either observe or write. Since it got embarrassing staring at people the whole time, she would end up writing a few things, then the real world would disappear and her inner world would roll out. She would set a time limit, usually around two hours; if she gave herself a longer time, procrastination and distraction would inevitably take over.

Today, the rest of her time would go into research, answering and writing emails, a little accounting, and updating her blog. She had neglected it for too long; her readers might get fed up with her intermittent posts and head for someone more reliable.

For her Scotland guide project, she had already identified the itineraries she wanted to include, asking some Scottish acquaintances to give her feedback on the feasibility of each. Then she had gone through a painful process of corrections and checking, and now the raw material was ready to shape into something readable and interesting. Only, she wasn't inspired.

She wrote, she deleted. She wrote again, she deleted again. She recited her mantra internally. *Keep the words flowing. You can edit later, just write whatever pops into your head. Let's start with a wee introduction to sum up itinerary number one.* But the words failed to come.

Giò opened the photo album on her

laptop. Photos were always her best source of inspiration. She took another sip of her cappuccino, ordered a cornetto, ate it without any pleasure and collected the last breadcrumbs from the plate on the end of her finger, then slammed the laptop closed.

Leonardo, startled by the noise, approached her.

"Are you having a hard time?"

"Indeed. There's too much sun, too much beauty around. I wish I were climbing the mountains or swimming in the sea rather than wasting my time with a stupid laptop."

"Carlo finds his inspiration by talking to people," Leonardo said, taking away her dish. "He talks and writes at the same time."

"I could never do that," replied Giò, feeling worthless once more – a feeling that had become second nature to her even in her best moments, let alone in times of crisis.

"On the other hand, Mr Scribacchio – a

famous Italian writer known only to Leonardo – would write in the evenings after a day of physical activities. He'd work hard in his garden, take a swim or run, chop wood for the winter. He used to say he could only write when his body was tired enough. In those moments, he felt he was the most creative because his inner critic was too exhausted to bother him."

"Leo, I didn't expect you to be so knowledgeable about the writing process." Giò was amazed to find a creative counsellor in the central café of Maratea. "Mr Scribacchio's idea is interesting indeed, I might give it a try." Dorian would have been scathing of her for that. She could almost hear his sneer in her head.

"You're always so naïve, as if you're a perennial beginner. You should be more assertive."

Yeah, bugger off, Dorian. I'm going to start every day with exercise.

A huge smile spread over Leo's face: he liked to give useful advice to his customers almost as much as he liked serving them the latest news.

"So what will you do?"

"I might go swimming, and when the water becomes too cold, I will jog. I actually hate jogging, but I can't think of another sport I can do here."

"Giovanni has opened up a beautiful gym."

"I will leave that for winter and rainy days. No, I'd rather spend time outdoors."

"How about kayaking?"

Giò's eyes shone. "I'd love that, but all the lidos are closed. Where could I hire one?"

"In Fiumicello, you can still hire one."

"Really?"

"Yes, Romolo has a lovely business there. He gives tours to groups, working with a lot of foreign visitors, but he will be more than happy to let you hire one. I'm sure he is there in the mornings, but you may want to call him first. Shall I give you his phone number?"

"Yes, please. And would you bring me

another cornetto and cappuccino?" Her appetite had returned.

As Leo disappeared inside the café, a tall man approached her.

"Hi. So you're still alive after all."

"Hello, Andy." Her heart skipped a few beats. He had a slightly scruffy air: his beard was not perfectly shaven, but he looked good in blue jeans and a tight t-shirt showing off his broad shoulders and perfect abs. He removed his sunglasses to greet her and she saw the deep shadows under his dark eyes.

But my goodness, what eyes!

"It seems impossible to get hold of you."

"You're right. But it's not been the easiest move-in ever. And I've done quite a few." She laughed to hide her embarrassment; she had been trying her best to avoid him.

"So are you settled now?"

"I am almost done with the house, but I need to start concentrating on my work again."

"Is that a cute way of trying to prevent me from asking you out?" He smiled sheepishly and her heart melted.

"Please sit down, of course not. I can't work 12 hours a day, except when I'm at the closing stage of a project."

He sat down. "And what stage are you at now?"

"The stupidest one: writer's block."

"Lack of inspiration?"

"Sort of. I can't seem to find my way around my old job here – I feel like that's what I did in London."

At that moment, Leo arrived with the cappuccino and cornetto for Giò. "Hi, Andy, can I bring you something?"

"An espresso macchiato, Leo, please."

"Will do. Giò, this is Romolo's phone number." He handed her a piece of paper with a number scribbled on.

"Should I be jealous of this Romolo?" Andy said. He was smiling, but his eyes were scrutinising hers.

She burst out laughing. "Maybe!" He was taken aback and didn't hide it. "I mean," she continued, "I don't know who he is. So he might be as handsome as a Greek god, or an 80-year-old full of rheumatism and arthritis. I asked Leo if anybody around here hires out kayaks and he gave me this contact number."

"Is that research for your writing?"

"Not exactly. Exercise will help me to concentrate and clear my mind. He is based in Fiumicello. Do you know him?"

"No, I don't. When are you planning your first outing?"

"I'm going to call him and ask if we can arrange something for this morning. I was intending to go to the beach anyway, so I'm ready."

"Are you going to call him now?"

"Why not?"

"Then ask him if he's got two kayaks free."

Giò looked first surprised, then embarrassed. "You mean you'd like to come along?"

"Not if you say it with so much enthusiasm," he replied sarcastically.

"Please, try to understand. I'm sure it would be fun to go together, but I need to be on my own. Let me get started with my work and then we can go for a ride together."

"OK, OK, I didn't mean to be intrusive. Stupid me. But don't run away from me as you seem to have been doing these last few days."

Sweat formed on her neck. She was probably blushing and she fought hard to contain it.

"And Romolo might not be there at all, or his kayaks," she said, trying to justify herself.

"Come on, give him a shout."

She did. Romolo was there that morning and had a kayak available for rental. If she planned to hire one a few times, he would be able to offer special rates. They would talk it over when she reached him.

"May I accompany you to your car?" Andrea was clearly expecting a no.

"Of course you can."

There was no way she would be able to pay for her coffees and cornettos as Andrea waved to Leo to indicate he would be paying. In southern Italy, men always paid, and all Giò's protests were useless.

"And apart from your work, how are you settling in?"

"I'm happy to be close to Agnese, the kids, Granny again. I missed them so much. But my work is part of my life, so I can only give a definitive answer to your question when I'm back to work."

"Can't you help Agnese in the shop?"

"For work you mean?"

"Aye."

"Nope. I'll be happy to help her if she needs me, but my writing means everything, and... and I'm terrified of most of her customers. Even worse, some of her customers are terrified of me." And she reminded him of her attempt to hide away from Mrs Di Bello.

"I remember," he said, shaking his head and smiling.

They had reached Agnese's car. She put

her bag inside. He bent to kiss her the Italian way, one kiss per cheek, but she moved her head and her lips brushed against his.

She pulled away, blushing. "Oh, I'm sorry," she cried and climbed into the car as fast as she could.

He laughed. "I'm not. Call me when you get back."

She nodded and drove off at full speed, her heart once again beating furiously. What was she doing? She felt like a teenager.

Come on, Giò, you're 38 and counting! You're not single by chance. You should really be over flirting and heartaches. If Agnese knew, she'd be mad. Worse, she'd be right, and knowing my older sister is right is not the most gratifying experience ever.

By the time she arrived at the beach in Fiumicello, she had found her cool again. Romolo was there waiting to give her a life jacket and a waterproof zip-up bag for her phone. She positioned her rucksack containing her food and a water bottle in the gap at the front of the kayak.

"I'll be back this afternoon. Do you need an exact time?"

"I don't have that many customers at this time of year, but I'll be around till sunset." He showed her his sanding machine and all the benches and tables waiting to be sanded. "I need to get that done before the bad weather sets in. You can keep your kayak till this evening."

The perfect paddling rhythm came quite naturally to Giò, as if it was an ancient skill that had always been within her. For the first few strokes, she followed the coastline, then she aimed at the first rock point in view and headed out to sea to cut the distance. The water was so calm, it felt like she was on a peaceful lake surrounded by imposing mountains, at least on one side.

Childhood memories of inflatable boats and paddle-boards were filling her mind by the time she reached the last rocky outcrop and the Acquafredda bay opened up in front of her. The majestic view was sadly marred by the dark patch on the mountainside: the forests lost to the summer fires. Now at least those burned pines, bare rocks, black soil knew the name of one of the culprits: Antonio. But he must have worked with a team, because the fires had been set at the same time in various locations along the coastline, far enough from the road that the fire brigade couldn't reach them in their jeeps, let alone their fire engines. The man who had cultivated his garden with such passion had destroyed the whole façade of the mountainside without a second thought. He knew he would never again be able to enjoy the green mantle covering the rocky wall just beyond his home, but he'd decided he didn't give a damn.

A dangerous idea weaved its way into her brain. And with her impulsive nature, there wasn't much time between idea and action.

The tip of her kayak aimed right at Anginarra beach, the longest beach in

Maratea. It was split into two parts by a group of rocks on which sat the Gabbiano Hotel. It was her favourite hotel on the whole coast; had she not had a home in Maratea, she'd have stayed there, no doubt. The hotel was just above sea level, the bedrooms facing a little path above the rocks and the great expanse of water beyond. When the sea was rough, it covered both the rocks and path, and the hotel restaurant looked out directly onto the waters. She loved it.

"Hello, Mario." She greeted the hotel bathing attendant warmly as she'd known him all her life. Tanned and slender with curly salt-and-pepper hair and grey eyes with swirls of dark blue, he had an expression that hinted at a greater wisdom than his simple manners would suggest.

"Hello, Giò, a perfect day for being on the water," he said, helping her to pull the kayak ashore.

"Amazing! You look younger than ever."

"Oh no, I'm getting older, and I'm

happy about that. It means retirement is coming closer."

"This place won't be the same without you."

"It will. The mountains and sea will carry on as they've done for ages."

"Not quite. The summer fires have done a lot of damage."

"It's been a devastating summer."

"Have you heard Antonio was involved in the fire business?"

"Yes, I heard, but I can hardly believe it. Unlike the seasonal workers, he had a steady job. I can't imagine what led him to do such a thing, it's so unlike him."

"Did you see him at all before he died?"

"Not really. He had kept to himself since his wife passed away, deliberately avoiding people. I heard he had gone back to drinking. The poor devil hadn't had an easy life, you see."

"No, you're right." While talking, they had secured the kayak on the shore and she was drinking water from her bottle.

"Would you mind if I left the kayak here for a while? I'd love to walk up to the cemetery."

"It's a long way up. You can use my scooter," he offered, handing her the keys. That was good news: she could now save her energy to paddle all the way back home.

"Thanks, I will be back in half an hour or so."

"I'm here till sunset. As for the scooter, it's the only one in the car park. The helmet is stored under the saddle."

She took up her rucksack, found the scooter, put on his helmet, and up she went. She passed Gerardina's place, but the old lady wasn't at the window. It was almost lunchtime – the perfect hour to pass by unseen. Nevertheless, Giò decided to take no risks and left the scooter in the graveyard's car park. Then, instead of entering the cemetery, she skirted around it to take the hidden path leading to Antonio's place.

The whole house had been cordoned

off by the carabinieri with red and white tape. She ignored it and tried the main door, but as expected, it was locked. She checked all windows: they were shut. There was only the annexed storeroom left to try. Paolo had told her it had an inner door that gave entry to the house.

On the outer door, a padlock was hanging. She smiled a complacent smile: locks had no secrets for her. Maratea children didn't have many games to play, so they had to invent new ones with whatever the place offered. Padlocks were amongst the most common objects at their disposal, and learning to open them was a basic skill for any boy. Since boys did more adventurous things than girls, she had always stuck with them.

She put her rucksack down, took out the can of cola she had taken with her, drank a sip and then another, then glugged it all down. With her Swiss army knife, she cut the top and bottom away, then cut the can open vertically and flattened it out. With the small scissors on the Swiss army knife, she managed to cut a T-shape from the aluminium. She folded the sides so as not to cut herself and to strengthen the T, then rounded the head so she could grip it better. The hard part was over: she could now try the padlock.

It took her fewer than two minutes to hear the familiar click: it was unlocked. Giò put all the pieces of aluminium back in her bag and cleaned the padlock with her handkerchief: better not leave tracks behind. Now, she was ready.

She pushed the door open and inside she went, using her mobile as a torch. In the storeroom there were all kinds of gardening instruments, including a motor hoe, a whole series of spades and rakes, and a number of old petrol tanks. On the other side of the room, a second door led into the house.

Only when she was pushing the inner door open did Giò realise she was doing something illegal. Not only was she breaking into private property, she was entering a crime scene cordoned off by the carabinieri. She visualised the angry red face of the maresciallo and shook her head. Frankly, she didn't give two hoots.

~

AGNESE WAS BUSY DOING AN inventory before setting up a new order when the door opened and young Cabiria came in.

"Hello," she said sheepishly.

"Hello," Agnese replied, without asking her usual, "What can I do for you?"

"I'm sorry if I was rather nasty last time…"

"I didn't take it personally."

"You should have," Cabiria whispered, looking around to make sure there were no other customers in the shop.

"Really?" Agnese's surprise was not entirely genuine, but she didn't want to give the girl the idea that she knew what was going on in her head.

"Yes. I know it wasn't you. But I was mad at you because after I sprayed those perfumes, my confusion seemed to grow rather than decrease."

"I can assure you, my purpose – if I had any – was to help you see things with more clarity..." With a gesture of her hand, she invited Cabiria to have a seat on the sofa.

"I'm afraid I need to go," said the girl, shaking her head. "I have very little time. But you're right, my confusion was greater because I didn't want to see things as they were. Those perfumes evoked visions which were so weird... but now I know I've got to dig deeper or I will be forever obsessed by what I refused to face."

"Is there anything I can do for you?"

"Oh yes!" Cabiria chuckled and her face brightened. "Please, would you sell me the full bottles of those two perfumes we chose? I promise I will not hold you responsible for any side effects."

"That's a relief." Agnese grinned and went to fetch the two perfumes. Cabiria paid and took the turquoise bag from the counter.

"I'll come back before I leave to say goodbye. If you don't mind, I mean."

"I'll be waiting for you. Be the brave girl you are. It's not easy, even when you get older, believe me."

∿

GIÒ FOUND HERSELF IN THE corridor of the house. Natural light from the windows allowed her to switch off her phone's torch.

In the living room, the chalk outline drawn by the carabinieri to mark the place where the body had been found made a shiver run down her spine. Her instinct was yelling at her that she shouldn't be there. She breathed in slowly, trying to calm herself.

Might not be pleasant, but it needs to be done.

The room was simple, divided into two areas. On the right side, a large table stood in front of the fireplace in the corner. On the other side, a little cabinet held the TV, but there were no DVDs or such. The room had a worn sofa and a single armchair; no bookshelves, but a couple of anonymous paintings of landscapes hung on the walls. Behind the sofa was a cupboard. She opened it to find a few plates and glasses and a drawer full of batteries, lamp bulbs and all the other things people generally don't know where to store.

She left for the kitchen, which was a rather small one with a little table. The cabinets contained what Giò recognised as everyday plates, glasses and cutlery. She felt sure, since his wife had passed away, Antonio had never used the *good* ones in the living room.

In the fridge, there were a few beers, a piece of cheese. The opposite cabinet contained little in the way of food, but a huge reserve of cheap wine, whisky and more beer. For someone who was supposed to have given up drinking, Antonio definitely had too much alcohol in his house.

She went back into the living room, and from that position she could see something sparkling between the irregular tiles on the floor. She took a picture with her phone, then picked the object up to look more closely. It was a golden cufflink, enamelled in dark blue with the initials CC. A single thought flashed through her mind: *Carlo Capello*. Could it be?

Keep your cool, don't jump to conclusions. Think later. Now is the time to look around and find things. But her heart was beating faster.

She took another picture of the jewel with her mobile then put it back almost where she'd found it, just a bit more in view. How had the carabinieri not seen it? They were clearly not too smart, so she'd better help them as much as she could. A pity she couldn't tell any of this to Paolo.

She felt triumphant – she had found the first hard evidence to suggest that Antonio's death wasn't an accident. Was that what she had come here looking for? In any case, she wanted to see upstairs.

She went back to the corridor and took

the stairs. The first floor was smaller than the ground floor. The bathroom contained a few products on the shelves and a medicine box in the wall cabinet. There was only one bedroom – maybe when the daughter had been alive, they'd lived somewhere else. On the bedside cabinet, she saw two photographs. One was the portrait of two smiling women – his wife and daughter – and the other showed the three of them when his daughter was only about five or six. They looked a happy family. Poor Antonio.

It was then she heard a sound that turned her blood to ice.

Someone was unlocking the door downstairs. She had not been aware of a car coming up the drive. Maybe she had been too deep in her thoughts. She was trapped – if she were to go downstairs to exit via the back door, she would come face to face with the intruder. She looked out of the small window in the bedroom, but it was too high to jump down onto the concrete path beneath.

Her brain, stimulated by rising terror, identified the only two places to hide: under the bed or in the wardrobe. She pulled back the bed linen, hoping to find room to slide under the bed, but it almost touched the floor. Only the wardrobe, then. She opened the doors as slowly as she could, anxious not to make any kind of noise. There were a few clothes hanging up and several sweaters and blankets piled on the bottom. She stacked these on top of herself, praying that whoever was in the house wouldn't search the wardrobe.

Placing her fingers on the bottom of both doors, she gently pulled them closed. She couldn't hear much from the ground floor – whoever was there was moving silently too.

Who could it be? And why were they there? Could it be Carlo, who had realised his cufflink was missing and come looking for it? Was he the killer? Was he a psychopath disguising himself as an artist, his resentment growing after the humiliation he'd suffered at the hands of

Mrs Rivello at the Pink Slippers dinner? But why would he kill Antonio? Maybe the poor devil had surprised him when he was dislodging the rock?

However, if it was Carlo, she could be in luck. Chances were that if he found his cufflink downstairs, he'd leave right away. After all, it would be risky for him to be found at Antonio's.

She was sweltering with all the clothes on top of her. She waited – no noise whatsoever. Had the intruder found what he or she wanted and gone? Shouldn't she find out if it was really Carlo? Otherwise she would only have her speculations and no proof except her photo.

She removed some of the layers that were covering her up and slowly pushed the doors ajar, her ears pricked to catch any little noise. And then she heard the intruder. He was climbing the stairs. He was coming.

She pulled the wardrobe doors closed in horror and dived into the clothes again, even covering her head. This man had killed twice, he would not hesitate to do it a third time.

He was in the bathroom. She could hear him moving things around. It wouldn't take him long. There wasn't much there. In fact, now he was in the bedroom: she could hear him searching the drawers of the bedside cabinet. What was he looking for? Maybe he hadn't seen the cufflink on the floor.

He seemed to have a system. She heard him opening one drawer at a time then closing it. Four drawers searched and he was coming over to the wardrobe.

He opened it and examined the hanging clothes, searching the pockets of each. She had buried herself so deeply, she could hardly breathe, her heart bumping so hard she was terrified it would give her away.

The man had pushed all the hanging clothes to one side and was rummaging through the stuff on the floor when he gave a loud gasp and jumped back. With horror, she realised he had touched her stiff knee. She heard a suspicious click, a pause, then slowly he started to remove the stuff around her head. When her face emerged from the covers, they both cried out. Giò was blinded by the sunlight, but she kept screaming as loud as she could.

The man stepped back angrily. "What the hell are you doing here? Oh my goodness!" He lowered one hand, and Giò's eyes, adjusting to the light, saw he held a gun.

"Paolo, don't shoot," she begged.

He sat down on the edge of the bed, putting the safety catch back on the gun. Breathing heavily, he sat there for a couple of minutes before giving her his hand to help her out.

"What the hell are you doing here?" he repeated.

"I... I wanted to look for evidence." Her legs were all pins and needles; she couldn't stand, so she sat beside him. "I thought you were Carlo."

"I was going to fire!"

"Into my legs, I hope."

"Yes, your legs. It becomes instinctive: shoot to wound, not to kill... if you can."

"I'm relieved. Not that I would like to receive a bullet in my knee, but at least I would be alive. Lame, but alive."

"I thought it was a dead body hidden in the wardrobe." Paolo was no longer shouting, but his voice was still louder than usual. "Then when I realised it was alive, I feared it might be the killer." He shook his head again. "You said you thought it was Carlo... did you find something downstairs?" As he recovered his composure, his carabiniere brain was already at work.

"I've found a cufflink with his initials on. I guess not too many people are stylish enough in Maratea to wear cufflinks on their shirts. How did you miss it during your inspection?"

"I have no idea. Where is it?"

"Well, it's not exactly where it was..."

"You mean you touched it and moved it around?"

She waved the handkerchief she had

used to handle the jewel. "I didn't leave or erase any fingerprints."

"Let's go downstairs, I want you to show me where you found it."

On shaky legs, Giò followed Paolo back into the living room. She showed him the photo with the cufflink in its original position. Paolo put it back where it had been, took the same photo, then carefully slid it into a plastic bag.

"It's not all that visible, but still, it's weird we missed it. Carlo has some questions to answer, and Sara too. Let's get some fresh air – I need to question you as well."

Once outside, Giò saw a pump and washed her hands and face to get rid of all the signs of fear. She drank too, a few fresh sips to relieve her dry mouth.

"That's better," she said, inhaling air deep into her lungs while Paolo was making a couple of phone calls. He wanted to interrogate Sara and Carlo separately, so he gave instructions that the two were not to be allowed to meet. But there'd be no formal charge – yet. He then turned back to Giò.

"I'm giving you five minutes to explain what you were doing here. You know it's against the law, don't you? How did you get in?"

She told her story completely truthfully, then continued in a frenzy of words, "Now if it was Carlo, he had a motive. Mrs Rivello had offended him and his mother publicly. Of course, he must be a sort of psychopath... And the threatening letters? They're so much more in line with him and his obsession with transforming real life into literature, and vice versa. But why would he bother to pick up Elena's mobile?"

"Simple: he thought he had killed Mrs Rivello, and maybe they had exchanged bitter messages. Maybe he had sent threatening texts directly from his mobile and wanted to make sure no evidence was left. If we charge him, we'll get hold of his mobile and PC and check them out. We will also question Mrs Rivello again with a little less tact this time. She's been hiding important information from us."

"Maybe she didn't know it was Carlo threatening her. After all, her husband hid the first letter from her."

"Hmm."

"But why would Carlo murder Antonio?"

"Maybe Antonio saw him on the day of the murder. Carlo may have feared that Antonio might put the pieces together."

Paolo's mobile rang. "I'll be there in about 15 minutes." He put down the phone. "How are you getting back?"

"I've got Mario's scooter, and then I'll kayak back to Fiumicello."

"Are you OK?"

"Exercise will settle my nerves. I might have a bite to eat at the hotel, too. Frankly, I'm starving."

"Promise me you'll never do anything as stupid and dangerous as this again. From this moment, you're no longer on the case. I should have known better.

Anyway, I believe we may have finally got to the bottom of it."

"Oh, come on, Paolo, you can't kick me out like that. Let's discuss it later."

He was already in the car, shooing her away. She didn't need him to remind her. She walked up the path to the cemetery, took Mario's scooter, ate a sandwich on the beach, and made her way back on her kayak, which seemed to take much longer than the outward journey.

Once she was settled at home, she found a message from Andrea on her phone. *"Are you back? How about having dinner together?"*

She had no doubts about refusing this invitation.

"I'm at home, but I'm less fit than I thought I was. I'm exhausted. Sorry!" She didn't add anything nice like, *"Let's do it tomorrow"*.

He interpreted her abruptness correctly and sent back a simple, *"OK"*.

Giò felt guilty and stupid. Why was she so good at spoiling things when they were... well, just perfect? Carlo was the murderer, and Andrea, as she had wanted to believe from the very beginning, had nothing to do with the crime. Just like her, he had been in the wrong place at the wrong time. But somehow she had managed to screw things up with this guy.

She felt too exhausted to think on it any longer and headed instead for the shower.

19

SETTING UP TRAPS

After dinner, Agnese knocked on her sister's door, and Giò gave her a sugar-coated version of all that had happened.

"I can't believe Paolo pulled me off the case so brutally. After all I've done for him."

"I need to confess," said Agnese, "that I suspected Andrea. I never thought it could be Carlo."

"Not even when we overheard him speaking to Sara?"

"No, I concluded that something weird

was going on between the two of them, unrelated to the homicide."

"Why did you suspect Andy?"

"Because of his closeness to Mr Rivello, the argument with Mrs Rivello, his way of life…"

"His way of life?" cried Giò, exasperated.

"I mean, he loves the good life."

"As does Carlo, and I do too."

"But Carlo has always been rich, whereas Andy's wealth has mostly come about thanks to his collaboration with Mr Rivello. It seems to me he lives beyond his means…"

"Which is one more reason why he'd want to protect his friendship with Mr Rivello, not kill his wife."

"I know. That's what I'm saying: you were right and I was wrong, so don't get so defensive." Agnese was getting tired of having to pick and choose the right words to soothe her sister. You can love your sister with all your heart, but there will still be things about her that will irritate you beyond reason, and Giò's quick temper was one of those things for Agnese.

"I'm not defensive. But it seems you've decided there's something between me and Andy, and you've been overprotective ever since. I mean, I'm no longer a teenager. Can't you reserve your maternal instincts for Lilia and Luca?"

"I'm just looking out for my sister. Plus I'm admitting I was wrong. But since you're this touchy, I'll leave you to it. Goodnight!"

"You're touchy at times as well," blurted Giò.

"Goodnight," repeated Agnese, choosing to ignore her sister's last remark and shutting the door behind her.

"Goodnight," Giò growled. She hated arguing with her sister. She slammed books here and there, prowling through to the kitchen like a lion in a cage. Then she took her jacket and headed out. She wouldn't sleep until she'd calmed down. It had been such a long day – when would it ever come to an end?

She set off towards the parish church. The square was empty, just a few cats were playing hide and seek. The full moon illuminated the walls of the buildings on the square better than the yellow lamplights, but the clear night meant the air was cool, and she was relieved to find a warm scarf in her bag to knot around her throat.

She went down towards the main square. Leo's bar was still open and Paolo was there, sitting by himself, drinking a beer.

"May I join you?"

"You're still up? I thought you would have had enough for one day." He pulled up a chair beside him.

"It looks like I won't get any sleep at all tonight, as much as I need it."

"A beer might help?"

"I think it might."

"I'm not going to tell you a thing, though," he warned her seriously.

"I don't want more things to think about," she replied sulkily.

"I can't believe my ears." This time a cheeky smile appeared on his face.

"That doesn't mean I won't change my mind tomorrow," snorted Giò.

They talked without once mentioning what had happened, just reminiscing about the good old times. They were laughing heartily in the almost deserted square when Andrea passed by. He pretended not to have seen them, but she was sure he did. She had refused to see him, telling him she was too tired, only for him to catch her laughing merrily with Paolo in a bar after midnight. Damn!

THE NEXT DAY, SHE WOKE UP TO find out that one, she had overslept, two, rain was pouring down in buckets, and three, her muscles hurt all over because of the long kayak ride. It was not a brilliant start to a new day. Giò had breakfast inside, looking gloomily at the terrace being swept by the violent rain and howling wind, then left her mug, dish and Moka pot in the sink. She'd leave the washing-up for later.

She switched on her laptop. No news on the local newspapers' pages. She opened her Scrivener project about Scotland. Her research folder was full of information, and the project folders, where she was supposed to do the real writing, showed 12 chapters, but each chapter folder had nothing more than a temporary title.

She would write the introduction at a later date. Starting with Edinburgh and its surrounding area, she'd suggest day trips from the capital. She read her research material again, noting a few things on a piece of paper as if she were creating an outline for the chapter. What should she call it? What adjective would define Edinburgh's character without being too obvious? Elegant Edinburgh? That was true, but it missed out on the mystery that identified the city... to her eyes, at least. In Edinburgh, she had always had a sense that a city existed beyond the city. That even somewhere as famous as Victoria Street would be a very different place when there were no passers-by late at night or very early in the morning. But she was positive her editor wouldn't approve of her going beyond the obvious. They had already reminded her that writing a travel guide is much closer to science than literature. You have rules to follow and you have simply to list and categorise all the worthy attractions. You could include a couple of boxes quoting a legend or an anecdote, but that was all. So, no matter what, millions of tourists would pick up their favourite guide, which would not be too different from all the other guides in the marketplace, and see exactly the same things as all the other visitors. Their short stay would be spent fitting in as much stuff as they could: a museum after a church, after a castle, a monument, a view. Was that the true meaning of travelling? Just a long list of must-see attractions?

She could not work when her inner critic was so vocal, so she switched off her laptop defiantly, put it aside and opened *Edinburgh* by Robert Louis Stevenson. She lay down on the sofa and buried her nose in the musty scent of the yellowish pages.

A KNOCK ON HER DOOR SOME TIME later woke her with a start and she realised that, much as she enjoyed the book, at some point she must have fallen asleep. She got up and opened the door.

"Auntie, will you be coming down for lunch?" Lilia smiled shyly.

"Did your mum ask you to invite me?"

"We all want you to come, if you're not too busy working, Mum said."

"Well, I can take a break. How long have I got?"

"How long do you want?"

"Fifteen minutes?"

"I'll tell Mum," and Lilia ran away.

Giò showered hurriedly, looked outside and saw it was raining just as heavily as it had been earlier. It was rare that it rained in Maratea, but once it got started, it was hardly ever a short shower. It would carry on all day long.

Nando hugged and teased her, Luca was kind, Granny didn't ask about her work, Agnese was sweet. It felt good to have a family who would accept her with all her imperfections, little demons and bad temper. After lunch, Nando and Luca offered to clear the table and the kitchen. When everything was clean and tidy, the kids went to do their homework, Nando left for his office, and the three women lingered in the kitchen.

Granny said, "I hope the carabinieri aren't closing the case and simply charging Antonio with the homicide."

"But there's plenty of evidence against him," Giò replied, wondering if Granny had heard the news about Carlo's cufflink.

"It's easy to blame someone who can't defend himself."

"So what's your theory?"

"A very simple one. Antonio was involved in something illegal and therefore he could be blackmailed, so if he knew something about the murder, he couldn't speak up. But since he had started drinking again, the killer decided it would be safer to get rid of him in case he spoke out when drunk."

"Who is the killer then?"

"That I don't know... yet!"

"While you carry on with your investigations, Granny, I'd better go upstairs and get back to work."

Giò feared that in front of her shrewd grandmother, she might give away secrets Paolo had asked her not to share. Maybe it wasn't smart to keep quiet, though; Granny had a powerful imagination.

Before she reached the door, Agnese called to her and asked softly, "No hard feelings?"

Giò melted. "How could there be?" she

said, hugging Agnese, and added, "I have a bad temper, but I didn't want to hurt you."

Back in her room with her books, she almost felt like calling Lilia and Luca to do their homework with her, but resisted the temptation in the interests of actually getting something done.

I will go back to reading. Inspiration will come, but at the moment I can't stand the thought of looking at a blank page.

She picked up her book where she had left it.

AGNESE WAS BENT OVER THE lipsticks drawer. It was amazing how difficult it was to keep the long lines of small boxes in order; they would fall like dominoes, one knocking over the next, and the numbers would get mixed up, tricking her into believing she had run out of one shade when the stock was simply in the wrong place. Patience – she needed lots of patience and hard work to keep a perfumery running.

She heard the door open and she rose up from her uncomfortable position. The big smile and "Good afternoon" on her lips faded away in an instant.

Mrs Tristizia stood in front of her, puffy eyes surrounded by dark shadows. A red nose, a heaving chest and a handkerchief in her hand completed the picture.

Agnese gently approached her. "Good afternoon, Mrs Tristizia. May I help you?"

Mrs Tristizia tried to speak, but she just gulped. Holding her words in seemed to be the only way she could hold back her tears, too.

"Please, have a seat," said Agnese, pointing at the sofa and running to lock the door and put the 'Back Soon' sign in place. "I've just made a nice, spicy tea, it will do you good." She prepared a mug of hot turmeric, ginger and orange tea, added a spoonful of honey and handed it to Mrs Tristizia.

The woman held the warm mug in her

hands, breathed in the scent and took a couple of slow sips. Agnese could see the tension in her body dissipate a tiny bit.

"It's good," Mrs Tristizia managed to say finally, nodding at the mug.

"I find it so comforting when the days get a bit cooler or my mood is low." Mrs Tristizia nodded again, but made no indication that she was about to start speaking, so Agnese asked her, "How are you?"

With a shaky voice, fighting hard against her tears, the other woman answered, "Miserable. The perfume didn't work... at all! And it is all so bad, so very bad."

"What's so bad?"

"Come on, you know as well as everyone else in Maratea. We all know it. My husband is in love with that obnoxious young girl."

"It will pass," Agnese replied instinctively.

"I don't think so, not this time. And even if it did, how could I accept it?

Actually, how have I put up with it for so many years?"

Now tears were running down her face, but they were quiet, desperate tears without gulps or sobs.

"But I had two kids, and I had left my job to look after the family. Every time he strayed, I said to myself, 'He's just a man, he can't help himself. He will come back to me and his family, it's just a flight of fancy.' But it was hard, believe me. He took my dignity away.

"And with this young lady – if she is young! – he knows no shame. In the past, at least he tried to keep his affairs secret, though it's sort of hard in a village like Maratea. Here people always seem to know everything. But this time he's made no attempt to hide anything. I hear people whisper, 'How can she bear that?' Some think I'm stupid and don't realise what's happening. Others think I'm simply not bothered and only care about my husband's money. Neither is true. I know what he's like, but I love my husband,

and my family. I must do, to put up with him.

"But there is no end to how bad things can get. Yesterday he asked me for a divorce."

She had to stop. Agnese felt her heart aching with sympathy and said the first thing that came to her mind.

"He will change his mind and realise it is just a phase. Men do that all the time, only to realise when reality strikes who's stood by them throughout the years, who they have to thank for where they are, who they really love."

As soon as the words were out of her mouth, Agnese realised that she didn't believe a single thing she'd said.

Mrs Tristizia shook her head. "He won't come back this time, I know him. But even if he did, I can't make a fool of myself anymore."

Between the gulps and sobs, Agnese spotted something firm in Mrs Tristizia's tone, and a look of resolve in the older woman's eyes she hadn't seen before. This time she didn't reply. She wouldn't lie to Mrs Tristizia again.

"I told him at first that I would never consent to the divorce, but then I changed my mind. There is no way back, but I wonder... where should I start to rebuild my life?"

"A lawyer would definitely help. You have rights for sure, and since he is the one asking for the divorce, and he was quite happy for you to give up your career years ago to look after him..."

"Yes, I spoke to a lawyer. We are going to have a more in-depth meeting tomorrow. I just came over because I think I shocked you the other day. I recognise it was so stupid of me."

"Oh no, I understand." Agnese patted her back softly.

"I must have looked ridiculous."

"Well, let's just say I didn't understand what was going on. But we could have a proper perfume session this time."

Mrs Tristizia was surprised. "What for?"

"Last time, you chose a perfume for him. But perfumes never work that way. This time, we will choose a perfume for you. You need strength, you need to discover more of yourself. I'm sure I can help... a tiny bit."

Mrs Tristizia was a little baffled, but accepted the proposal. She chose a candle with a delicate milky scent. The first accord she picked out had an unusual wheaty scent, the second a delicate fruity one.

"This reminds me of apricot skin," she told Agnese. "When I was a child, I loved to caress apricots – they were so smooth and had such a velvety fragrance."

Agnese smiled. This time the session had been an honest one. She took the table of perfumes that corresponded with the accords Mrs Tristizia had chosen and handed her the colourful spinning top. When it stopped, Agnese pinned its position and turned the table-top upside down.

"Jeux de Peau, that's a perfect choice."

She couldn't help a satisfied grin. "It's a comforting scent. It will be a good companion for you."

Agnese went towards one of the cupboards and picked up a tester.

"Can I spray it directly on your skin?"

"Please, I'm rather curious," Mrs Tristizia replied. She smelled her wrist and gave a gasp of surprise. "It's... it's the smell of... of bread. It reminds me of when my granny used to bake a special sweet bread in the family oven and I couldn't wait for it to cool down. I would try to break the caramelised crust as soon as Granny turned the other way. Its smell was so good when I held a piece of it in my hands, and that perfume reminds me of the smell of that bread between my fingers."

Agnese nodded in approval, and Mrs Tristizia continued.

"I was never a pretty child, not ugly either, but I knew for my gran, I was the cutest child ever. She simply adored me." A few tears came into her eyes and she let them run freely down her face. "How different I was then. I was confident I would do something special with my life. My parents believed in me... how stupid of me to end up where I am."

"Please don't judge yourself. It's so easy to blame ourselves when in reality we are the victims of circumstance. Just stick to that childhood feeling."

"Yes, Agnese, thank you. It was something I had forgotten about. I don't know how a perfume can conjure up the past so suddenly and vividly."

"This is the real power of perfumes. There's no magic, but they appeal to the most instinctive part of our brain without giving our rational side a chance to meddle."

Mrs Tristizia's eyes were still watery, but she had a sweet smile on her face. "I think I'll buy the perfume and go home, have a soothing bath and listen to my favourite music. The family are all away today. I will enjoy my freedom and have a good sleep, and think it all through tomorrow."

"That sounds very much like Scarlett O'Hara." Agnese smiled and Mrs Tristizia laughed, probably for the first time in weeks, maybe even months. Then she smelled her wrist again.

"You know what? Maybe after all, there is something I can do."

There was a note of determination in the way she said it. She wasn't out for revenge, wasn't chasing a dream; she just wanted something simple and concrete. Or at least, that's what Agnese hoped.

IT WAS SIX O'CLOCK IN THE evening when an SMS alert rang on Giò's phone. Andrea, perhaps? She opened it up. No, it was from Paolo.

"I've got news. Can I come over in 30 minutes or so?"

"I'll be waiting," she texted back.

It was actually gone 7pm before Paolo

rang her buzzer. She opened the door and waited for him to climb the stairs.

"Coffee, beer, wine?"

"I'd better not drink, I have to think clearly. A glass of water will do."

Giò cut a lemon and put a slice in each glass of water, then made room on the table by pushing all her research material aside.

"I know I don't want you involved anymore, but after what we discovered, I thought it was only right to let you know the latest developments."

"Is it about what happened when you spoke to Carlo and Sara?" asked Giò, pleased that Paolo still felt the need to share his investigation with her.

"I interviewed Sara first. I made her nervous by reminding her that this is a murder case and she would be charged as an accomplice if she didn't tell me everything she knew. She burst into tears, then confessed that when she arrived at the car park the morning Elena died, Carlo's car was already there. Apparently he'd asked her to back his statement that he'd arrived after her."

"But that makes no sense. It would have been a better alibi for him if a witness had said he'd arrived and gone before Sara. Why would he ask Sara to lie?"

"Exactly, but we'll get to that in a moment. Sara admitted that they'd had a discussion about it, which was when you overheard them. She was begging him to let her tell us the truth, but he said that since she had already made her statement, she'd better stick to that version or we would suspect she was a liar, and we might even think she had a role in the murder.

"At this point, I had enough to question Carlo. When he heard Sara had confessed, he told us his story. He had been in Sapri since the day before – he'd spent the night there with one of his lovers, but he didn't want his fiancée, who was away visiting her parents, to find out. He had called her the night before, pretending he was in Maratea."

"Men can't ever be trusted!" Giò

grumbled. Paolo ignored her outburst and continued.

"When he heard about the accident, he realised that there was a very real risk of his private movements being made public if the gossips got hold of the fact he hadn't travelled from Acquafredda that morning as he usually does. He justified his lies, saying that at the time of his first statement, he believed it had just been an accident, not a murder. He thought there would be no repercussions to convincing Sara to say he had arrived after her. She too saw nothing wrong with it at the time."

"So what did he really do that morning?"

"With his fiancée away for a few days, he left for Sapri at six o'clock the evening before the murder. He dined with his lover, and then he spent the night at hers."

"And, I imagine, she is the only witness?"

"No, there's also a mechanic. He left the scooter with him as soon as he arrived in Sapri because it had a problem starting. His lover went to pick him up from the garage."

"That could be an attempt to build up an alibi."

"I've asked the carabinieri in Sapri to check his story: restaurant, lover, mechanic. They will let me know."

"Do you believe he might be speaking the truth?"

"Yes, I'm confident he spent the night in Sapri."

"He could have reached Acquafredda from Sapri that morning. His lover might have driven him or he might have used another means of transport."

"She owns a car, but she used it to go to work. I was sceptical when he reported his story, but we're checking all the details. And, it would explain his and Sara's weird behaviour. It also confirms that Gerardina is a trustworthy witness – she was adamant Carlo's car didn't pass her house that morning, and she was right."

"But how about the cufflink?"

"He swears he's never been to Antonio's house. He recognised the cufflink at once and said he'd lost it a few days after the accident. It could be that somebody planted it in Antonio's house after the homicide to frame Carlo, perhaps when you spread the news that the carabinieri didn't believe Antonio was the murderer. This would explain why we didn't find the cufflink during the first inspection: it wasn't there."

"So you need to start the investigation all over again?"

"Not exactly. You see, we had five suspects: you, Sara, Carlo, Andrea, Antonio. We cleared you first, then Sara…"

"Is she not on the suspects list again?"

"No, remember Gerardina saw her arriving after 7 and the bus driver confirmed she was on the 7.15 bus. That was before Elena arrived."

"So, why was she so eager to cover for Carlo?"

"I suspect she has a crush on Carlo, and in the beginning, it looked like it wouldn't matter. Only when it became a murder case, she realised the implications of what she had done. On the other hand, she thought that the lie gave her an alibi."

Giò gave him a quizzical look.

"Remember, the suspects don't realise we have a witness and know the exact time of the murder. Sara felt that since Carlo stated he had arrived after her, he would confirm her innocence. That's how he convinced her not to give him away when she became uneasy' about the whole thing."

"But Carlo, didn't he feel his remedy was worse than the disease?"

"Only later, but by then he feared it would sound even worse to confess to the whole thing. He considered it better to stick to the made-up version."

"I'm sorry to keep interrupting you, but... Sara and I are both in the clear. And you say you might have the evidence to clear Carlo, too."

"I'm waiting to hear from the Sapri carabinieri tomorrow, but my instinct says we can remove Carlo from the suspects list."

"In which case, you're left with Antonio and Andrea."

"Not quite."

She gave him another quizzical glance.

"You remember, we said we were setting a trap for the real murderer, and…"

Paolo paused as if he couldn't find the right words to continue. Giò drummed her fingers on the table.

"Why aren't you finishing your sentences today?" she demanded.

"And he fell in. He cleared Antonio…"

Again, words seemed to fail him.

"My goodness, what's with the stopping in the middle of an explanation? Who cleared Antonio? How? Why? Where? Should I add more questions so you can string a few sentences together?"

He looked at her with a rather piteous expression that drove Giò even madder.

"Let's start with your first question:

who? Our murderer cleared Antonio for us, which is precisely what we wanted him to do. Second question: how? Answer, the cufflink. Who apart from the murderer has an interest in framing Carlo at this point of the investigation? He heard that the carabinieri concluded it was a second murder and not an accident, so he had to act fast and give us a suspect before we were led to him. Either by chance or design, he found the cufflink. He knew how to break into Antonio's house since he had already gone there to kill him, so he returned and hid the item."

Giò's face was as white as a sheet. "Are you telling me you suspect Andy is the murderer?"

"Evidence has excluded all the other suspects one by one. The one who's left has to be the culprit."

"What was his motive?"

"We're working on it. But I wanted you to be prepared, to know where our investigations are leading us."

"Are you going to arrest him?"

"Not yet. It might be better to leave him free to act. We don't expect he will try to harm Mrs Rivello again, but just in case, she's under carabinieri protection. We're waiting for him to make another mistake..."

"So, you didn't tell me all of this to help our investigations. It was a warning, wasn't it?" Giò was clearly disappointed.

"Got me! I don't know whether there is something going on between the two of you, but yes, I wanted you to know he is under suspicion for having killed Elena, mistaking her for Mrs Rivello. He had been with Mr Rivello's team on the mountains when the road was closed. He could easily have noticed the large stone and its position, and he knew where Mrs Rivello parked. After the first attempt, he tried to kill Mrs Rivello again on the day of Elena's funeral. I suspect Antonio saw something when Elena was murdered, and he had to be killed too."

"But what could he have seen?"

"Maybe Antonio went to the graveyard

when he came home at 7am and saw Andrea. If he had a hangover, maybe he needed the comfort of a visit to his wife and daughter's graves. On the night of his death, Antonio would have let Andrea in without suspicion because he trusted the man. When he knew we suspected murder, Andrea tried to frame Carlo. He's spent plenty of time with Carlo recently, so it would have been easy for him to take the cufflink. I'm sorry, Giò. I wish you and Andrea hadn't got close, but you'd better stay away from him till we've finished the investigations."

"We're not that close. He is... ahem... an attractive chap, but I have avoided him recently. You surely know I had to call off my wedding, so I'm in no hurry to start another romance. So no hurt feelings, if that's what you feared." But as she spoke, she realised she wasn't being entirely honest.

"I'm glad to hear that, but it's not only hurt feelings I'm worried about. He's a dangerous man, he might feel he's been pushed into a trap and overreact. Keep away from him. And this time, no jokes, no games, no entering locked houses, or wardrobes. It's a matter of life and death."

"I understand. Still, are you totally satisfied you've looked at all the angles?"

"What do you mean?"

"Well, I've always had a strange feeling about the whole story. When I was on the kayak yesterday, I thought of at least two things that aren't very clear."

"Are you going to share them with me?"

"The first one is the threatening letters. There's always been something weird about them. Why would the killer write a threatening letter to his victim and then try to pass the murder off as an accident? There were lots of easier and more reliable ways to kill Mrs Rivello, so the killer must have chosen the falling rock because he had a good chance of passing it off as an accident. If it hadn't been for Mr Faraco, nobody would ever have found out that the rock had been dislodged deliberately. So writing threatening messages makes no sense.

"Andrea is an architect, he's got a rational mind. I can imagine him plotting clever ways to get away with murder, but not writing ridiculous letters that give his plan away. And the same applies to the flowerpot accident. The murderer writes and threatens Mrs Rivello, then he tries to kill her. Why is he alerting his victim every time?"

"It's a good point, but killers are not as smart as they look in books. They are often led by instinct and fear."

"Well, I confess this was my stronger point. The second is more about why the killer would steal the phone. Didn't he realise he had killed Elena, not Mrs Rivello?"

"It could be that he couldn't see enough of the body. Elena's face was hidden by the crushed car roof, but her bag was easy to reach from the passenger seat of the car through the broken window."

"OK, but the killer should have known

the carabinieri nowadays can gain access to calls, messages, emails without actually having the phone, so why take it?"

"Maybe he thought we wouldn't make a search. Remember, he was trying to pass it off as an accident."

"Then we circle back to the threatening letters. But OK, let's stay with the phone. What if he wanted it to destroy other content on it?"

"What do you mean?"

"Imagine if there were photos that would incriminate him. If he destroyed the phone, he would be safe. Unlike messages and calls, photos cannot be tracked without the phone."

"That's an interesting theory, but unfortunately the phone will probably be at the bottom of the sea by now. I'm sure the killer disposed of it."

"Duh, Brigadiere, I thought you were smarter than the maresciallo. The phone is right under our nose. We only need to fetch it."

This time, Giò had totally lost Paolo and he didn't even try to hide it.

"Paolo, we're looking for *Mrs Rivello's* mobile, not Elena's. And she's still got it. Elena's phone might be on the seabed, but the real victim's phone is still with its rightful owner."

He looked at her, flabbergasted. "You're right! I wonder if the coroner would grant me access to the phone records. I frankly doubt Mrs Rivello would hand us her mobile willingly."

"Well, you know, I'm not the carabinieri." Giò stood up, her clenched fists against her hips. Paolo looked at her in horror, but she returned a blank gaze. "I could 'borrow' her mobile for a while, pretend it dropped from her bag or something. Before returning it, I could scan her messages, phone calls, recent numbers and photos. I'm sure the mystery is in the pictures."

"I can't believe I'm having this conversation with you," he said, but his voice sounded anything but irritated.

"I will ask Agnese and Granny to invite the Rivellos for an aperitivo at ours. I need them to feel relaxed," Giò concluded.

When Paolo left, she remained deep in thought.

I need to know the truth. Andrea Aiello, I still can't believe you're a cold-blooded murderer. I'm giving you one last chance...

20

APERITIVO AT THE BRANDOS'

Giò had it all planned with her family. She told them why she wanted to invite the Rivellos round for an aperitivo, sharing the fact that she needed to be able to browse Mrs Rivello's mobile for as long as possible. She just hoped that either it wasn't protected by a PIN code, or she'd have the opportunity to spot the code when Mrs Rivello used her phone.

That morning, Granny shut herself in the kitchen to prepare home-made panzerotti. The filling included plenty of mozzarella, a few spoonfuls of tomato sauce, provolone cheese cubes to complement the sweeter taste of the mozzarella, a little parmesan to tie all the ingredients together, a sprinkle of oregano and fresh basil leaves. The mix had to be a perfect blend of flavours and tastes. Granny had already prepared the pizza dough, which was well kneaded and elastic. She insisted on doing the kneading by hand rather than using any kind of mixer.

"There's nothing to beat the warmth of your hands for kneading!' she protested every time Agnese or Giò invited her to use a machine.

Once the dough had risen, she cut little pieces out of it and rolled them into round shapes with a rolling pin. She added two to three spoonfuls of filling to one half of them, then wet her fingers in a cup of cold water and ran them around the edges before folding the empty side over the filled one. With a fork, she crimped the edges closed.

At that point, each half-moon-shaped panzerotto was ready to be fried. They had to be thin enough to be light to eat, thick enough not to break while frying.

Granny lined a few on a wooden board she only used for making pasta or pizza dough. She covered them with a slightly damp towel so they would not dry out, then finally took a break. She would only start frying them just before serving them.

The doorbell rang and Lilia ran to welcome the guests, followed by the rest of the family. Camilla and Raimondo Rivello were all smiles, although Mr Rivello looked a little tired, as if the events of the past two weeks had taken their toll. Camilla, on the other hand, seemed just as full of herself as ever.

Luca offered to take their jackets, but Mrs Rivello kept her bag and phone with her. As they sat down in the living room, Granny appeared from the kitchen. She had been Raimondo's teacher when he was a little boy, and goodness! How deferential he was with her. No matter how important a person may become in adult life, a teacher will always exert a certain degree of authority over them.

They were chatting amiably when Mrs Rivello's mobile rang. "I don't recognise this number," she said, looking at the caller ID. She refused the call, but typed in her code to see the details, and Giò followed the movement of her finger: 1598. Easy-peasy. Giò winked at Lilia who was sitting on the other end of the sofa with an angelic smile on her face.

A couple of minutes later, the conversation was again interrupted by the ringing of Mrs Rivello's phone.

"The same number again," she said. "I wonder who it is?"

"Let it ring, you can call them back later," replied her husband, looking guiltily at Granny whose brows had risen to her hairline in disapproval.

"Oh, sorry," Mrs Rivello said.

"Don't worry about Granny," whispered Agnese. "She does it with us too, we're obliged to switch off our mobiles at lunchtime. She's so old fashioned."

"But that's a very healthy attitude," replied Camilla Rivello. "And a good example for your kids," she added, sliding her mobile back into her bag in silent mode.

"That's the main reason we do it." Agnese nodded – there were not a single mobile around.

Granny said she would go back into her kitchen to start frying the panzerotti. Nando opened a bottle of Grottino, a dry white wine from Roccanova, and invited the Rivellos to join him at the table.

"You know how messy panzerotti can be, so we thought it would be better to sit down."

The table was laid with plenty of salads, tomatoes, olives, and bruschette. As the Rivellos left the sofa to join Nando, quick as flash, Lilia jumped up.

"I'll take your bag and store it with your coat, Mrs Rivello. Then Granny won't be grumpy with you."

Mrs Rivello looked a little taken aback, but Lilia had already left the room, so she could only smile in acceptance.

"Oh, I'm sorry," Agnese smiled back sympathetically, "but you know how it is with these kids. The rules have to be obeyed by the adults too. I hope you don't mind?"

"Of course not."

The panzerotti arrived. They were hot, crunchy on the outside, the dough was thin and light, and long strings of melted mozzarella stretched out with every single bite. Silence fell on the room, broken only when the last panzerotto was gone.

"They are delicious," said Camilla Rivello. "Very different from the ones we make here."

"Granny's mother came from Apulia, which has a cooking style altogether different to Basilicata's," Agnese explained.

As the kitchen door opened and Granny came in with a second tray of panzerotti, Agnese looked towards her sister.

"Giò, dear, is something wrong with you?"

"Just stomach cramps again. I'd better go and take my medicine." She rose, leaving an untouched panzerotto on her dish, which took all of her willpower. Why couldn't she have thought of another excuse for her temporary disappearance?

"Isn't Giò feeling well?" Mrs Rivello enquired.

"For a couple of days now, she's been experiencing stomach pains whenever she eats. I guess she shouldn't have eaten any of the panzerotti, but they are so hard to resist…"

They forgot Giò and fell upon the new batch of panzerotti. Absolute bliss!

GIÒ CREPT INTO THE CORRIDOR where Lilia had left Mrs Rivello's bag and searched for her phone. Finding it, she ran upstairs to Lilia's bedroom and opened Mrs Rivello's latest phone calls. Andrea's name was registered, but no recent calls to him were listed. Carlo and Antonio's names weren't among Mrs Rivello's contacts at all.

Mrs Rivello didn't have WhatsApp installed, so Giò went to her photos folder. A few photos of flowers, her daughters, her nephews, pictures with her friends. Giò scanned through them with care, a cable on hand so she could download the pictures onto Lilia's computer, but frankly it seemed pointless. She didn't know what she'd expected to find, but there was nothing worthy of interest.

The email! Giò opened Mrs Rivello's emails too. The usual magazine subscriptions and newsletters popped up, mainly related to fashion, clothing and accessories. The reading recommendations she received tended to be sweet romances, which took Giò by surprise. There were a lot of emails from her school colleagues discussing the more problematic students and gossiping about other colleagues.

Giò made a search for the surname Aiello and then Capello, but no results came up. Whatever Mrs Rivello had argued with Andrea about, they hadn't carried on the conversation in emails. Either that, or Mrs Rivello had deleted the messages. But that wasn't very likely as the full inbox showed Camilla Rivello tended to keep every email. Maybe she'd only deleted the compromising ones.

Whatever reason the killer had had to take the mobile, it wasn't obvious from the content of Mrs Rivello's mobile. Apparently he'd been overcautious.

Giò took one more look at the few dull apps on the phone, then finally decided she could drop it back where she had found it. She had missed out on Granny's panzerotti for nothing!

After wiping the phone clear of fingerprints, Giò slid it back in Camilla Rivello's bag, zipped the bag closed and returned to the living room, feeling disappointed. Agnese recognised her defeated look.

"Are you feeling any better?" Camilla enquired.

"I'm OK, but I'd better not eat anything else." How Giò hated having to say that with the delicious aroma of panzerotti filling the flat.

Mr Rivello, his moustache stained white and red from the panzerotti filling, murmured, "Such a pity, they are delicious." It was the first time he'd seemed to relax – good food can cause the most careful person to drop their social façade, at least for a while.

Lilia was trying to catch Giò's eye, and Giò feared her niece would give the game away if she wasn't careful. She glanced at the two guests and saw they were each tucking into their umpteenth panzerotto, then shook her head and mouthed, "Nothing". Lilia looked disappointed, too; she had played her part extremely well, making the anonymous phone calls to Mrs Rivello, ready to say it was a silly joke if she was found out, then taking possession of the woman's bag so that her auntie could search it. The plan had worked brilliantly, but it had all been for nothing. They had drawn a blank.

Granny came out of the kitchen feeling a little tired, but she was instantly uplifted by all the compliments she received.

"But you didn't eat anything," Mrs Rivello said to her.

"I lose my appetite when I'm cooking," Granny replied. "And at my age, I'm better off avoiding fried food anyway."

Agnese looked at her dubiously, knowing full well that Granny had tried at least a couple of panzerotti in the kitchen to check they were good enough. But she let Granny play her game for once. After all, for various reasons, none of the family had been acting completely honestly during the meal.

"It's been a delicious lunch, not just an aperitivo," said Mr Rivello, admiration in his voice for his former teacher.

Agnese smiled. "Whenever Granny

prepares panzerotti, we don't need anything else for lunch."

Mr Rivello approved. "A good choice indeed."

"I take it you'd like a cup of coffee?"

Apart from the children and a reluctant Giò, they all replied that they would. They moved back to the sofa while Agnese served the coffee, asking the Rivellos whether they'd like sugar.

"So, any more news about poor Elena's homicide?" asked Nando.

There was a subtle but clear change in Mr Rivello's demeanour. He was once again the efficient manager.

"No. At least, the carabinieri haven't mentioned anything."

Giò pressed for more information, looking at both wife and husband. "Do you really think Antonio was involved?"

"Alcohol is a weapon of Satan," Mrs Rivello said, accepting her coffee from Agnese with a small smile of thanks. "I believe since he went back to drinking, he was no longer himself. Raimondo had helped him put his life back together, but as they say, you can't save someone who doesn't want to be saved. I alerted my husband to Antonio's drinking so many times."

"But why would he want to kill you?"

"I don't know. I'm not even sure he did want to kill me. You see, in his drunken state, he probably didn't realise what he was doing."

"I'd say that whoever caused that rock to fall knew exactly what they were doing," Giò said.

"Maybe he just wanted to hurt somebody – anybody – because life had been so hard on him."

"But he sent you two threatening letters, so he clearly intended to hurt you," Giò insisted, longing for a drop of coffee too.

"As I said, I believe alcohol drove him out of his mind. And I told my husband many times to get rid of him. I felt he was a dangerous man to have working for us."

Mr Rivello was quietly nodding.

"But what if it wasn't him? The murderer, I mean."

"I'm sure it was, but it's up to the carabinieri to find out what really happened," Mr Rivello said. Giò felt sure he and his wife weren't sharing everything they knew.

"Well, the whole village has been whispering another name recently..."

"In Maratea, all kinds of hypotheses have been aired. People have mentioned Carlo Capello, but of course that would be absurd. My wife and his mother don't get on too well, but you're unlikely to find any two people in Maratea who haven't argued at least once. We're a small community with strong ties, so in the majority of cases a reconciliation follows sooner or later. Although at times, it's quite a lot later."

"What about Andrea? Did either of you ever argue with him?" Agnese casually slipped this in before taking a sip of her coffee.

"Not that I can remember," Mrs Rivello replied drily. Then, she added with a twinkle in her eye, "Agnese, I'm sure in the perfumery you have a difference of opinion with your customers every now and then. At times they might be just too demanding. Maybe they won't come into your shop for a while, then they return as if nothing ever happened and it's all peaceful... until the next argument."

Agnese laughed. "That's exactly how it is. At times, I'd love the not-turning-up interval to be a little longer."

But Giò had noticed that Mrs Rivello's expression had not been as relaxed as her husband's when Agnese had mentioned Andrea.

"What do you think of Andrea Aiello?" she asked.

"He is a cunning guy, more than my husband thinks. At times, Raimondo trusts people more than he should do, really."

Mr Rivello looked at his wife in surprise. "What's this about?"

"Nothing in particular. But you gave him the chance to work here, in Maratea where it's not easy to gain trust within the community. But he did, since you introduced him into the circles that matter and told them you trusted him."

"He's a serious chap. He is precise, meets the deadlines…"

"But he has been using the relationships you helped him to cultivate for his own benefit. He cares about himself, not your company."

"This is the problem with freelancers, but after a few failed projects, they always come back to me." He smiled, but there was something hard behind his smile. He looked at his watch, and nodded to his wife.

"Time to go, I'd say. It's been a delicious lunch."

"And it's been pleasant to be able to chat so freely," Mrs Rivello added, rising from the sofa. "Giò dear, would you show me where my coat and bag are?"

As they went into the corridor together, Mrs Rivello said to Giò, "Listen, dear, I've heard you're getting closer to Andrea."

Giò blushed beyond control.

"Be careful, he is not what he seems."

Giò managed to swallow her natural defensiveness and ask, "Why? What has he done?"

"As I said, he uses people. He takes what they give him and believes he can drop them anytime in favour of the next 'important' person. He is an ambitious social climber. I wouldn't like him to use you – you don't deserve it after all you've gone through already."

"I wish you would give me a definite example of something he's done so that I can understand what you mean," said Giò, helping Mrs Rivello into her light jacket.

"I can't tell you any more. But keep your eyes open." Camilla Rivello took her bag and searched for her mobile. She had no idea whatsoever that it hadn't remained in its place all through lunch.

As the Rivellos left, Agnese and Giò complimented Lilia on playing her part so well.

"But I couldn't find anything strange –

no messages, no photos, not even suspect phone calls," Giò said.

~

"WHAT DO YOU THINK?" GIÒ ASKED Agnese while placing the plates in the dishwasher. Lilia had gone to play a game on her computer, Granny was taking a nap and Nando had returned to his office.

"Nothing useful came out of their mouths. It's like they were telling all while not telling us anything. Still, I believe we gathered some evidence, even if it is that there's no evidence, if you know what I mean."

"But the fact remains that the killer wanted his victim's mobile," Giò mumbled as Agnese handed her the last cups and cutlery from the table.

"Mrs Rivello mentioned Andrea, didn't she? It seems to me she doesn't share her husband's positive attitude towards him. Did you notice?"

"Of course I did. I tried to get more

detailed answers from her, but she wouldn't tell me any more," Giò said, waving the washing-up brush in the air while a pool of water formed at her feet.

"Reading between the lines, I think she discovered Andrea stole some of Mr Rivello's clients for himself," Agnese replied, mopping the water up from around her sister's feet.

"Depending on Mr Rivello for his livelihood is certainly not a favourable prospect for someone who wants to build his own career."

"But Mr Rivello was quite cool about it."

"Far too cool for my liking. He looked like a cat playing with a mouse – you can run wherever you want, but you're still under my own control." Giò passed a cloth over the kitchen surfaces with exaggerated energy. "Still, it seems to me Mrs Rivello knows something about Andy that her husband doesn't..."

"Whatever it is, it seems it's not on her mobile, unfortunately." Agnese looked at the kitchen with a critical eye, but it was sparkling clean, just as Granny liked it.

"My head is spinning. I need to tell Paolo what we've discovered, or rather not discovered, but I don't want other people to know I'm speaking to him. I guess I will have to wait for this evening when he's finished work," Giò said, pulling off the rubber gloves she had used. "Meanwhile, I think I will go out on the kayak again. It soothes my nerves."

Before Giò left, she texted Paolo. "*Got the phone, nothing there at all. It was a wild goose chase.*"

"*Well done anyway,*" he replied. "*We now know we need a better theory.*"

21

LOVE ALL, TRUST FEW

Giò opened the driver's door of Agnese's car, threw her bag inside and headed for Fiumicello, where Romolo was happy for her to hire a kayak. Since her arms and back still hurt from her previous excursion, she'd decided to take a shorter route this time, maybe heading towards the harbour and the Spiaggia Nera. The latter was one of the few sandy beaches in Maratea, but since the rocks around were of an unusual black colour, the sand was similar. Hence the name: Black Beach.

The regular splash of the paddle in the

water put her in a good mood. As soon as she pulled away from the coast, she stopped to take in the full view, looking all the way up to the statue of Christ the Redeemer, then back to the Santa Venere Hotel, its green meadows reaching down to the sea. It was then that she noticed another kayak leaving the beach.

A kindred spirit, she thought. *There aren't many people on the sea in October.*

Giò headed south towards the harbour. She had almost reached it when she heard a whistle. She turned around sharply, fearing she might be in the path of a larger boat. No, the whistle had come from the other kayak.

It took a short while, but then she recognised it was Andrea who was paddling it.

"What are you doing here?" she called when he was within earshot.

"You've been running away from me recently, so I decided I had no other choice but to follow you. Mind you, I didn't realise it would take this much effort to reach you." He pretended to be out of breath. "I've wasted time and money going to a gym only to find out a simple lassie can out-paddle me."

She laughed. "I'd certainly complain to my personal trainer."

"You can bet he will be hearing from me. My goodness, couldn't we have gone by motorboat?"

"But that's too easy. You don't get the same sense of achievement as you do when you're travelling under your own steam."

"So, my captain, where are we heading today?"

"To the Black Beach."

"My goodness, I thought you'd be happy just to reach the harbour."

She laughed again. "But that's just around the corner! Anyway, did I ask you to come along?"

"No, you didn't. I won't complain again, even if you head towards Pino Island or the Eolie."

"I might consider visiting Pino again

one day; I do have my share of quirky memories from there. As for the Eolie, I'm afraid we haven't got enough time."

"Thank God!"

Their regular strokes touched the water. They were silent, but kept in sync without effort. Moments later they were in front of the small and rocky Santo Janni island, and beyond lay the Black Beach.

"Let's leave the island for another time," said Giò finally. "I can't resist the beach – looks like we'll have it to ourselves."

"I'll be grateful to avoid the snakes for the present." Word had it that vipers lived on the island.

"You've got your shoes on, haven't you?" Giò asked.

"But such succulent bare ankles."

As they pulled the kayaks onto the beach, Giò said, "Your precious ankles will be totally safe here."

"I know."

The beach was no longer than 300 metres, contained by the forest all around it. There was a rather steep walk leading to the Illicini kiosk which sat among the holm oaks with their shining dark green leaves. A pity the kiosk was closed for the season.

Giò took a few steps on the black sand. "I adore it," she said, feeling the gravel under her feet and between her toes. The waves were breaking along the shoreline, and for Giò it was simply impossible to resist the temptation to walk through the foam.

"Shall we?" She pointed to the rocks on the northern side of the beach. He nodded. "The water is colder today," she said as the waves embraced her legs up to the knees.

"Autumn is coming, I'm afraid."

"But the weather is still so beautiful."

"Things change. Even if they look exactly the same from one day to the next, there're small changes creeping in. You might not be even aware of them, then suddenly, you're in a totally different season."

She stopped in surprise. "Are you

thinking about something other than summer and autumn?"

"You're right."

"What are you thinking of?"

"Just silly thoughts. But that's a pattern in my life. Maybe I'm just too stupid to look beyond face value and understand what's going on underneath..."

"Are you talking about your marriage?"

"Well, no." He paused to consider what she'd said, then added, "But actually you're right. It happened with my marriage too. On the surface, it all seemed as joyful and happy as it had in the beginning, but underneath things started to change. And one day, the season changed."

"How about your life here in Maratea?"

"You get straight to the point, don't you?"

She shrugged. "May I remind you that you've led the conversation so far?"

He laughed. "Oh no, I've only done the muscular part of it, as with paddling. But it was you who led the direction."

She opened her mouth to protest, but for once couldn't find the right words.

"You were the one to talk about things seeming not to change then changing suddenly," she said eventually. "I didn't lead you there."

"But you didn't stop there either. I could have just meant summer quietly turning into autumn." His eyes twinkled teasingly.

"Well it didn't sound as if you meant that."

They had reached a part of the beach enclosed by rocks and caressed by gentle waves. She turned around as if to go back.

"Shouldn't we have a look at the grotto?"

"What grotto?"

"Just behind this." He took two steps into the water to bypass a small group of rocks and gave her his hand. Hesitantly, she stretched her hand out and took it, loving the feeling of his skin against hers. It was a strong but careful grip; it felt good.

With a couple more steps, they were inside the grotto. It was 10 metres long and narrow, ending in a little elevated beach.

"I've got a few sweet memories from here that I'm afraid I'm not going to share." He quickly added, "From my youth, I mean." He led her a few steps forward to show her an opening on the left. It was short and low, giving the waves another place to explore.

"The tour is over." He smiled gently, taking her back outside. The sun felt good after a few minutes in the damp shade. He lifted her hand to his lips and softly kissed her palm, then pulled her body into his arms.

"You are a beautiful soul," he said, and he kissed her passionately, sweetly, disarmingly. Her heart beating tumultuously, Giò for once was unable to think clearly.

He pushed her away smoothly. "I should have waited until things were clear. I'm sorry, I couldn't resist you."

She shook her head as if to dispel a dream, ready to contradict him.

"What things?"

"Carlo told me the carabinieri called him in, suspected him. He was obliged to give them all the details of his private life."

She felt a pang in her heart as she asked, "Do you have something you didn't mention to the carabinieri?"

"It's not like that – no secret love affairs. But yes, there are things, a few mistakes I've made, and I'd hoped the carabinieri wouldn't have to look into those." He let go of her hand. She didn't like that; she'd enjoyed his firm caress.

As he was moving back towards the kayaks, he said, "Shall we go?"

"Yes, let's."

He helped her into her kayak and pushed it into the waves, then with a few strokes, he was behind her. She had partly recovered from the kiss, although she feared her romantic side had just been released, despite all her attempts to keep it safely under lock and key.

"Can we talk about it? What is it that you don't want the carabinieri to find out?"

"It's just business stuff. Things are not as clear cut as I'd like them to be. I signed some papers for my clients before it dawned on me that it wasn't the wisest thing to do..."

"What papers?"

"Projects, construction plans that were pushing the limits of what you can do on certain types of land." He realised she was looking at him with a shocked expression. "Mind you, it wasn't strictly illegal. But you know, when you don't come from a place, you're not the best judge of the locals. I realised later I shouldn't have agreed to work with some of them. They might be involved in all kinds of stuff."

"I hope you can get out of the projects."

"Yes, they had been using me, I can see that now. I'm just afraid that if Mr Rivello finds out, he will strike me off his list of partners. Without his endorsement, it will be almost impossible for me to work in Maratea."

"Is that why you argued with Mrs Rivello?"

Before Giò could stop herself, the words were out of her mouth. He stopped abruptly, his paddle suspended in mid-air, dripping water onto his head.

"How did you know about that?"

"Do I have to remind you that Maratea is a small place where everybody gets to know about everything?" She kept paddling, leaving him a few metres behind.

"Everything... except who murdered Elena and Antonio," he shouted. "If it's true that he didn't kill her, which I don't believe..."

"You mean you believe Antonio was the killer and that he conveniently fell and hit his head so as not to disturb Maratea's quiet way of life anymore?" she said, looking at him wryly as he rowed his kayak parallel to hers. He noticed the sarcasm in her voice.

"Well, when you put it that way, I don't

know what to believe. But, I'll be frank, I can't see who else might want Mrs Rivello dead and have had the opportunity to do her in."

A sudden thought crossed her mind; she saw the recent sequence of events. Andrea knew he was on the suspects list, and maybe he had also learned that Carlo had been cleared. He was the next suspect in line, so had he held her and kissed her, then confessed that he had run into trouble by working with people of dubious reputation to make an accomplice of her? Had he planned it all now that he was swimming in rough waters? The thought really hurt, because... because for a moment, she had fancied...

There was no getting away from it: she had fancied him.

Whenever Giò felt hurt, she blurted out the first idea that came to mind, regardless of what it was.

"Did you know that Carlo was suspected because the carabinieri found his cufflink at Antonio's?"

"Really?" Andrea seemed genuinely surprised. He slowed down.

"Apparently, when the killer realised the police didn't believe Antonio was the murderer, he tried to frame Carlo. He didn't know Carlo had a cast-iron alibi, so he tried to frame the wrong person!" Her tone angry, she gave a few strong strokes with her paddle. She wanted to hurry back; she'd had enough of Andrea's company.

"Will you slow down a bit?" he asked.

She ignored him and kept going until he caught up with her.

"Hey, what's happening?"

"Nothing much, I just want to get home. It's later than I thought."

"Can you hold on a second?"

"No, I can't."

She kept paddling furiously. He caught up with her again and grabbed the hook on the outside of her kayak, obliging her to stop. She was alone in the middle of the sea with a man who may well have killed two people mercilessly. This was exactly the situation Agnese and Paolo had told her to avoid. Only this time, it wasn't really her fault that she'd been caught out.

The two kayaks stopped, far away from anywhere and anyone. He looked straight into her eyes, despite her attempts to look away.

"How do you know everything about these investigations? And don't just tell me that it's because everybody knows everything in Maratea."

"That's precisely how things are," she replied stubbornly.

"Oh no, remember I've seen you with Paolo on a number of occasions."

"So that's why you wanted to speak to me today."

"Do you think I kissed you so you would bring me goodies while I'm in prison?" he growled.

"As you asked, that's exactly what I think!"

He moved his kayak alongside hers, took hold of her chin and lifted her face, looking into her eyes again.

"I was very stupid to do what I did, I

grant you that, but it wasn't planned. It just happened, but it wasn't the right thing to do, nor the right moment to do it." She was looking at him, looking for something in his eyes that would signal a lie. Frankly, she didn't see anything of the sort, but a sudden shadow did cross his face as he added in a lower tone, "Yes, not the right moment for a number of reasons. Please, forget it. At least we stopped in time. Let's go now."

Not a single word was spoken till they reached Fiumicello. They were still pulling the kayaks up when Paolo and two carabinieri rose up from nowhere and approached them.

"You are under arrest for the murders of Elena Errico and Antonio Fiorenzano," said Paolo in a colourless voice. "You have the right to remain silent. Anything you do say may be used against you in a court of law. You have the right to an attorney. If you cannot afford an attorney, one will be provided for you."

For a long moment, Giò wondered if

Paolo was speaking to her. Then she saw the two carabinieri approach Andrea and take him to their car.

He looked over his shoulder at her and whispered, "I'm sorry."

Paolo glanced at her too, silently nodded and turned towards his car. She sat down on the beach, too befuddled to think.

THAT AFTERNOON, A MIDDLE-AGED woman with ash blonde hair entered the perfumery. She had a perfectly oval face, so beautiful it reminded Agnese of a Madonna of the Renaissance paintings. Maybe not quite that stunning, but definitely a classic beauty.

"Good morning, madam, may I help you at all?"

"I'm just having a look, thanks," the lady murmured, browsing clumsily through the shop cabinets. After a few minutes, it became obvious she couldn't find what she was looking for.

She approached Agnese's counter and whispered in a barely audible voice, "Can I have a love potion, please?"

"I beg your pardon?" Agnese was sure she had misunderstood her words.

"I asked if you could give me a love potion," the woman repeated sheepishly, looking down at her feet.

"Oh, I'm sorry, I don't think I sell those." Agnese tried to sound as cool as if the lady had asked for a common perfume brand she didn't stock.

"But they told me... they told me you could help me," the woman babbled, disappointment clouding her face.

"A love potion? What for exactly?"

"Well, there's a man... He is so good and sweet. But I'm not sure he loves me."

"You mean you're in a relationship with him, but you're not sure you can trust him?"

"Well, we're not really in a relationship..."

It was extremely hard to extract words from this softly spoken lady.

"Maybe you should speak to him and clarify things," Agnese suggested.

"Oh no, we've never really had a conversation," she replied. "He comes to the library every Saturday to return his books and stops by to choose new ones. I'm always there at about the same time."

"And you've never spoken to each other?"

"Once I was sick and two Saturdays running I couldn't go to the library. When we saw each other again, he asked me if everything was OK... And I said yes."

"And that was all?" Agnese uttered in disbelief.

"Yes, but he asked me very sweetly."

"How long has this been going on?"

"Two years next month."

Was this real? Even for a traditional village like Maratea, this story sounded like it belonged in the 19th century rather than the 21st: two grown-ups having a silent relationship of stares. Agnese's brain worked like lightning – who else had mentioned going to the library on a Saturday? Then a sudden flash of inspiration zig-zagged across her brain.

I've got it!

"People in the village told me you make love potions, that's why I came over... I thought that you could give me something to induce him to speak to me... because at times I believe he cares. But I'd better go. Thanks for your help, and please don't tell anybody what I confessed to you."

"Rest assured, nobody will know. But please don't go... I think I can do something for you. Today is Saturday, so are you heading for the library?"

"As soon as I leave, I'll be going there. We meet at half past five and I don't want him to worry if I turn up late."

Agnese had an impulse to bang her forehead with her right hand, but she resisted and headed towards the shelves behind her. She picked up a bottle of Villoresi's Musk and turned back to the Shy Lady.

"As I said, I don't sell love potions. But I do sell perfumes that have great powers over people." She knew she was cheating a little, but what else could she do? Agnese sprayed the perfume in the air, forming a large cloud.

"Quick, step in, close your eyes and turn around three times, pronouncing these words: 'Perfume Powers, help me to win my love'. Be quick!"

While the Shy Lady did precisely as she'd been told, Agnese prayed nobody would enter the shop just then, particularly her sister, otherwise they might think she'd lost her mind. Fortunately, nobody did come in.

"Please join your hands and bend your head to thank the Essences that will work for you."

The Shy Lady once again did exactly as she was told. She was the most docile student a teacher could wish for.

"Now, you need to create a pretext to talk to him."

The Shy Lady withdrew in horror. "I can't!" she cried.

"Do you want the Perfume Powers to work for you?" Agnese was implacable, but inside she felt as bad as she did when she had to be harsh on Lilia or Luca for their own good.

"Yes, but…"

"There's no other way. You need to get close enough to him for the perfume to release its powers on him."

"But what should I say?"

"Ask him how he is, whether he has had a good week at work, what he is doing over the weekend, what he has been reading, what he plans to read in the future. And you don't only ask questions, but also tell him about you. The important thing is that you engage with him for at least 15 minutes; this way the perfume has a chance to work on him. Then, if silence falls, it means that the Perfume Powers are starting to work. That is the moment you need to act fast and kiss him."

"Kiss him?" The Shy Lady pressed her hands against her heart.

"Of course. That's the only way the Perfume Powers can enfold him entirely and finish their job."

The Shy Lady stood in front of her, dumbfounded. She started to tremble so violently that Agnese wondered if she had pushed things too far. But, hey! Two years of looking at each other – that really called for some strong medicine.

"And after that?"

"He will be your man forever and ever."

"Are you sure?"

"I'm positive. But remember, you only have one chance: if you do not accomplish your mission today, the Perfume Powers will refuse to help you in the future."

For the first time, she saw something akin to a spark of determination in the woman's eyes.

"It's twenty past five. I think you'd better go."

"Shall I buy the perfume?"

"Only afterwards, if things work out

well. Now, don't waste your time. You can't be late!"

Shaking like a leaf, the woman said, "I'm going, and thank you. I will not spoil what you've done for me."

"Good girl. Remember, no second chances: it's now or never."

AS IT TURNED OUT, AS SOON AS THE Shy Lady stepped into the library, she found herself face to face with the Shy Man. She couldn't speak, or smile; her heart was thundering like a herd of wild bison, a lump obstructing her throat. Just another failure.

But the library was small, and she ended up so close to him that he instantly recognised the perfume. He was so astonished that he spoke instinctively.

"Hello, hem... is this... hem... beautiful perfume you're wearing a musk?"

She nodded. In her mind, the fact that

the conversation had started on the subject of the musk meant only one thing: the Perfume Powers were already working their magic on him. She was so encouraged that she kept him talking for a good 10 minutes. The librarian was unable to believe it – she would have to silence them if they carried on. But as the good woman looked around the hall, she could see only two elderly readers, both rather deaf, and she realised they wouldn't be disturbed by the Shy Couple's chatter.

All of a sudden, the dreaded silence fell between the two. The Shy Lady heard Agnese's words in her head and a terror seized her: she didn't want to wait another couple of years to speak to Shy Man again. A courage she had never experienced in her life came upon her. She closed her eyes and moved her face gently towards his, her chin and lips lifting into an unmistakable position. The Shy Man didn't even have time to feel surprised before he was kissing her with all the love he had been bottling up for two long years.

The librarian gave a little cry of both awe and happiness, then returned to the other side of her small desk, pretending to be busy with some paperwork.

THAT EVENING, AFTER AGNESE HAD closed her shop, she was passing through the Main Square when her attention was caught by two figures sitting at one of Leonardo's outside tables. The Shy Couple were talking to each other so intensely, they only had eyes for each other; they didn't even acknowledge her. But she saw two things that delighted her: he was holding her hand tenderly, and she... she was wearing the necklace from the perfumery.

22

EARLY DELIVERIES

G iò and Lilia were walking together. Agnese had asked her daughter to stay close to Auntie Giò following Andrea's arrest, and Lilia was taking the job seriously. This afternoon, she had invited Auntie Giò to go out with her, once she'd finished her homework, to enjoy a bocconotto together. This was a sweet, fragrant pastry traditionally made in Maratea, filled with either sour cherries, sometimes with custard, or custard and chocolate.

The best artisanal pastry shop in town was Panza in one of the paved backstreets around Piazza Buraglia. Giò loved the place. It was tiny, but it had three cabinets full of biscuits, cakes and sweets. The owner was a dear old man with a round face and straight white hair, always smiling at his customers. Behind his thick glasses, his eyes sparkled each time a client congratulated him on the excellent flavour of his pastries. This was something that happened very often, but every time the old man seemed to be as happy as if it was the first time he'd ever received a compliment.

His granddaughter worked with him, and in the kitchen a young pastry chef had taken over from Mr Panza when he got too old to do all the work by himself. He had taught the young man all the secrets of the ancient art. On the shop walls, framed as pictures, were a few old recipes handwritten by Mr Panza's ancestors. Each time they visited, Giò and Lilia had fun reading them aloud, deciphering the old calligraphy and laughing at the amount of ingredients that were needed. The sponge, for example, had no baking powder, but it required over 24 fresh eggs. Even today at Panza, the pastry chef would never use egg or milk powders, but only the freshest ingredients.

Giò chose the dark cherry bocconotto, and Lilia the chocolate and custard one, both still warm from the oven. Mr Panza's granddaughter sprinkled the sweets with powdered sugar before handing them to Lilia and Giò, who went to sit outside on a wooden bench in front of the pastry shop. They simply loved to sit there, and looked at each other with dreamy eyes while biting the crunchy crust and savouring the warm filling.

"They are delicious!" Lilia said.

"Hm, I have been dreaming of these," Giò agreed.

"Auntie, what's your wildest dream?" Lilia enquired spontaneously. Giò laughed.

"I've got so many! I'd love to visit Iceland for a month, or even better, two. I'd love to spend Christmas, or maybe the week before Christmas, on the island of

Ærø. I'd love to hike the West Highland Way in Scotland again in drier weather than last time."

"But, Auntie, are your dreams only about travelling?"

"You said my wildest dreams, didn't you?"

"But don't you fancy having a boyfriend or a hubby?"

"Not at this moment, dear." Giò thought about how to put it nicely for a nine-year-old. "You know, I really loved Dorian, and it still hurts a bit. It's like when you broke up with your friend Lavinia. You didn't fancy finding a new friend the next day…"

"But I'm friends with Lavinia again now."

"That's good. I'm afraid I will never be friends with Dorian again."

"Did he hurt you beyond forgiveness?"

"It's not only that. You see, for two adults to love each other, they need to share an ambition, a dream. Like your mum and dad, they really wanted to have a family. They dreamed of having a Luca and a Lilia, a home for you two filled with love. But Dorian and I started to have very different dreams, and if a couple don't have shared dreams... Well, we realised we were just wasting our time with each other."

"But if you were to meet a charming man, would you marry him?"

"Of course I would, but I can't take it for granted that I will meet Mr Perfect. So in the meantime, I'll cultivate my dreams even though I'm alone. I'll enjoy my gran, my sister, my niece and nephew, my house and my beautiful Maratea. That's more than enough to be grateful for, don't you agree?"

A big smile crossed Lilia's face from ear to ear. "You talk to me as if I'm a grown-up. I love you for that."

"I love you for at least a tonne of things!"

"I love you because you will buy a tray of bocconotti to take back home for dinner."

"That's cheating!" Giò grumbled, but in they went to order their tray of bocconotti anyway.

"They're still warm," said Mr Panza's granddaughter. "If you don't want to eat them straight away, you'd be better off leaving them to cool down. Could you come back to fetch them in 20 minutes or so?"

"Yes, we'll do that, but I'll pay now."

They were in Piazza Buraglia, the little square with its pastel houses and bar tables, when Giò remembered.

"I need to get a few magazines from Nennella."

"Okey dokey, I will see if there's a *Winx* book for me."

They crossed the square, and with a few steps reached the newsstand.

"Hello, hello. How are you doing?" Nennella asked cheerfully.

"We're both fine, I guess. We just treated ourselves to a bocconotto."

Nennella's Jack Russell Annina came to say hi, and Lilia caressed her. Giò wasn't a big fan of small dogs, but Annina wasn't the annoyingly yappy type. And she was undeniably pretty.

"Did you go to Panza?"

"Where else?"

"No one can bake as they do," Nennella said, closing the door they had left open. "Annina is in heat," she explained. "I don't want a herd of stray dogs piling up in front of the shop." Then she gave Giò a rather sly look and asked, "Can you believe Andy's been arrested?"

For a moment, Giò wondered if Nennella had seen them kissing passionately. *Come on, Giò, we were on a deserted beach. Not even Nennella could be this good!* Nonetheless, she felt herself blushing and bent down to caress the dog, hoping Nennella wouldn't notice her embarrassment.

"Yes, I was there when the police took him away. But you know him better than I do; I only met him recently. Did you ever suspect him of murder?"

Answer a question with a question – return

to sender, as it were. That's what they say you should do, isn't it?

"My goodness, no, of course not. He's always been a charming fellow. He would come in and crack a joke or two..." Since Lilia was absorbed in the *Winks* books, Nennella got closer to Giò and whispered, "But I heard he was playing at the casino and lost quite a large sum of money."

Giò gasped, still stroking Annina's tummy. Was this true? Most likely, Andrea had believed that nobody in Maratea would know if he'd always gone to distant cities to satisfy his gambling addiction. But Nennella knew everything, and therefore so did most of the good folk of Maratea.

The newsstand owner continued, "Gambling can put you through hell. I've seen respectable men ruining themselves and their families. They shouldn't allow people to play with money, I say."

"I suspect they'd then turn to some other addiction."

"I can't understand it," said Nennella, shaking her head. "Send them bungee jumping if they need an adrenaline rush, it's safer! Anyway, I can't believe Andy did such a thing..."

"Do you suspect anyone else?"

"I'm not convinced it wasn't Antonio. If Andy had a little problem with gambling, Antonio was out of control with drinking. The day before the murder, he'd had to leave his car at the warehouse overnight, he'd been so drunk. Mind you, he used to be a good man, but he never recovered from the loss of his daughter."

"But he can't be the murderer since the cops suspect he was murdered too." Giò was speaking rather mechanically; she couldn't help feeling her attention should have been on something else.

"That's the carabinieri overcomplicating things. The poor devil was so drunk, he fell and died. That's all."

Giò was browsing through a travel magazine while Annina jumped up at her legs, asking for more caresses. Absentmindedly, Giò bent down for cuddles, but her thoughts were elsewhere.

Something had passed right before her eyes. Maybe something important...

Then suddenly her heart beat faster, her emotions almost choking her. She breathed deeply; she had to be careful not to show Nennella any trace of excitement. The woman was a better sleuth than Sherlock Holmes.

"What do you mean Antonio left his car at the warehouse the night before the murder? Which murder?"

"I mean the night before Elena was killed. In the morning, I took an early delivery to Mr Rivello. I usually go in through the main entrance, but that day, after collecting the papers from the distributor, I had a flat tyre. I didn't want Mr Rivello to complain that he hadn't got his delivery, so I left the car where it was and walked the short road to the back. It was not yet 6am, but Antonio's car was already there. And he wasn't a morning person, so I checked he wasn't in his car, sleeping. He wasn't, so maybe a kind soul had given him a lift home the night before, planning to pick him up for work in the morning."

"Did anybody see you?"

"Of course. I greeted a couple of workers and left the daily papers at Mr Rivello's office door. He wasn't there at that time, the lights inside were all off, so I left."

Was the kaleidoscope's pattern changing yet again?

Lilia joined Giò with a book. "Can I get this?"

"Of course you can," Giò said, then turned to Nennella and pointed to all the stuff she had piled on the counter. "How much do I owe you?"

"That's 18.50 Euros with Lilia's book."

Giò handed her the money and forgot her change, she was in such a hurry to leave. Once outside, she handed the pile of magazines to Lilia.

"Lilia dear, I need to take a few notes for my guide. Can you manage to pick up the bocconotti and take everything home?"

"Of course I can. Do you have an inspiration for your book?"

"Exactly!"

As Lilia left, Giò walked the whole length of the village. She needed a little peace and quiet, and she knew she would get it in the park at the entrance to Maratea. It was a wonderful little park full of huge old trees; it was a mystery to Giò why Maratea people hardly ever used it, except for young couples after school hours.

She sat on a bench and took out her notebook, browsing her notes. At the warehouse, Mr Rivello had held the morning meeting from 6am to 6.30, then retired to his office. Antonio must have arrived at work around 8.15. She and Paolo had assumed he had driven there, but according to Nennella, somebody had gone to pick him up. So why did Gerardina see Antonio's car coming back at 7, then leaving again at 8? Why didn't his colleague just pick him up in their own car, then Antonio could have driven his car home from work that evening? And why did it take him or her so long to leave again with Antonio? If Antonio had overslept, it seemed unlikely that he'd need a whole hour to get ready, even with a bad hangover from the night before.

What if the car driver had arrived at 7am to commit murder, building themselves the perfect alibi in the process? Could this mean there was another suspect the carabinieri weren't currently aware of – was the murderer the mysterious driver?

She went through all her notes again patiently, stopping at the threatening letters. They had bothered her right from the beginning. Again she experienced the same feeling she'd had at Nennella's newsstand, but now it was stronger. Much stronger. Her heart beat faster and faster as a sudden flash of inspiration crossed her mind. She was thunderstruck: the kaleidoscope had received its most violent shake-up yet, creating a totally new pattern of colours and shapes, something neither she nor the carabinieri had ever suspected.

What if it's true? Impossible!

She tried to reconnect with reality – this sort of thing only happened in books, didn't it? But if she assumed, just for argument's sake, that... well, that she could explain the threatening letters. Her breath was again cut short by her violent emotions – that meant she could explain the disappearance of the mobile phone, too. It made sense. She didn't know what was on the phone, but the reason why it had to disappear was now clear.

Only, it seemed too awful to be true.

Should she call Paolo? No, she had to check one more detail, just to make sure her theory could hold water. She knew the questions he'd ask her.

She looked at her watch, nodded to herself, then left the park to fetch Agnese's car as the first few raindrops of a brewing storm fell.

AGNESE WAS RETURNING HOME with three heavy bags full of groceries when she felt the rain start. She would have to cut through a backstreet to reach home before the storm soaked her through.

She was halfway along it when a skinny figure jumped on her, actually hugging her in ecstasy.

"Oh my goodness, is that you, Cabiria?" Agnese hardly recognised the girl, she looked so different from the composed young lady who had visited the perfumery the first time. She was wearing a khaki parka, fastened at her thin waist over long flared trousers that made her look much taller than she was, the hood up to shelter her from the rain. Her outfit was so simple, but so very stylish at the same time – Cabiria really put her personality into whatever she did.

"Sorry if I scared you, but the perfumery was closed and I wanted to say goodbye before leaving."

"Are you going back to Milan?"

"Nepal, actually."

"Nepal?" Agnese was so shocked, she had to put her bags down.

"Come on, you can't be as surprised as my father was. After all, you are the one who gave me Dzongkha!"

"Well, I've sold quite a number of perfumes with exotic names, but none of them has ever been taken so literally."

"Maybe it's because you reinforced it with *Eat, Pray, Love*."

"Are you going into an ashram?"

"Not really. Not to start with, that is. I've joined a small local NGO building schools, and they certainly don't mind having an engineer with them."

"So you're giving up your Master's? What did your father say?"

"He's not happy, but I'm taking a year out. I need to leave the perfect bubble I was in, measure my strengths, know who I really am. It may be that this time next year, I'll be happy to join my Master's, but if that is the case, it will be because that's what I really want to do." Cabiria bent to catch some of the large round tomatoes that were rolling down the hill from the bags Agnese had left on the ground.

"Oh dear, I hope I haven't been a bad influence on you," Agnese gasped, taking the tomatoes the girl handed back to her and knotting the bags closed.

"Of course you have," Cabiria chuckled, "but it was the best thing that could ever have happened to me. I need to go and finish packing now, but if I find any sort of internet point in Nepal, I will email you every now and then. If that's OK with you, of course."

"Please do, I'd be so happy to know you're doing fine."

"By the way, I'm scared to death about whatever I may find in Nepal – I've never been outside Europe before. But at the same time, I'm so happy. Thank you, Agnese," and Cabiria hugged her again.

Agnese returned her hug with a strong, motherly embrace, her eyes slightly damp. "Take care of yourself, and if things don't turn out the way you hope, don't hesitate to come back home."

"I'll find my way through, whatever happens, and spend my year out there." Cabiria was smiling as she walked away. Then from a distance, she called out, "Agnese, I almost forgot. I tried really hard to explain to Dad that you had nothing to do with my choice, but I've told you how stubborn he is. I hope he won't bother you…"

Agnese waved her hand. "I can deal with your father, just take care of yourself."

And Cabiria ran down the little alley till she disappeared from sight.

23

DANGER!

Despite the rain on the windscreen, Giò managed to find the little road at the back of Mr Rivello's warehouse that Nennella had mentioned. It was actually more of a bumpy track that the municipality no longer took care of. She left Agnese's car behind the warehouse, half hidden by vegetation. This was where Antonio had parked his car the night before Elena's murder, according to Nennella.

The gate was locked. She walked all the way around the fence to check if the main entrance was open. It was. There was somebody inside.

She pushed the gate open, hoping there would be no guard dogs. Her ears pricked up as if she was a wild animal herself. Everything was silent.

She walked on. There was a small building on the left that had to be Mr Rivello's office. The lights were on. Was Mr Rivello in there, or somebody else?

On her right was the warehouse building where the machines and materials were kept, waiting for the staff to return. From here, the staff could see the main door to the building housing their boss's office.

Giò went around the office, keeping out of view of the windows, and approached the back fence and the gate behind which she had parked Agnese's car. From a low balcony at the back of the office, anyone could have easy access to the back gate while remaining hidden from the warehouse area.

"His staff know not to disturb him once his office door is closed, so no one spoke to him until 10am." Paolo's words echoed in her head. She now knew the sequence of events; it was all falling into place. It was the strongest theory she had come up with, but still she had no proof. But gathering evidence was a problem Paolo and the carabinieri would have to deal with. Or would it be one of those cases where they'd know the truth, but couldn't do anything about it? Would the carabinieri free Andrea, at least? Maybe, but then she thought of the maresciallo. He would never believe her theory, and Paolo would be powerless against his superior.

She switched on her mobile and, sheltering it from the rain, texted, *"I know who the murderer is, and it's not Andy."*

Paolo replied immediately. *"I'm just finishing a training course, where are you?"*

"Behind Mr Rivello's office."

"I'll call you back as soon as I've finished."

"I'm going home now, so come over when you can. I need the blackboard to explain. It's rather involved."

She put the phone on airplane mode; she didn't want an unexpected call to betray her. She was about to slip her phone into her pocket when a voice cut through her thoughts.

"Who's there?" Mr Rivello came forward a few steps and recognised her. "Is that you, Giò?"

She babbled, "Yes, yes, it's me."

"What are you doing here?" He was evidently disturbed by her presence.

"I'm sorry, I should have called out, but I was texting and got lost in my thoughts." She tried to sound cheerful and relaxed, smiling at him. He did not smile back.

"What are you doing here?" he repeated.

That was a difficult question to answer – a *very* difficult one.

"Well…" Her mobile was still in her hand and a silly idea flashed into her head. She pressed the 'record' button before sliding the phone into her pocket.

"Well?" he growled, his tense jaw

jutting forward, his lips slightly raised to show his teeth.

"Someone saw Antonio's car outside your office the night before Elena's murder." If attack was the best form of defence, she must have taken him by surprise. And in fact, he gave a slight gasp and stood still for a moment.

"Then what?" he demanded.

"You see, the next day, someone else saw Antonio's car returning to his place in Acquafredda at 7am, then going out again at 8am."

"Maybe he slept off his boozing session from the night before and went home for a shower before coming back to work."

"But he didn't sleep in his car. Most likely, someone took him home the night before and went to fetch him in the morning."

"So?"

"I suspect that someone was the murderer. It was perfect – he could travel to the scene of the murder without using his own car. In fact, he lingered around

Antonio's house for an hour at the time Elena was killed. I personally don't believe in coincidences, do you?"

"I don't," he confirmed.

"Exactly. There was never a question of coincidence, was there? The woman who had to die wasn't your wife, it was Elena all along. The way you planned the crime was admirable, but you made a bad mistake with the threatening letters."

He must have been a poker player. If he was surprised (and she would have been very surprised in his place), he didn't show it. He finally smiled a rather sinister smile and looked at her questioningly.

She explained, more to herself than to him. "Whoever committed the murder wanted to pass it off as an accident, so he had no reason to write a threatening letter. Unless..."

"Unless?"

"Unless the threatening letter was written after the accident story failed. You didn't mention the letters until after Mr Faraco had made it clear it wasn't an accident, leading us to believe the victim should have been your wife and not Elena, and that changed the whole course of the investigation. But the only person who saw the first threatening letter was you, so we only had your word for that. This made me think." Was she bragging a little? Maybe, but she needed to provoke him into a confession. So far, she had been the only one to speak about the murder.

"You're going a little too far, don't you think? I've heard you fancy Andrea and you're playing the sleuth in order to save him. All very noble indeed, except you're blaming it on an honest citizen."

"Come on, Mr Rivello, it's obvious you killed Elena because she was blackmailing you."

His eyebrows rose slightly in alarm. She knew this was the moment to strike hard, and strike she did.

"I have a USB with all the evidence. It wasn't enough to have destroyed her mobile, nor to have ransacked her home to steal her laptop. The girl was smart, she made copies."

She extracted a sparkling new (and empty!) USB from her pocket. Again, Mr Rivello was poker-faced.

"An interesting story, have you told the police?" There was something malevolent in his stare, a feral expression she had never seen in human eyes. And again, the question wasn't simple to answer. The wrong answer would put her in serious danger – or had she already crossed that line?

"I was just texting Brigadiere Rossi, he's coming over," she lied.

"That's a pity because it leaves us very little time!" He took a gun from his pocket with the same nonchalance as if it were a cigarette box.

"You can't kill me like that!" Giò cried.

"No, not like this if you're a good girl. So you've been nosing around and playing the detective, which is never a good idea. Go towards the warehouse," and with his gun, he pointed the way.

Giò's knees seemed to fail her. Now she was terrified, but she knew the only thing she could do was to buy time.

"So what made you do it?"

"Haven't you listened to the recordings yet?"

"There was no time. Elena gave the USB to her father, but he didn't connect it to the homicide until I spoke to him today. I guess it's about the fires..."

"You're smarter than I thought." They had reached the main warehouse, but he waved her to keep going along the wall to the left. "But hurry up, I have little time to waste."

She kept going as slowly as she could – so slowly he approached her and pushed her forward.

"You paid Antonio to light the fires on the mountains this summer. You would then get the contract for the reforestation and road security works."

"Yes, and even if I didn't win the contract, an associate company would. That's how we distribute the work."

"And take control of the votes in the next elections."

"Now, that's an even more lucrative line of business: direct control over politicians."

"But you didn't realise Elena was recording your meetings and discussions."

"She was stupid, I thought her smarter. If I hadn't killed her, somebody else would have."

"Elena endangered the whole system you had set up..."

Giò stopped. She had seen something she didn't like and her situation had suddenly become far more important than Rivello's affairs. In front of her stood an iron-fenced enclosure, and inside was a powerful Rottweiler. She stood, unable to move, gasping as panic climbed up her limbs and throat.

"I'm not going in there. You'll have to kill me using your gun and the carabinieri will know it was you."

Seeing she wouldn't move forward, he passed her quickly, keeping the gun pointed at her, and walked the 10 metres separating them from the enclosure.

"You were trespassing on my property. I didn't recognise you and fired, fearing it was the murderer: self-defence." He reached the gate. "But, it will be better if it is Apollo who does the job."

The dog was growling deeply, watching her and his master. She looked around, but there was no escape, nothing to climb on to. The exit was far too far away; running would mean her death for sure.

Rivello opened the gate. "Attack!" he shouted. The Rottweiler marched towards her, growling, his hair standing up on his back.

"In case of an attack from a dog, don't act like prey. Don't look at him; speak softly as if another human is around." Giò recited what she had learned in a dog rescue centre where she had worked as a volunteer. Her voice firm, almost cheerful, she continued, "Without crossing his eye line, turn about 45 degrees from the line of attack. Don't raise your arms – the gesture tells the dog you're his target. It's the signal he's been trained to act upon." She was doing exactly what she was preaching. The dog stopped as if in doubt.

"Attack!" Mr Rivello cried again, more ferociously.

The dog resumed walking, his eyes fixed on her, ready to attack. He was now just a couple of metres away.

"Move gently as if he is no threat to you. No sudden gestures. Don't give off adrenaline." This was the toughest part – how could you control your adrenaline in such a situation? She couldn't see an off button on her body, but she kept speaking softly, as if the dog wasn't there.

"If the dog attacks, protect your head and neck, and try not to fight back. Play dead."

The dog had reached her. He was sniffing her and growling, but at the same time, his stumpy tail was wagging vigorously. That wasn't supposed to happen. Had the dog not decided what to do yet?

"Attack, Apollo, attack!" Raimondo Rivello was crying almost hysterically.

The dog finally jumped on her, his legs embracing hers. But he wasn't biting. Oh no, he was using her legs for something that was far more fun, just like a thousand randy dogs had done to hapless passers-by before him, much to the embarrassment of their owners...

Then she remembered: Annina, Nennella's dog, was in heat. And she had been caressing Annina just a short while ago.

Rivello took Apollo by the scruff of his neck and pulled him off, red in the face with rage. Giò had escaped one death to face another. But better to be shot in the head than mauled to death by a Rottweiler.

"Thanks, God, you were merciful with me. I'm very sorry if I screwed up my life and did nothing too good with it, but I tried hard."

She closed her eyes.

"Stop there, Rivello! Stop there or

you'll be facing three counts of murder, not two. It's too late."

When Rivello turned towards the voice, Paolo and another carabiniere emerged from the shadows of the building and were on him like a flash, taking the gun away from him. Apollo, seeing his master attacked, went to help, but Giò raised her right arm with palm open, afraid Paolo would shoot the dog.

"HALT!" she shouted as firmly as she could. The dog, already confused, actually obeyed and sat down, waiting for another command.

Rivello knew the game was up and for once did the right thing, giving Apollo the command the dog was waiting for.

"Go home, good dog," he said, and Apollo went back into his enclosure. Paolo closed the gate, and while the other carabiniere put handcuffs around Mr Rivello's wrists, he recited the charges against the man and advised him of his rights.

Then, nodding to the carabiniere, he said, "Let's take him to the station."

Giò's legs gave way and she dropped down onto the ground, her back against the warehouse wall.

"My goodness, I thought I was dead."

"It looks like Apollo rather liked you," said Paolo, sitting beside her.

"It's thanks to Nennella's dog. She's in heat and I was stroking her earlier, and poor Apollo got very confused." Giò started to smile, but her body was still shaking. Paolo laughed.

"Poor Mr Rivello. He had planned the murder of the century, but he didn't account for the Brando sisters."

Surprisingly, Paolo's laugh was contagious. She had faced death and survived, and a sort of intoxicating hilarity took over. She had never felt as alive as she did in that moment.

"We've defeated the murderer. But how come you came here rather than going to my flat?"

"Cop's hunch. I wondered what had

brought you over here. We finished the course just after you texted, so I texted back asking if you were putting yourself in danger, but you never replied. Then I called you, but it went straight to voicemail. So I asked the carabiniere in the car with me if we could stop by and check that you weren't here, perhaps in danger..."

"I put the phone in flight mode after the last text so it wouldn't ring and give me away. I guess it was a rather stupid move."

"That was a very stupid move. Fortunately, there was a smart carabiniere already on his way."

GIÒ DUCKED BEHIND A TREE. SHE knew the man was hunting for her, but she wasn't certain how to hide her tracks from his dog. She kept running in the dark of the forest, doubling back on herself in the hope that would be enough to confuse the animal. Piercing her mind was the memory of merciless and unreasonable eyes.

She had just thrown herself into the undergrowth when she heard a knocking sound, followed by another more impatient one. She turned around and opened her eyes, gratefully recognising where she was.

"Just a dream, thank goodness," she whispered with relief, adding, "Coming!" in a louder voice. She opened the door to find the whole family behind it: Agnese, Lilia and Luca, Granny, and beyond her, Nando.

"Breakfast time," Luca said, waving a bag of warm cornetti.

"Let's have breakfast together," Nando added, showing Giò a basket full of Granny's marmalades, brown bread, and special breakfast biscuits still warm from her oven.

Agnese was already laying the table. "We're sorry to wake you up this early, but we didn't want you to start today alone."

"Did you sleep well?" Lilia asked.

"You just saved me from Mr Rivello and Apollo: they were hunting for me. I guess it will take a while to forget his eyes."

"Apollo's eyes?"

"No, I dread Raimondo Rivello much more than the dog."

"I wouldn't have been able to have your control, I would have run away," admitted Nando.

"I couldn't. My legs were like marble when I realised the death Rivello intended for me. Then my volunteer work at a farm in Scotland where they kept aggressive dogs for rehabilitation came in handy."

Agnese put a jug of hot milk in the centre of the table while the Moka pot growled, spreading the aroma of coffee around the room.

"Paolo said he needs you at the carabinieri station," she said. "He will come to fetch you at 10am. Do you need me or Nando to come with you?"

"I think I can handle it on my own." Giò smiled.

"You'll have to explain to us what happened. How did you find out that Rivello was the killer? He wasn't even a suspect. You were too shocked last night, but today is gonna be explanation day."

"Yes, Auntie, you should explain everything so that I can answer my friends' questions at school. None of them has ever had an auntie come close to being murdered and helping the police to arrest a killer."

Giò promised them a full question and answer session after lunch, complemented by a multimedia lecture.

"A multimedia lecture?"

Giò turned the blackboard around to reveal the notes from her investigations. "Ta-dah!"

The kids had huge smiles on their faces.

After a while they all left, and Giò got ready for the carabinieri, wondering if she would have all the answers to their questions. She still felt confused by all the alibis, times, fakes... she wished she could take the blackboard with her.

At 9.30, the doorbell rang. Paolo was early. She released the lock on the downstairs door without bothering to look at the videophone, but when she opened the door to her flat, she found herself face to face not with Paolo, but with Andrea. She couldn't help gasping.

"What are you doing here?"

"The carabinieri let me out first thing this morning. I had nothing to do with the murder, and now they believe me... thanks to you."

He stood on the threshold, looking at her. She felt embarrassed without knowing why.

"Please come in, don't stand there. I'm expecting Paolo at 10 – the carabinieri want me at the station."

They sat down at the table where earlier the family had consumed the rich breakfast.

"I won't take much of your time. But I

had to pass by and say thanks... before I go."

"Where are you going?"

"Back to Rome. But I need to tell you a few things."

"I'm all ears." Her tone sounded sarcastic, even if she hadn't meant it to be... at least, that's what she told herself.

"I will sound rather stupid, I'm afraid."

"Don't you worry about that, we all sound stupid more often than we like to think." Her voice still resentful, she offered, "Do you fancy a cup of coffee?"

"Yes, please." He smiled back sheepishly.

While she prepared the Moka pot, Andrea began.

"In prison, I had time to think. I ran away from my family, coming to Maratea because I knew here I'd be free from my responsibilities, like when I was young. But I did a lot of stupid things, the worst one being gambling. I was earning good money thanks to Mr Rivello, but I wasted it all on the cards.

"Because I was constantly in debt, I had to ask for advance payments for my work, and I also started to accept a few customers who were not people I really wanted to deal with. Mrs Rivello found out through her friends that I owed a heavy debt to a ruthless loan shark who was pressurising me into signing technical documents for houses in areas that are not safe. Once she found out, she threatened to reveal the whole thing to her husband. That would have ruined me forever, because without his support, I would never get any more work here in Maratea.

"This was the argument that Mariella overheard – I'm guessing she was the one who told you about it. That morning I ostensibly called for Mr Rivello, but I knew he wasn't at home. In fact, it was Mrs Rivello I wanted to speak with. When she told me she'd have to tell the truth to her husband, I got mad and threatened her. Then we calmed down and talked it through, and I promised I'd quit gambling."

"Mrs Rivello has a passion for setting people on the right road," said Giò.

"She said she'd wait and see what I did. I didn't like it at all, she kept me under her thumb. Mind you, it was nothing compared to the threats from the sharks, but she loved having control over my life, and I... I couldn't bear it.

"Then when I was under suspicion of murder, she felt her power over me was stronger than ever. Behind her Good Samaritan façade, she loves to play God and destroy people. I believe Antonio's life would have been better without the Rivellos' help."

"I know what you mean," Giò replied, rather more sympathetic now. "So you're going back to Rome?"

"I'm very sorry. I feel I misbehaved with you. I wasn't cheating, though; I really like you, but... I miss my daughter so much. I don't think my wife will put up with me again, but I want to be close to my daughter in the future."

He seemed very contrite. In any case, what could she say?

"Do you think you'll get any work in Rome?"

"I will have to be humbler than I used to be, start from scratch, but I have my strengths. I don't want to be a puppet in anybody's hands again." He stood up. "Before I go, I just want you to know that it was good getting close to you, seeing your love for your family, and the happiness you derive from the smallest things. I mean, you loved that kayak more than my yacht..."

"Andy, I think you'd better go," she interrupted him briskly. "I don't want to be another Good Samaritan." She smiled, hugged him good luck and sent him away with a weird tingling in her heart.

This isn't fair. I don't want to inspire feelings of friendship in a guy like Andy. I'd rather have him love me passionately. What's wrong with me?

She didn't have time to answer her own

question before the buzzer rang again. This time, it was Paolo.

"Come on up, I'm not ready yet."

After they'd greeted each other, she asked, "Did he confess?"

"Well, we told him we had the recording, meaning your recording, but he thought we were referring to the USB you passed off as Elena's and he confessed to everything. His only worry was how his wife and daughters would be affected by the news. It's so weird to think how a human brain works at times."

"How about Apollo?" she asked.

"We consulted a vet. According to him, his training wasn't as brutal as some guard dogs suffer, where their aggression is pushed beyond limits. This is why you managed to confuse him. The vet said Apollo is actually a very friendly animal who can be re-educated. He will help us find both a trainer and a new owner – Mrs Rivello and her daughters are not the right people to look after him. But now let me ask you, how did you know it was him? How did you solve the whole puzzle?"

"I don't know," she admitted frankly. "There were a few things I was never comfortable with, starting with the threatening letters and the disappearance of Elena's mobile, especially after I checked Mrs Rivello's phone and found nothing on it..."

Paolo interrupted her gently. "You'd better skip that part at the carabinieri station."

"Oh... yes. When Nennella told me that Antonio's car was at the warehouse before 6am on the morning of the murder, I had a flash of... can I call it intuition? I combined that piece of information with what we knew from Gerardina about the comings and goings of Antonio's car that morning and wondered if it hadn't been Antonio driving the car. It couldn't have been any of our suspects as they were all driving their own cars, so it was someone we hadn't suspected before."

"It could have been any other worker at the warehouse," said Paolo.

"But the threatening letters were very convenient for the Rivellos because they put the whole murder into a new light, taking the attention away from Elena, making Mrs Rivello appear to be the real victim."

"The flowerpot incident helped to convince us," Paolo confirmed.

"Did he plan that too?" Giò asked.

"He gave away all the details as he confessed. While pretending to search for his keys, he looked around to make sure he had witnesses and saw you coming. He had tied a transparent nylon thread around the vase and down to his door, and pulled it just at the right time. Nobody would ever have noticed it."

"Then he got down on his knees as if examining the pot. He must have been removing the thread then."

"Yes, he made the whole thing up, pretending to run after an intruder who was never there just to convince us that someone wanted to kill Mrs Rivello. He has a cunning mind, he deceived us from the beginning. We were manipulated all the way through the case and never realised it. He was like a magician, showing us only what he wanted us to see."

"But why did he kill Antonio?"

"He was involved in the fire business, but since he had taken up drinking again, Rivello feared he would give him away when drunk. When he accompanied him home that night, he'd already realised Antonio had to die, too, so he checked how he could murder him and get away with it. But when he got home that evening, his wife told him about Elena taking her car to Acquafredda the next day, and Mr Rivello saw the chance to kill his more dangerous enemy. He seized the opportunity, and had Antonio's car at his disposal. The next morning, he had the meeting with his workers, retired to his office telling them not to disturb him, left from the balcony at the back and drove to Acquafredda using Antonio's car.

"He parked at Antonio's house, when Gerardina recognised the car at 7am, walked through the cemetery and killed Elena when she arrived. He then returned to Antonio's, thinking Antonio would still be sleeping off the booze, but he found him up and waiting, and he didn't like that. A few days later, Antonio told him straight up that he knew he'd killed Elena, and Rivello knew he had to kill again, soon.

"And kill he did, again trying to pass it off as an accident. But when he heard the rumours in Maratea saying the carabinieri suspected it was another murder, he panicked. He had to keep us on the wrong track, and since it seemed at the time the most likely suspect was Carlo Capello, he managed to steal one of his cufflinks when they met in a bar and plant it at Antonio's house."

"It's so weird to think he killed a man he had apparently saved."

"He had no choice. From his confession, we know he killed Elena without any remorse. She had blackmailed him, she deserved her death – in his view, I mean. He was sorry about Antonio, but his life and his family came first, and Antonio was lost to alcohol anyway."

"I wonder what Mrs Rivello will do now. She was always on the side of the pious and the righteous, thinking herself superior to the rest of the human race. Will she disown her husband now?"

"I have no idea. She is such a bigot, a puritan when it comes to others, but she's much more mellow about her family. Double standards are often the norm with people like her. I wouldn't be surprised, though, if she were to move away from Maratea, perhaps to live with one of her daughters."

"It will be very hard for her to stay here, after she has preached to half the population about how they should behave..."

"It's time to leave for the station and

explain all of this to the maresciallo. He is still extremely confused."

Giò sighed and nodded sadly. She wasn't looking forward to meeting Maresciallo Mangiaboschi again and hoped she would be back home soon. Maybe conditions were finally right for her to get started on her Scottish travel guide.

EPILOGUE

Mrs Tristizia came into the perfumery with a little bundle in her hands.

"Good morning, Agnese, I have baked some of my grandmother's special bread. I couldn't resist the temptation to see if it really matched the perfume as I remembered. And of course, I wanted to share it with you."

"That's so very thoughtful of you, Mrs Tristizia," said Agnese, stretching her hand out to receive the gift. "It smells delicious!"

"Please call me Amanda, I'm no longer

Mrs Tristizia. That's my husband's name, so I'm reverting to my maiden name, Triunfo. We're not divorced yet, but I don't want to keep that surname a day longer." And unexpectedly, she smiled.

"Is your husband determined to file for divorce then?"

"I certainly am. I said to him and his mistress that I will keep the house. He's got plenty of money and can buy whatever he wants, wherever he wants. The kids are grown up, but not financially independent, and a tribunal will decide on alimony. I also asked him to let me work as an associate legal consultant in his firm for a year."

"Are you sure you want to see the two of them every day?"

"I'm no longer bothered, really. I sacrificed my career for my family, now I want a chance to be back in business. No other firm will take me on in my 50s after I have been out of work for more than 20 years. I've also signed up to do a Business Master's two days a week in Salerno. Once

I feel I'm 'valuable' enough for the employment market, I might go to work somewhere else, but for now I'm asking him for a chance to be independent again, and he owes me much more than that."

"And do you think he will agree?"

"He asked his mistress, who of course doesn't like the idea a tiny bit. But I reminded the two of them how many husbands have been completely ruined by their former wives, having to pay them huge monthly allowances. To show them I meant business, I hired one of the best divorce lawyers in Campania. I think they got the message."

At that moment, Giò dropped into the shop on her way home from the carabinieri station.

"Good morning – is that you, Mrs Tristizia?" The woman looked exactly the same, but her overall demeanour was completely different – the straight back, the uplifted chin.

"Hello, dear, I'm doing fine. And as I

was saying to your sister, I'm Amanda Triunfo from now on."

"OK, Amanda. I hope I'm not intruding."

"Not at all, we had just finished." Amanda interrupted Agnese, who was inviting her to stay longer, and added, "I didn't come to bother you with details of my divorce, it's just as awful as they say. But I do want you to enjoy my sweet bread, and thank you for that perfume... I don't know how it's possible, but it showed me that I did have a future."

They hugged each other, and Amanda Triunfo left.

"Is she really the same wretched soul I met a couple of weeks ago, unable to choose a lipstick for herself?" Giò asked her sister.

"She is, and she isn't. And I'm so proud of her," Agnese replied with a smile.

THAT EVENING, AGNESE TOOK DOWN

her journal. She didn't write in it every day, only when she felt she had something worth writing about and enough time to do it. After all, now the crime had been solved, it was the end of a rather peculiar time in the history of Maratea and her family.

Lilia popped her head into the bedroom. "Mum, it's Claudia's birthday party today. Had you forgotten?"

"You're right, dear, but give me 15 minutes. I need to rest for a short while."

Lilia shut the door and Agnese sighed. Then she made a bullet list:

- Giò has solved Elena's murder (and Antonio's too), and managed to save herself from a brutal death (my God!).
- Mr Rivello was the cold-blooded murderer (I would never have imagined it was him).
- Giò was a bit hurt by Andy, but I believe that has helped her to get over the called-off wedding

and Dorian. Actually, I think the whole murder story helped to heal her. Life is so strange sometimes.

- I believe Giò is settling in nicely. I really hope she decides to stay in Maratea (and travel as much as she wishes to).
- My young Cabiria is going to experience the world. She is a strong girl, even if she is shy and looks like a fragile little thing. I need to remember that her father might be mad at me.
- ~~Mrs Tristizia~~Ms Triunfo seems to have found a new equilibrium. She has a very tough path ahead, but my goodness, how different she looks. She's got her dignity back and is ready to fight hard for her independence. What a great example for us all.
- Mrs Di Bello no longer bores everyone to tears with stories about herself and her family,

ignoring anyone else's point of view. Thanks to Giò. I wonder, though, if it's a permanent change.

- Mr Shy Man and Ms Shy Lady are together. After two years of secretly loving each other, the musk worked its Perfume Power perfectly!

- Mrs Lavecchia is the same unbearable lady. I don't think all the Perfume Powers on the earth (or in the sky) could sweeten her manners and bad temper. Even I can't figure out the perfume that would suit her. Nor do I wish to.

THE END

I REALLY HOPE YOU ENJOYED THIS

book, my debut novel I've cuddled for 18 months, and now I'm letting him walk on his own two feet.

Is there any way a reader may help a newbie author? Yes! Please leave a review on your favourite e-store, Bookbub and/or Goodreads. It doesn't matter how long or short; even a single sentence could say it all. We might be in a digital era, but **this old world of ours still revolves around word of mouth.** A review allows a book to leave the shadow of the unknown and introduces it to other passionate readers.

GRAZIE :)

GLOSSARY

ANAS: the company responsible for construction and maintenance of motorways and state highways in Italy. ANAS is under the control of the Ministry of Infrastructure and Transport.

ANGIPORTO: an alley or side street.

APERITIVO: this is a convivial social event, often in a bar with friends before heading home for the family lunch or dinner. Let's say it's a sort of appetiser before the real meal. It can be simple or lavish, merely a drink or a variety of finger food. In Italy, we also invite people home for an aperitivo, which is not as formal as a proper meal, but beware! Like Granny's panzerotti, it can be delicious, moreish and *very* filling.

BOCCONOTTO – **plural bocconotti:** a sweet typically made in Maratea, this fragrant pastry is filled with either sour cherries, sometimes with custard, or custard and chocolate. And in this at least, I agree with Giò – my favourite place to eat bocconotti is Panza in Angiporto Cavour 9.

BRUSCHETTA – **plural bruschette:** a slice of toasted bread (possibly cooked on the barbecue or grilled or roasted in a pizza oven), seasoned with garlic, olive oil, sliced fresh tomatoes, anchovies, olives, etc...

BRIGADIERE – **plural brigadieri:** this can be loosely compared to a detective sergeant. In the carabinieri ranks, a brigadiere operates below a maresciallo.

CARABINIERE – plural carabinieri. In Italy, we don't only have the polizia (much like the police in most countries), we also have the carabinieri. Essentially, this is another police force, but it's part of the army and is governed by the Ministry of Defence, whereas the polizia depends on the Ministry of the Interior. The two are often in competition with one another (though they will never admit it), so never confuse one with the other (especially if you're talking with Maresciallo Mangiaboschi, he is rather touchy). For me, the only difference between the two is that we have a number of cracking jokes about the carabinieri and none about the polizia. Don't ask me why.

In Maratea, there's only the carabinieri and no polizia. But Paolo would have been a carabiniere and not a policeman in any case. By the way being a military corps carabinieri tend to wear their uniforms more than the police corps even when investigating crimes.

CORNETTO – **plural cornetti.** This is the equivalent of a French croissant. I have to admit it was the French who invented them, but they're very popular in Italy too.

CRODINO: a popular non-alcoholic soda used in Italy for the aperitivo.

GIANDUIOTTO: this is a popular Italian chocolate, originally from the Piedmont region, made of cocoa and nut paste. The production of nuts is a speciality of Piedmont, and it's said that the first Gianduiotto was made in Turin in 1865.

MARESCIALLO: this rank is similar to detective inspector. A maresciallo is superior to a brigadiere, carabiniere semplice and appuntato.

MOUILLETTE: see 'TOUCHE' below.

PANZEROTTO – **plural panzerotti:** small calzones made with the same dough as pizza, filled with mozzarella, tomato and fresh basil leaves, and deep fried.

SALUTE! – **or CIN CIN** (pronounced chin chin)! This is the equivalent of "Cheers!" When celebrating an event with a glass of wine or prosecco, we love to accompany the word by clinking our glasses together.

TOUCHE: this is a French word that refers to paper strips onto which you can spray perfumes for people to smell. They're also called *mouillette*, again a French word.

VONGOLA – **plural vongole:** means clam(s), so spaghetti alle vongole means spaghetti with clams. In a real restaurant in Southern Italy, you will always find spaghetti alle vongole on the menu, but (TIP!) if it offers spaghetti Bolognese, then the place is only run for the sake of tourists. Italians do not eat spaghetti with their Bolognese sauce, which is not a common sauce in the southern part of the country anyway.

If you have found other Italian words in the story and would like to know what they mean, please let me know.

Contact me on:
    Twitter: @adrianalici
    Join the Maratea Murder Club:
    www.adrianalicio.com/murderclub

ABOUT THE AUTHOR

Adriana Licio lives in the Apennine Mountains in southern Italy, not far from Maratea, the seaside setting for her first cosy series, *An Italian Village Mystery*.

She loves loads of things: travelling, reading, walking, good food, small villages, and home swapping. A long time ago, she spent six years falling in love with Scotland, and she has never recovered. She now runs her family perfumery, and between a dark patchouli and a musky rose, she devours cosy mysteries.

She resisted writing as long as she could, fearing she might get carried away by her wild imagination. But one day, she found an alluring blank page and the words flowed in the weird English she'd learned in Glasgow.

Adriana finds peace for her restless, enthusiastic soul by walking in nature with her adventurous golden retriever Frodo and her hubby Giovanni.

Do you want to know more?

Join the **Maratea Murder Club** at www.adrianalicio.com/murderclub

You can also stay in touch on:
www.adrianalicio.com

f facebook.com/adrianalicio.mystery

twitter.com/adrianalici

a amazon.com/author/adrianalicio

BB bookbub.com/authors/adriana-licio

JOIN THE MARATEA MURDER CLUB

You'll get exclusive content:

- **Book 0,** *And Then There Were Bones,* the FREE eBook prequel to the *An Italian Village Mystery* series
- **Giò Brando's Maratea Album** – photos of her favourite places and behind-the-scenes secrets
- **A Maratea Map** – including most places featured in the series
- **Adriana Licio's News** – new

releases, news from Maratea, but no spam – Giò would loathe it!
- **Cosy Mystery Passion:** a place to share favourite books, characters, tips and tropes

Sign up to:

www.adrianalicio.com/murderclub

MORE BOOKS FROM ADRIANA LICIO

An Italian Village Mystery Series

Book 0 – And Then There Were Bones, prequel to the *An Italian Village Mystery* series, available in Print an Large Print or **you can get the FREE eBook only by signing up to www.adrianalicio.com/ murderclub** – You can unsubscribe any time you like, but of course, I hope you will stay.

Book 1 – Murder on the Road is the first book in the series, and it lets you know how and why Giò Brando decided to come back to Maratea (and what else life has in store for her).

Book 2 – A Fair Time for Death is a mystery set during the Autumn Chestnut Fair in Trecchina, a mountain village near Maratea, involving a perfume with a split personality, a disappearing corpse, a disturbing secret from the past and a mischievous goat.

Book 3 – A Mystery Before Christmas A haunting Christmas song from a faraway land. A child with striking green eyes. A man with no past. A heartwarming mystery for those who want to breathe in the delicious scents and flavours of a Mediterranean December.

Book 4 – Peril at the Pellicano Hotel – A group of wordsmiths, a remote hotel. Outside, the winds howl and the seas rage. But the real danger lurks within.

They say that...

Those well informed on Adriana's movements say she is working at **a new series that will take us through small villages all across Europe**, starting from

Castelmezzano in Basilicata. Let's wish her luck with the Muse!

ACKNOWLEDGMENTS

I frankly feel intimidated when I see long lists of names in other authors' 'Acknowledgements' pages. It looks like you need an army of people to write a book, which isn't really compatible with the hard-won reputation writers have of being lonely creatures, locking themselves in a dark corner of their neglected houses. (Of course, they're so busy building new worlds, they don't have time to take care of trivia such as housework!)

But on the other hand, not having such a page would prove I'm a newbie to the art, so I started one, thanking my family, Giovanni (my hubby) and Frodo (the doggy), because they trust in whatever venture I happen to be pursuing. If I were to announce that tomorrow I'm going to become an astronaut, they'd not only believe that's the best idea I could have come up with, but they'd be totally confident I'd succeed.

Then there's my brother, whose attempts to turn me into a sensible person invariably end up with him saying, "OK, next time" and "Let's go with this idea for now."

Thanks to my best friend Maria Gerardi, who couldn't read the book since she doesn't speak English (and that, I believe, is the only thing on earth she can't do). She's one of the few people with whom I discussed the book while I was writing it, and she took an active role in designing my website too. But mostly, she supports me in whatever silly or massive (or both) project I start.

A word apart goes to my editor, Alison

Jack. She has had to deal with an Italian woman's funny interpretation of English and turn it into something that makes sense to the English speakers around the world, also finding time for encouragement, appreciation, critique, advice. I think her work would be listed as the thirteenth Herculean labour, if we had been born in those times. How a single person can offer this much is still a mystery to me. But, of course, she's English.

I must mention Joanna Penn of the *Creative Penn*. I started to listen to her inspiring podcast, and all of a sudden, it dawned on me that yes, I wanted to write a book if I'd ever wanted anything in my life. So I joined her course 'How to Write a Novel', and you've just read the result. If you didn't like the book, you know who to blame!

Then there's Debbie Young, whose *Sophie Sayers Village Mysteries* gave me great inspiration. She's also the one who sent me directly to Alison Jack, and if, as they say, finding a good editor is like dating, Debbie is definitely one of the rare successful matchmakers. But mostly I'm grateful to her because she's full of advice for all authors and wannabe authors. She's UK Ambassador for the Alliance of Independent Authors and keeps encouraging us with her enthusiasm.

Talking of the Alliance of Independent Authors, Orna Ross created this here thingy. It's an incredible place where experienced authors, instead of keeping the secrets they've learned over years of trial and error to themselves, share them with newbie authors everywhere. I guess it's a result of Orna's hospitality and generosity, for which the Irish are so well known, trickling down to all the people who have joined the Alliance. You couldn't start from a better place if you want to become an author.

I'd like to thank Shirley Holder Platt, a romance author who doesn't mind reading cosies in her spare time, and Theresa Taylor, an upcoming cosy mystery author.

They both volunteered to beta read this book of mine, encouraged – should I say pampered? – me a lot, and gave me a precious *reader take* on what I had written. Thanks again to DY, who most unexpectedly ended up beta reading my book – what an honour, I mean! – and gave me invaluable advice to improve it. Love you all for taking the strain and the pain!

Thanks to Julia Gibbs, my lovely proofreader, who had to face a long list of questions from a rather touchy author. It's testament to her patience and bionic eye that this manuscript has improved beyond my expectations.

Thanks to my Advanced Reader Copy (ARC) team: 40 enthusiastic people who, after having read *And Then There Were Bones*, came forward to join my team and return precious feedback on this book. In particular, thanks to Anne K and Pete B; you've been awesome!

Wait a second, I'm counting how many paragraphs I've written for my

'Acknowledgements' page. Perhaps I'd better stop here.

[Adriana pats herself on the shoulder, smiles in satisfaction, turns her back and moves away. She's got other books to write now – it looks like she's a real author!]

A Q&A WITH ADRIANA LICIO

How do you pronounce Giò?

The same way you'd pronounce Jo.

Why did you call your main character Giò?

My instinctive reply would be because it works well with the surname Brando, a surname that captured my imagination a few years ago while I was sipping a cappuccino at Iannini's bar in Maratea. But I have to acknowledge that my life has always been full of Giovannis. It was my grandfather's name (and my great-great-grandfather's), and it's now the name of my brother and the man I've shared my life with for the past 20 years. My dog's first son was named Giò, too.

And of course there's Jo – Josephine March, whose deeds will accompany me forever, and now Joanna Penn, whose writing course I joined when I decided I really wanted to write a book. Without Joanna, this book would not even exist.

Maratea – is it real?

Yes! Have a look on Google Maps. Maratea is there, as well as Acquafredda, the Maratea harbour and most of the places I talk about. But... and it's a big but... the Maratea of *Murder on the Road* is a fictional version of the real village.

For example, in Maratea we have experienced quite a number of rockfalls, almost in the place I described, but a bit further up than the graveyard and the last houses where Gerardina lives. And there would be no buses running to Sapri from the closed road, but I needed to tweak things for my story to get going. An author's brain works in a weird way – we turn and twist things without even realising what we're doing. While we're creating, all we are writing is just as real as you and me right now.

In that case, why not create a totally new village with an imaginary name, location and businesses?

I have at least three reasons for not wanting to do that. The first one, I'm almost ashamed to confess, is that I'm a strong believer that the best lies are the ones that are the closest to the truth. You may shake your head in disapproval and remind me that lies are not a good thing at all, but I'll pretend you're all agreeing with me and carry on.

The second reason is that I love travelling (sometimes in slippers and pyjamas from an armchair) and there's nothing like exploring (in person or on the web) the places where my favourite novels are set. That may be Camilla Lackberg's Fjallbacka, Beatrix Potter's Hilltop, Anne of Green Gables' Prince Edward Island, or Viveca Sten's Sandhamn. As a reader, I also love it when authors name a few businesses, real places where the locals live and spend their time, so it was natural for me to do the same with Maratea. In the story, 90% of it is as it is, 10% comes from my imagination, but no – not even under torture will I reveal where the line is between the two.

Do you take inspiration from real people?

For people, things are completely different. In order to stay creative, you don't want to involve real people at all. I might combine the traits of 10 different people to create Mrs Lavecchia, for example, but the end result is a new person (often an exaggerated one) who bears no resemblance to anyone I know.

A person who fires my imagination may be the stranger on the bus, a lady I've never spoken to, someone making a weird remark in a café. From that spark I can create a fictional character. But on the whole, unlike places, real people bog down the imagination. The more I know them, the less I have the freedom to do with them as I wish.

The fires – is that a true story?

Yes and no. Almost every summer, fires do destroy Maratea's wild beauty. It's painful beyond limits. You wake up with the acrid smell of smoke in your nostrils, you hear the crackling flames and the terrifying dull roar of the advancing fire. I've never heard anything more menacing, not even a storm.

Firemen say that the fires are mostly caused by people, but who they are and why they do it has always been a mystery. If you ask local people, they will reply, as Giò found, that the culprits are the shepherds. But I went through a few articles and documentaries on the causes of fires in Italy in general and Southern Italy in particular. Apart from stories about a few mad arsonists, most hypotheses seem to revolve around the fact that the system plunges money into the fighting of fires rather than the prevention of them.

From there, I created my own imaginary hypothesis of a pool of men making money out of the fire business, but this is not backed by any evidence in the specific case of Maratea. I'm applying what I have seen in the rest of the country to my little (imaginary) corner of Southern Italy. It's not speculation; it's – I guess – my own way of expressing my anger and trying to make sense of the problem.

Do you live in Maratea?

Unfortunately not yet. I live on the Apennines in a little town that's not as quaint as Maratea. In fact, some say it's a rather boring, anonymous place, but I like it nonetheless.

In my ideal life, I'd spend the off-season months in our house in Maratea to write, two to three months travelling (mainly in Europe – we love home swapping), and the rest of the year where I live (writing some more and walking in the mountains).

Why are Italian words not italicised in the story?

In the first draft of this book, I did, as is normal writing style, use italics for all non-English words. But when I saw the words *carabiniere, maresciallo, brigadiere* in italics over and over again, I felt they were like a punch in the stomach. I asked Giò, and she said that since she speaks Italian and lives in Italy, she couldn't see the point of highlighting words that she would use over and over again. She also said she wanted you, the readers, to feel as close to Maratea as possible, and italicising Italian words might have the opposite effect.

Giò's argument convinced both me, and Alison Jack, my heroic editor. "So be it," we said. We also included a Glossary to help you out. But the last word is for you, the reader. Please let us know if you (don't) agree with Giò's choice.

More questions?

If you have any other questions you would like to ask me, feel free to contact me. I might even add your question to the FAQ section on my website – www. adrianalicio.com – or the Q&A page in my next novel.

Contact me on:

Twitter: @adrianalici

Join the **Maratea Murder Club**:

www.adrianalicio.com/murderclub